EUROPE IN TRANSITION: THE NYU EUROPEAN STUDIES SERIES

The Marshall Plan: Fifty Years After
Edited by Martin Schain

Europe at the Polls: The European Elections of 1999
Edited by Pascal Perrineau, Gérard Grunberg, and Colette Ysmal

Unions, Immigration, and Internationalization: New Challenges and Changing Coalitions in the United States and France
By Leah Haus

Shadows over Europe: The Development and Impact of the Extreme Right in Western Europe
Edited by Martin Schain, Aristide Zolberg, and Patrick Hossay

Defending Europe: The EU, NATO and the Quest for European Autonomy
Edited by Joylon Howorth and John T.S. Keeler

The Lega Nord and Contemporary Politics in Italy
By Thomas W. Gold

Germans or Foreigners? Attitudes toward Ethnic Minorities in Post-Reunification Germany
Edited by Richard Alba and Peter Schmidt

Germany on the Road to Normalcy? Politics and Policies of the First Red-Green Federal Government
Edited by Werner Reutter

The Politics of Language: Essays on Languages, State and Society
Edited by Tony Judt and Denis Lacorne

Realigning Interests: Crisis and Credibility in European Monetary Integration
By Michele Chang

The Impact of Radical Right-Wing Parties in West European Democracies
By Michelle Hale Williams

European Foreign Policy Making toward the Mediterranean
By Federica Bicchi

Sexual Equality in an Integrated Europe: Virtual Equality
By R. Amy Elman

Politics in France and Europe
Edited by Pascal Perrineau and Luc Rouban

Germany after the Grand Coalition: Governance and Politics in a Turbulent Environment
　Edited by Silvia Bolgherini and Florian Grotz

The New Voter in Western Europe: France and Beyond
　Edited by Bruno Cautrès and Anne Muxel

The Mobilization of the Unemployed in Europe
　Edited by Didier Chabanet and Jean Faniel

Germany, Poland, and Postmemorial Relations
　Edited by Kristin Kopp and Joanna Nizynska

Liberalization Challenges in Hungary: Elitism, Progressivism, and Populism
　By Umut Korkut

Lessons from the Economic Crisis in Spain
　By Sebastian Royo

The Europeanization of European Politics
　Edited by Michael L. Mannin and Charlotte Bretherton

Parliament and Diaspora in Europe
　By Michel S. Laguerre

Politics and Society in Contemporary Spain
　Edited by Bonnie N. Field and Alfonso Botti

The Discourses and Politics of Migration in Europe
　Edited By Umut Korkut, Gregg Bucken-Knapp,
　Aidan McGarry, Jonas Hinnfors, and Helen Drake

The Discourses and Politics of Migration in Europe

Edited by
*Umut Korkut,
Gregg Bucken-Knapp,
Aidan McGarry,
Jonas Hinnfors, and
Helen Drake*

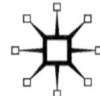

THE DISCOURSES AND POLITICS OF MIGRATION IN EUROPE
Copyright © Umut Korkut, Gregg Bucken-Knapp, Aidan McGarry, Jonas Hinnfors, and Helen Drake, 2013.
Softcover reprint of the hardcover 1st edition 2013 978-1-137-31089-7
All rights reserved.

First published in 2013 by
PALGRAVE MACMILLAN®
in the United States—a division of St. Martin's Press LLC,
175 Fifth Avenue, New York, NY 10010.

Where this book is distributed in the UK, Europe and the rest of the world, this is by Palgrave Macmillan, a division of Macmillan Publishers Limited, registered in England, company number 785998, of Houndmills, Basingstoke, Hampshire RG21 6XS.

Palgrave Macmillan is the global academic imprint of the above companies and has companies and representatives throughout the world.

Palgrave® and Macmillan® are registered trademarks in the United States, the United Kingdom, Europe and other countries.

ISBN 978-1-349-45678-9   ISBN 978-1-137-31090-3 (eBook)
DOI 10.1057/9781137310903

Library of Congress Cataloging-in-Publication Data is available from the Library of Congress.

A catalogue record of the book is available from the British Library.

Design by Newgen Imaging Systems (P) Ltd., Chennai, India.

First edition: June 2013
10 9 8 7 6 5 4 3 2 1

To Dave Allen (1949–2012) and all of our loved ones

Contents

List of Illustrations   ix

Foreword   xi
Martin A. Schain

Acknowledgments   xv

Immigration and Integration Policies: Assumptions
and Explanations   1
Umut Korkut, Gregg Bucken-Knapp, and
Aidan McGarry

Part I   Construction of the Foreigner

1. Whose Interests Do Radical Right Parties Really Represent?
The Migration Policy Agenda of the Swiss People's Party
between Nativism and Neoliberalism   17
Alexandre Afonso

2. Domestic Work, Gender, and Migration in Turkey: Legal
Framework Enabling Social Reality   37
Hande Eslen-Ziya and Umut Korkut

3. Struggling with the US Safe Country Practices in Asylum   53
Sarah Craig

Part II   Host Nations

4. The Politicization of Roma as an Ethnic "Other": Security
Discourse in France and the Politics of Belonging   73
Aidan McGarry and Helen Drake

5. "Good" and "Bad" Immigrants: The Economic Nationalism of
the True Finns' Immigration Discourse   93
Mikko Kuisma

6 "A Two-Way Process of Accommodation": Public Perceptions
   of Integration along the Migration-Mobility Continuum   109
   Kesi Mahendran

Part III Law and Order

7 Asylum Policy Responsiveness in Scandinavia   135
   Frøy Gudbrandsen

8 The Multilevel Governance of Migrant Integration:
   A Multilevel Governance Perspective on Dutch
   Migrant Integration Policies   151
   Peter Scholten

9 Ideology and Entry Policy: Why Center-Right Parties
   in Sweden Support Open-Door Migration Policies   171
   Andrea Spehar, Gregg Bucken-Knapp, and Jonas Hinnfors

The Discourses and Politics of Migration: Policy,
Methodology, and Theory   191
Umut Korkut, Jonas Hinnfors, and Helen Drake

Bibliography   199

Contributors   227

Index   231

Illustrations

Figures

6.1	The 10-Point Migration-Mobility Continuum	111
7.1	Probability of Policy Changes by Share of Government Supporters Who Oppose Refugee Immigration	148

Tables

7.1	Descriptive Statistics of Refugee Attitudes of Government Supporters	145
7.2	Ordered Logit on Asylum Policy Changes	145
9.1	Swedish Parties, 1989–2011: Immigration Entry Policy Stances	173
9.2	Immigration Policy Decisions in Relation to Several Strategic Contexts	186

Foreword

This fine collection of chapters focuses on the impact of political discourse on the politics of immigration in Europe. Indeed, discourse is understood as an integral part of the political process. Most of the authors in this volume understand discourse as a way to define and/or frame issues of immigration, such as entry, immigrant integration, asylum policy, the securitization of immigration, and the role of immigrant labor in the economy. While institutions may be important to understand policy and its implementation, ideas and the framing of policy tell us much more about the way that institutions actually function. The key point, then, is to understand how immigration problems are framed in specific ways, and then why one definition prevails while others do not.

Such a perspective of politics is rooted in the idea of E. E. Schattschneider, first developed more than 50 years ago. Schattschneider associated the initial struggle about policy to the way policy issues are portrayed through the arguments and strategies of political actors. How issues are defined in policy debates, he argued, is driven by strategic calculations among conflicting political actors about the mobilization of "the audience" at which they are aiming (Schattschneider 1960, Chapter 2). From this point of view, political leaders skilled in formulating issues to their own advantage strongly influence how (and who in) "the audience"—voters, militants, and other leaders—becomes involved.

The motor force behind policy portrayal is issue-driven conflict among political elites, and different formulations of issues can mobilize different coalitions of supporters, each of which has its policy bias. The way these issues are defined by public authorities is a crucial aspect of policymaking that is also linked to which publics are mobilized and within which political arenas policy decisions are taken. The construction of the issue of immigration may be related to pressures of public opinion, pluralist pressures of organized interests, initiatives within administrations, or to all the three. The point is that issues do not generally just emerge. They are constructed within specific institutional arenas in specific ways for specific purposes linked to political conflict.

Also, an analysis of conflict among political actors trying to gain political advantage does not help us to understand cross-national differences in policy *content*. For example, at various times, in their framing of immigration policy, political party actors in Britain and France, on one hand, and the United States, on the other, were all driven by the possibility of electoral advantage. However, the policies themselves were very different in Europe compared with those in the United States, and the dynamics among the party actors were very different in Britain compared with those in France.

Although questions of framing are often analyzed in terms of winners and losers, the losers do not generally disappear. Schattschneider emphasizes that policy definition is a continuing struggle, often among the same actors in an evolving institutional context. The way policies are framed, therefore, is important, whether we are dealing with political actors using policy to gain political advantage, responding to conflicting interests, or using policy as a way of dealing with perceived, ongoing problems.

Consider the framing of immigration issues by political parties for vote maximization. There are often striking differences between the ways that European and US parties have tended to frame immigration issues, in each case with a different electoral logic. In Europe, immigration has often been framed in terms of identity politics, even among parties of the left, and immigrant populations have been objectified as a challenge to cultural and/or political stability. The logic is to mobilize anti-immigrant sentiment, and perhaps gain votes from the opposition party or parties. This tendency is particularly strong when both the right and the left are challenged by a party of the radical right. For the right, the radical right challenges their hold on voters who tend to prioritize identity issues; for the left, the radical right is a powerful magnet for working-class voters who would otherwise vote for the left.

In the United States, there has been a greater tendency to see immigrant populations as a potential political resource, capable of altering the rapports de force between the parties (Schain 2012b). The logic is that immigrant-ethnic mobilization is more strategically beneficial than a loss of identity voters. This near consensus on framing the issue of legal immigration emerged less than 20 years ago, but the logic of its electoral frame has been used since the nineteenth century.

Nevertheless, in both cases, there have been other ways of framing immigration issues that are consistent with a different electoral (and policy) logic. As Andrea Spehar, Gregg Bucken-Knapp, and Jonas Hinnfors have demonstrated in this volume, parties of the center-right have more or less steadfastly framed immigration issues in terms of labor market utility, and have supported policies that tend toward more open immigration. However, for these authors vote maximization is less important than ideological consistency. We might add that ideological consistency may be related to the maintenance of loyalty and cohesion within the party.

For similar reasons, French center-right parties and governments supported open immigration policies during both the Fourth and Fifth Republics, and for almost a decade prior to 1973 even encouraged undocumented immigrants to come to France in search of work; most were later legalized through a series of amnesties (Schain 2012a: 94–98). Prior to 1962, the British Conservative Party had supported free access to the United Kingdom from other countries of the British Empire/Commonwealth (now 54 countries), and had framed the issue in terms of empire identity (Schain 2012a: 171–174). In each of these cases, the apparent dramatic change of frame was an altered political-economic environment that permitted a frame that had been advocated by a different group within the party to gain ascendancy.

In the United States, the recent presidential election campaign revealed a growing tendency in the Republican Party to frame immigration as a challenge to identity. Of course, the focus of Republican candidates (as well as governors) was on undocumented immigrants and the need to enforce law and order, but the rhetoric was so raw that it was widely perceived as more generally anti-Latino and anti-immigrant. The framing of immigration as a challenge to national identity has a long history in the United States. After all, the United States was the first country to have a successful anti-immigrant national political party (the American Party in the nineteenth century). It was also the first Western country to exclude a class of immigrants on the basis of race.

The authors in this volume also confront important challenges to the use of discourse and framing analysis. Scholten, for example, analyzes policy discourse as a multilevel struggle. Examined only at the national level, it might appear that the Netherlands has had an evolving multicultural discourse that has nurtured its policies on immigrant integration. Nevertheless, he has presented an impressive case that the very different political environments in localities with large immigrant populations (Amsterdam and Rotterdam) have led to quite different frames for understanding integration policy and different policies as well. These multilevel differences can also be seen in a highly centralized system like the one in France (Schain 2012a: 77–87).

Another issue that emerges in the chapters in this book is the relationship between policy frames and actual policies. In Alexandre Afanso's analysis of the Swiss radical right party, the SVP, he argues that there is a considerable gap between the discourse of the SVP and the actual policies that it supports. He argues that this discrepancy is the result of an attempt to appeal to diverse interests. For its working-class voters, the nativist rhetoric is highly appealing. However, its neoliberal policies that have been developed to attract low-skilled labor cater to its business clientele. There is a parallel here with Kuisma's analysis of the anti-immigrant True Finn Party, which has approached immigration by differentiating between "good" and "bad" immigrants for the labor market. This is an approach adopted by the French government under Nicolas Sarkozy. Each case, however, demonstrates, once again, the importance and power of rhetoric, even in the absence of consistent policies.

Although each of the chapters in this book stands by itself as an impressive piece of scholarship, the collection has a coherence. These chapters demonstrate the continuing importance of Schattschneider's work for more than half a century now, which was developed through the seminal idea that the discourse around which policy issues are portrayed is an essential part of the policy process.

MARTIN A. SCHAIN
New York University

Acknowledgments

We would like to acknowledge the generous support extended by the Glasgow Caledonian University Institute for Society and Social Justice and Professor Jackie Tombs as the Head of Institute to host the workshop that gave birth to this edited volume in November 2011. We also would like to thank Professor Martin Schain for providing the ideas that inspired this project as well as his later engagement. Some chapters in this volume received valuable comments from Dominik Geering, Ken Bryan, Nicola Magnusson, Stephanie Taylor as well as the participants of the "Political Parties and Migration Puzzles: The European Scene" conference organized at University of Gothenburg Centre for European Research in June 2012. We would like to thank them all. Finally, we would like to thank all our loved ones for their continuous support during the process of writing and editing this book.

Immigration and Integration Policies: Assumptions and Explanations

Umut Korkut, Gregg Bucken-Knapp, and Aidan McGarry

Migration is one of the key issues in contemporary European politics and society, placing high on the political agenda in local, national, and transnational political contexts, and widely debated in the media. All European states must grapple with the challenges posed when people move across borders. However, little is known about the relationship between the construction and elaboration of political discourse and its impact on institutions and actors associated with immigration, as well as the lives and everyday realities of frequently vulnerable migrant populations. This book engages with politics and political discourse that relate to and qualify immigration in Europe. It brings together empirical analysis of immigration both topically and contextually, and interprets such empirical evidence with the use of policy and discursive analyses as methodological tools. Thematically, this volume focuses on how discourse and politics operate in issue areas as varied as immigrant integration and multilevel governance, Roma immigration and their respective securitization, the uses of language in determination of asylum applications, gendered immigrants in informal economy, perceptions of integration by the migrants, economic interests and economic nationalism stimulating immigration choices, ideology and entry policies, and asylum processes and the institutional evolution of immigration systems. These issues are analyzed with empirical evidence investigating the discursive formulation of immigration in political contexts such as the Netherlands, France, United Kingdom, Turkey, Switzerland, Scandinavian states, and Finland. Overall, this volume constitutes a unique effort to elevate the underlying but implicit discursive frames that affect politics of immigration, and that inevitably have institutional, legal, and policy implications. Finally, we offer a portrayal of the public philosophy that emanates from how political and social actors approach the issue of immigration and politics that affect the functioning of immigration systems as a result.

It is essential to study how formal and informal countervailing factors have an impact on immigration. We are witnessing an emergence, albeit uneven, of a new kind of transnationally envisioned, transnationally protected, and transnationally mobile citizen-subject (Sparke 2006: 157). The Western variant of this mobile citizen-subject is relatively free, while the non-Western one is restrained and at times constructed as a form of deviance or even a threat. Vulnerabilities are particularly acute in the latter case. The problems of inclusion of people who speak different languages or who have different religious or cultural values raise policy issues of what should be done with respect to groups of such newcomers or immigrants (Hardin 2005). On the one hand, the host state's control over immigrants is stronger than ever, and the policy aspect of immigration research provides a vast array of formal mechanisms to deal with state control on migration, immigration, and asylum and related issues of residency, employment, welfare benefits, and citizenship. On the other hand, migration often provokes the deeply negative, exclusionary side of community against those who, in some sense, do not fit with the native population of the host state in terms of language, ethnicity, and religion.

The expression of discourse both within the formal institutional mechanisms and through informal ideational mechanisms on the topic of immigration deserves our attention as policies and political rhetoric on citizenship, immigration, asylum, and nationality have substantial consequences for public life. Policy and decision makers impart an ideational impact on the policies that are set up to regulate immigration: in short, they set the tone of the message. Under the common circumstances of structural, social, political, and economic disadvantage that unite migrants, the relative power of the host nation often allows it to dominate the definition of the "common good" in ways compatible with its own experience, perspective, and priorities. The ability of the host nation to impress its particular views regarding language, ethnicity, religion, and manners into authoritative knowledge without being challenged by those who have reason to see things differently is certainly a consequence of its social and political privileges. Such an ability to make authoritative claims about the common good is not limited to the host nation as a whole. Subnational actors, be they political parties, interest groups, epistemic communities, or the media, contribute to setting the boundaries of acceptable discourse about migration and integration, be it matters of identity or economics. Henceforth, the processes that produce and reproduce discursive action illustrate how structural relations become inscribed in policy and ideational environments (Young 2000: 108).

In this context, discourse emanates from people who hold different opinions and interpretations and who learn and refine their ideas as they share them with others. Viewing politics as a discursive process means that it is not a mechanical process whereby actors formulate a goal, devise a strategy to achieve the goal, and struggle with others as they employ their strategy. Rather, drawing on existing cultural and ideological symbols, actors develop a set of ideas and share them with others, who may challenge these ideas and provide some alternatives. The discursive interactions prompt them to refine, reframe, and reinterpret these ideas. Not only is this iterative and sometimes contentious discourse in play between political and social actors, but it informs the evolution of political institutions. The ideas upon which institutions are formed are also subject to discursive revision as actors reinterpret and debate the meanings of the ideas upon which existing institutions are constructed. The ideas that define institutions, as well as those shared by political actors, are in flux, often at odds, and malleable (Béland and Cox 2011: 10). The study of immigration, considering the discursive mechanisms that substantiate its operation, is certainly a fruitful exercise insomuch as we look beyond the linear evolution of discourses into institutions, but acknowledge that more often discourses may trump the institutions (Korkut and Eslen-Ziya 2011).

Equally noteworthy, the direction, content, and intensity (Schain 2010: 228) of formal institutional impacts on immigration policies inform this volume. Governments are required to control their borders, the territorial boundary of identity, and to defend national interests (Kastoryano 2010: 89), that is, the gamut of policy responses to immigration can shift from a permissive and proactive state action (Schain 2010: 230) to state action to "trace, detect, and eliminate parasites" (Zylinska 2005: 530). In this context, policy analysis reveals various routes open to the state including, first, the long-term stability versus instability of administrative traditions; second, the internal consistency versus inconsistency of ideas, institutions, and practices as the three constitutive levels of an administrative tradition; and, third, the dependence versus autonomy of an administrative tradition from external, mainly foreign, pressure and influence-seeking (Meyer-Sahling and Yesilkagit 2011: 311).

These three routes are especially central to public administration in the European states, considering the scope of Europeanization in immigration and citizenship issues as well as the scale of migration. A further point is human rights of migrants, given the pervasive institutionalization of human rights within the members and partners of the European Union (EU). Migrants can avail of international human rights standards in order to protect them as they move across borders but the rights of migrants are not group rights and are not special rights over and above what citizens can expect. Instead, they are exercised by individuals that sometimes act together. Thus, expressions in support of or dissent in respect of civil rights (Hattam and Yescas 2010: 142) and social rights availed to migrant populations closely relate to policy research on immigration. The discrepancy between human rights and migrant rights can be quite striking and it is the duty of policy research to qualify why this happens to be the case. Overall, the political discourse surrounding immigration in Europe is burdened with what is sometimes a seemingly intractable debate centered on a "Christian Europe and an 'intruding' Islam" (Kastoryano 2010: 79) where defending emancipation of people, the Republican idea of an enlightened, Cartesian citizen supporting the Republic, attached to the three major values—liberty, equality, and fraternity (Body-Gendrot 2010: 194)—are all figure prominently. Even when such sweeping cultural markers are absent from the discourse, as in the case of concerns over the impact of labor migrants on wage levels and the resilience of welfare state services, notions of difference can still figure prominently, as in the case of the British Labour Party's defense of "British jobs for British workers" in the mid-2000s. Despite this, normative policies should be able to disengage from this rhetoric and bestow rights to all that live under their jurisdiction. We advocate this point while noting that ideas can trump institutions, that is, while the institutional framework of rights can be robust, prevalent ideas regarding how to handle immigration systems may prevail (Korkut and Eslen-Ziya 2011). Therefore, in this volume, we are interested in the underlying and interlinking mechanisms that qualify politics and political discourse of immigration in Europe, bearing in mind their expressions in multiple thematic and contextual forms.

The themes and issues that this volume looks into have been featured in the past and recently in a few other books on migration. Hence, this volume contributes to the existing scholarly work on migration, welfare, integration policy, and the underlying politics and discourses fundamental to these issues. Nonetheless, it takes the debate further on several fronts. Previously, Ireland situated the discussions of migration, security, and welfare regimes in proximity to each other through depicting both political expressions and public feelings emanating from their intersection (2004). Accordingly, welfare states could have provided processes by which immigrants and those of immigrant origin engage with and become part of the host society (Ireland 2004: 15). However, it appears more and more that rather than providing accommodating processes, the politics and discursive frames of welfare have turned into mechanisms of exclusion toward the outsiders. We elaborate on this point further by exploring how this theme is featured in various other works as well.

Sainsbury explores the social rights of immigrants in a comparative perspective in diverging welfare regimes such as the liberal, corporatist, and social democratic. He elaborates on politics of inclusion and exclusion (2012). It is a notable work exploring the situation of immigrants and immigrant rights within welfare states that at times lead certain political and social actors to question the raison d'être of welfare states with chauvinist presumptions. The functioning of the welfare state under the impact of newcomers and their respective needs from welfare regimes feature in our book extensively. Along with political debates of future welfare state arrangements, we elaborate on emerging narratives and discursive frames that mold the relevant public actors' perception of how immigration is situated in the welfare state debate. Givens and Maxwell (2012) reflect on the representation of ethnic minority immigrant origin communities in contemporary European politics. Bringing together media discourses, public opinion data, and elite interviews, Givens and Maxwell present how European publics feel about nonwhite politicians, how political parties reach out to nonwhite communities, and eventually how nonwhite communities feel about their political influence in selected EU states (2012). Taking this crucial debate significantly further, this volume shows how the convictions of the host nations about both the integrated and outsider communities, and how such public sentiments frame party politics, asylum mechanisms, gender regimes, and the functioning of welfare states.

Ideas, Institutions, and Migration Research

An interesting question arises here. Namely, to what extent do public philosophies on immigration simultaneously transmit the desire for migration, on the one hand, and a feeling of apprehension by the nation into whose territory migrants enter, on the other (Zylinska 2005: 528)? A related question is how do the understandings of integration models ignore the evolution of both public philosophy and public policy rooted in the evolving societal ideas that are relevant to immigration? If this is true, a question remains whether the concept of public philosophy has any meaning at all, apart from political rhetoric. It does as long as one can demonstrate empirically that "its principles continue to inspire government policy towards immigrants," and to alter the rhetoric would in itself weaken the social fabric (Schnapper 1994: 133–135 in Schain 2010: 206). Moreover, what are the mechanisms of this rather natural interaction between rhetoric and social fabric? We maintain that the discursive institutionalism literature helps to delineate them and serves to provide an understanding of how this interaction works in context.

Discursive institutionalism considers the discourse in which actors engage in the process of generating, deliberating, and/or legitimizing ideas about sociopolitical action in institutional contexts according to logic of communication. On the interactive dimension, it covers all works that focus on the discursive processes by which such ideas are constructed in a "coordinative" policy sphere by policy actors and deliberated in a "communicative" political sphere by political actors and the public (Schmidt 2010: 47–48). For discursive institutionalism, institutions are internal to the sentient agents, serving both as structures (of thinking and acting) created and changed by those actors. This internal capacity to create and maintain institutions derives from agents' background ideational abilities (Schmidt 2008). This is a generic term for what Searle (1995) defined as the "background abilities" that encompass human capacities, dispositions, and know-how related to how the world works and how to cope with it, or for what Bourdieu describes as the habitus in which human beings act following the institutions of a logic of practice (Korkut 2012). These background ideational abilities underpin agents' ability to make sense in a given context, that is, to get it right in terms of the ideational rules or "rationality" of a given discursive institutional setting (Schmidt 2010: 55). Bearing this in mind, we have two issues that relate to the interaction between policy and ideational spheres with respect to the topic of migration. First, as stated above, discursive institutionalism foregrounds the questions: "how can institutions make ideas actionable, if ideas create institutions?" and "do ideas have an effect on the content of interests as long as they remain mental modes?" (52). In order to answer these questions, the chapters concentrate on the framework set by Schmidt (52), which is elaborated further, and our conceptualization of how it relates to migration research.

The second issue, to locate policy objectivity in the field of migration, is somewhat complicated, especially as our conviction is that migrant rights should normatively relate to the field of human rights as defined within the context of EU integration. The European Pact on

Immigration and Asylum, passed by the European Council in October 2008, introduced three criteria in effect to acceptance and integration in Europe: linguistic competence of the receiving country; knowledge and commitment to the values of the receiving country; and access to employment (Schain 2010: 221). As a result of the Amsterdam Treaty, a set of standards, which we can use to evaluate the relative success and failure, has been formalized in the "Common Basic Principles for Immigrant Integration Policy in the European Union" and agreed in the Hague Programme in 2004 as part of a common program for integration. Among the 11 agreed-upon principles, the most important are employment, which is a key part of the integration process, and education, which is critical to preparing immigrants to be more successful and more active participants in society. Access for immigrants to institutions, goods, and services and participation of immigrants in the democratic process and in the formulation of integration policies and measures are also parts of the features of the integration process (Council of the European Union 2004: 19–24 in Schain 2010: 223).

As such, the key question for our purposes is why some policy ideas become policy while others do not. Mehta considers three prominent models: Peter Hall's view that successful ideas combine policy, political, and administrative appeal; John Kingdon's view that policy ideas succeed when entrepreneurs link them to "problem" and "politics" streams; and, finally, the work of historically sensitive scholars who argue that prevailing ideas are shaped by the contours of past policies such that longstanding models can continue to affect action and discussion even as underlying circumstances change (Mehta 2011: 28–30). In this sense, a new policy idea creates its own backers, either by forging new coalitions or by causing groups to see their interests in a different and new way. The most effective strategy for the losers in any political debate is to expand the scope of the conflict to bring in more of the uninvolved players on the previously weaker side (Schattschneider 1960). Here, interests and ideas are not really in tension and are difficult to disentangle, because some of the most promising ideas will attract strong partners willing to back them (Blyth 2002). Moreover, how problems are defined has a substantial impact on which alternatives are chosen as policy solutions (Rein and Schön 1977 in Mehta 2011: 32).

Therefore, one issue that guides us in this volume while searching for policy objectivity is procedures of problem definition. Once a problem definition becomes dominant, it excludes policies that are not consistent with its way of describing the issue. A problem definition is similar to a frame in that it bounds a complicated situation by emphasizing some element to the neglect of other (Béland 2005). The key questions for understanding problem definition are, first, how political problems become defined and, second, why one problem definition prevails over another in a particular dispute/context (Mehta 2011: 33). In contrast to approaches that view political problems as either imposed by hegemonic elites or as a reflection of the social psyche of the public (Gamson 1990), Mehta argues that problem definition is a contested process among players with varying levels of power and persuasiveness (2011). Hence, this specifies a role for active agents, allowing for a diversity of views within the population. In our case, this explains how many of the social problems that result from managing immigrants in receiving societies become political problems, requiring politicians to intervene with policy positions. Under the guidance of this introduction and review of literature in relevance to both political and discursive elaboration of migration, over the next sections, we will demonstrate the narratives that the contributors to this volume explore in order to shed light on how politics and discourses are interlinked. We propose three narratives to this extent. They are, in order, construction of the foreigner, host nations, and law and order.

Narratives at Play: The Discursive and Political Elaboration of Migration

Construction of the Foreigner

In this volume, the construction of who is foreigner within the receiving societies organically relate to problem construction with respect to immigration. Migrants often want to be integrated into society, without being assimilated, and as such they also want to be recognized as different by retaining their cultural or ethnic affiliations. The clash between universality and particularity is central to the construction of foreigners in host nations in juridical, cultural, social, and political arenas. The notion of universality proposed in official political discourses may entail a certain particularity. Indeed, the universal juridico-political acts acquire their "universal" value only if they draw on the particularity of the official and nonofficial regulatory mechanisms that are supposed to exclude whatever and whomever may pose a threat to the idea of universality (Zylinska 2004: 525). In this respect, for Simmel, the "other" is the "stranger"—and the "stranger" is an element of the group itself—an element whose membership within the group involves both being outside it and confronting it (1971 [1908]: 144 cited in Kastoryano 2010: 79). Thus, defining the "other" requires drawing real or symbolic boundaries (Lamont and Fournier 1992) in social, cultural, and moral categories.

Young states that those who reduce group difference to identity implicitly use a "logic of substance" to conceptualize groups (2000: 87–88). Under this logic a group is defined by a set of essentials that constitute its identity as a group. Individuals are said to belong to the group in so far as they have the requisite attributes. Therefore, the essentialist approach to defining social groups freezes the experienced fluidity of social relations by establishing rigid inside-outside distinctions among and across groups. According to this conceptualization, a person's social location in structures differentiated by class, gender, age, ability, sexual orientation, ethnicity, or nationality, among others, often implies predictable status in law, educational possibility, occupation, and access to resources, political power, and prestige. Not only does each of these factors enable or constrain self-determination and self-development, they also tend to reinforce the social structures (Young 2000: 95–96). For migrants, ethnicity or nationality retains no contextual or conceptual autonomy, that is, the internal and external processes that construct, challenge, and inhibit the position of migrants in the host society are constantly being negotiated. Boundary maintenance (Barth 1969) between "them" and "us" is crucial for identity formation, but it also helps to shore up a collective sense of "we," as either the migrant or a member of the host nation.

Cognitive processes are fundamental for such essentialization. For ideational scholars, cognition is a process of interpreting the world, not simply discovering it. Human cognition, therefore, has its own independent force, and the ideas our mental processes create as we interact and communicate with others wield power over our decisions and actions (Béland and Cox 2011: 11). Yet, the recognition of "otherness" comes along with specific rights in the public domain of fundamental rights (Fraser 1995 in Kastoryano 2010: 80). It implies the identification of the "other" and its inscription into cultural, social, economic, and juridical codes, requiring specific rights in the public domain. At stake are the principles of justice, equal citizenship as well as political, participative, linguistic, ethnic, or religious rights as markers of situational boundaries or diversities (Kastoryano 2010: 80). Sometimes, it is easier to incorporate a language than a religion—as the former may not carry the emotions, the historical strife, and the beliefs that the latter triggers (Zolberg and Woon 1999). Yet, it is difficult for these principles to take effect, if familiarity of the host nation with immigrant identities (sex, faith, ethnicity, status) is low. In those contexts, historical contingencies (Hattam and Yescas 2010) such as working-class status, poverty, and colonial past (Body-Gendrot 2010: 181) may have an adverse effect. In this respect, the question for social scientists remains how to interpret public policies if ideas are so ubiquitous and tend to adversely affect the recognition of otherness with due rights. A further question is how to appropriate democratic representation for all residents, both citizens and migrants, at local and national levels. The discourses and politics of migration provide an extremely relevant topic of research for these questions, policy issues, and theoretical debates. Our volume has ample contributions investing the issues fundamental to immigration and integration. The dominance of economic considerations manifest themselves in the case of the Swiss People's Party (SVP), as Afonso shows in chapter 1. Offering a nuanced picture of the migration policy preferences held by far right populist parties, Afonso details how SVP leadership must balance the competing preference of two core constituencies within the party: blue-collar workers who are chiefly suspicious of the economic impact of migration, and small business owners who see a potential benefit to carefully regulated labor migration. Chapter 2 by Eslen-Ziya and Korkut presents how overlapping gender and informality of immigrants in Turkey feeds into social and political interests overcoming the politics and political discourse around immigration issue in Turkey. In this respect, actors, based on the gendered and informal needs accruing from the Turkish labor market and economy, construct the acceptable foreigner. In chapter 3, Craig debates the procedures of asylum policy with respect to how they can be manipulated to exclude applicants from protection. Hence, even if procedures for the protection of refugees may be in place, given the non- or poor involvement of migrants themselves within the general framework of the treatment of asylum seekers, the lowest common denominator persists among the EU member states for the protection of asylum seekers. Hence, overall, this volume presents the variation in the construction of who is foreigner in different contexts, serving the interests of political and social actors. This brings us to a debate on host nations as arenas whereby varying interests and politics are situated.

Host Nations

The most widespread discourse relating to migration is the prevalent belief in host states that those who are coming into their country have duties and responsibilities that they need to understand and that their adherence to these expectations can facilitate acceptance and integration. But this is not one-way traffic because for its part the host nation has moral obligations while the guests have duties (Zylinska 2005: 530). Nevertheless, especially under the conditions of economic transformation and crises, when social inequalities and economic insecurities become heightened, societies may need someone to blame, someone to avenge upon for its disappointments; and those persons whom the public philosophy disfavors are naturally singled out for this role (Body-Gendrot 2010: 196). The clandestine "other" is predictably constructed as the cause or the scapegoat.

But then, even undocumented foreigners do not easily correspond to the stereotype of the "clandestine." They may have a certain legitimate claim to legal status based on the number of years they have resided in the host country, the services they have provided, the family ties they have cultivated, or the threats that would be faced should they return home. Therefore, the boundary between documented and undocumented is much less clear (Fassin 2001: 4). An elaboration of the moral obligations, duties, and apportioning of blame the migrants may face in host countries and societies is theme central to this volume and this debate is closely linked to the popular discourse on immigration. In chapter 4, McGarry and Drake demonstrate how Roma are constructed as not belonging to the host nation, in their discussion of the policy dilemmas in France with respect to who is responsible for Roma. Similarly, in chapter 5, Mikko Kuisma presents how this debate is the centerpiece of the ideology of True Finns. Yet, this does not manifest itself in terms of extreme nativism and hostility to foreigners, but welfare chauvinism and responsibility vis-à-vis social citizenship. The reception of such sentiments by the migrants is crucial. In chapter 6, Mahendran presents such perceptions using a dialogical approach that she employs to elaborate on how connected with the broader society the migrants feel themselves in cities such as Edinburgh and Stockholm.

Law and Order

The depiction by political forces of law and order as a tool against those usurpers of either social or individual rights is the main mechanism of discrimination through rhetoric. There are various ideational, institutional, and policy-related factors at play in this instance, and the chapters in this book address these factors. Bauman states that "building and keeping order means making friends and enemies, first and foremost, however it means purging ambivalence" (1992: 120). Thereby, this rhetoric directs its claims—or else its possession—of law and order against what these political forces consider as the culpable or the deviant. Beyond direct, as well as indirect, discrimination, these political forces deploy their interpretation of law and order in order to discriminate against those deviant others— and hence discriminate by means of rhetorical subjection. In this context, to give an example, the migrant becomes the "other" who threatens "our" wealth, promising no more than uncertainty, insecurity, and danger. Diken qualified this action as the theft of enjoyment, that is, the particular way the "other" enjoys and steals "my" employment (2004: 89).

But where do these reactions derive their legitimacy from? Political forces seeking law and order subscribe to two methods in their attempts to establish legitimacy. The first method is seeking legitimacy in the course of alienating the migrant through the active process of policing borders between them and us, a by-product of which is fostering a collective consciousness and solidarity. Strictly speaking, they do not attain legitimacy by attacking the migrants but by espousing rhetoric that plays on fear and by showing solidarity with those who feel threatened by immigration. By presenting a tough stance on immigration, political forces seeking law and order legitimate their position as the public authority to stem the tide of waves of migration. Therefore, to quote an example, certain political parties find legitimacy pursuing new types of rhetorical strategies in order to legitimate their actions. In an attempt to highlight the assumed cultural dangers posed by minority populations, populist parties move beyond the boundaries of political correctness and avail themselves of a political vocabulary and rhetorical devices generally considered unacceptable by mainstream actors. An additional strategy, set against the backdrop of welfare cuts and ongoing economic crisis, is to scapegoat migrants as bearing responsibility for the financial insecurity experienced by many in the host nation. Given the conditions of liberalization and decentralization of provisions of social policy, migrants, minorities, or health care dependents have become useful targets.

The contemporary welfare apparatus established new entrance requirements and set a new "needs talk" for those it admitted, meaning that newcomers would have to prove their need for assistance. Tighter boundaries formed around the welfare state. As the welfare system drew in clients on the basis of what they lacked as opposed to what they contributed, welfare policy became informed by negative principles. It has been premised on a poverty discourse that failed to acknowledge multiple needs; it rested on surveillance techniques and disciplinary practices that pathologized and stigmatized (Haney 2002: 234–235, 246). Along with increasing immigration, a metaphor of the undeserving "other" haunts the debates around the future of Western welfare states. Or else, the immigrants have filled in service roles that either welfare regimes could not deliver due to their costs or else did not deliver because of the interests intrinsic to the functioning of societies on multiple fields such as gender, economic competitiveness, and employment relations. While far right populist parties are the chief actors to have exploited this phenomenon, they are not the only ones. Indeed, parties of the mainstream left, historically ambiguous toward unregulated immigration, have openly voiced doubts across Europe about the ability of welfare states and national labor markets to absorb substantial numbers of newcomers. Here, it is important to stress that the opposition is not predicated on cultural differences, but on the assumed impact that migrants might have on institutions cherished by the center-left.

The recent surge of populist and extreme right parties to political dominance in several (mainly West) European countries has produced a vast and diverse scholarship in political science and sociology. Much of it has been focused on explaining the reasons for the electoral success of these parties (Hainsworth 2008; Mudde 2007). This volume also offers contributions to this literature particularly in terms of negotiating strategies and articulating discourse, but challenges some dominant ideas on populist party success or motivation. Often the discussion has turned to migration and globalization as underlying causes. As a result of the pressures caused by immigration, the citizens of European nation-states have become increasingly reluctant to share their welfare system with newcomers. This situation opens up an opportunity for xenophobic parties to mobilize that part of the population who considers itself under threat from outside forces. This "welfare chauvinism" can be considered a type of politics of fear, that is, fear from an external threat—either imagined or real. At the same time, such politics have offered several new political parties an opportunity to gain a new prominent position in a political landscape where traditional political allegiances are shifting and where it is electorally rewarding to distance oneself from the political establishment of the political middle, which is often seen as cosmopolitan, and in favor of further globalization. This sociopolitical development may indeed be reaching beyond Western Europe. As Judt argues,

> Globalization itself—the "flat" earth of so many fantasies—will be a source of fear and uncertainty to billions of people, who will turn to their leaders for protection. "Identities" will grow mean and tight, as the indigent and the uprooted beat upon the ever-rising walls of gated communities from Delhi to Dallas. Being "Danish" or "Italian," even "American" or "European" won't just be an identity; it will be a rebuff and a reproof to those whom it excludes. (*New York Review of Book* February 23, 2010)

This argument explains why people in Europe have in substantial numbers voted for parties that seek to restrict immigration, or even push out immigrant populations. But it brings out the issue of human rights of migrants as problematic in advanced democracies. In other words, the law and order rhetoric needs to be seen as a phenomenon both broader and narrower than what is usually captured under headings like racist mobilization, anti-immigrant politics, xenophobia, right-wing extremism, radical right, and populism. The concept is broader because we can see it as a rhetoric that is not only found among parties that are considered to be on the extreme right of the political spectrum; it is a discourse that pervades a variety of political campaigns of different ideological backing.

At the same time, however, it is narrower because it is a rhetoric that always seeks to reduce a broad range of societal phenomena to problems of security and control. Law-and-order politics inflates public anxieties and argues that there is an urgent imperative of control, to name a few, welfare, border, reproduction, public security, and zero tolerance policies.

In chapter 7, Gudbrandsen explores the sources of restrictive refugee policy in the Scandinavian states over the past decades. Questioning broad claims about the role of public opinion in general as a driver of restrictive policies, she shows that parties move in a restrictive direction on asylum policy when core-voting constituencies of the party at hand prefer such policies. In chapter 8, Scholten analyzes the shifting instruments deployed by the Dutch state and key municipalities seeking to integrate migrants granted residency. In contrast to the largely static literature on "national models" of integration, Scholten demonstrates that the policies of Amsterdam and Rotterdam not only have come to diverge from those of the Dutch state, but also from one another. The Dutch capital maintains a targeted and modified variant of the multiculturalist approach, while Rotterdam has opted for a decidedly more assimilationist route. Shifting the focus to political parties, Spehar, Bucken-Knapp, and Hinnfors show in chapter 9 not all mainstream political actors support restrictive entry policies. Examining the case of Sweden, which since 2008 has the most liberal labor migration policies in the Organization for Economic Co-operation and Development (OECD), they detail how such openness resulted from the concerted effort of center-right parties and the Greens to open Sweden's borders to third-country nationals, a preference stemming chiefly from ideological considerations.

PART I

Constructiono fth eF oreigner

CHAPTER 1

Whose Interests Do Radical Right Parties Really Represent? The Migration Policy Agenda of the Swiss People's Party between Nativism and Neoliberalism

Alexandre Afonso

Introduction

Since the late 1980s, right-wing populist parties—parties that combine authoritarianism (law and order and traditional values), nativism (the protection of the interests of the native-born over those of immigrants), and populism (a critique of the political and economic establishment) at the core of their ideology—have emerged as a significant electoral and parliamentary force in Western Europe (Mudde 2007). In a number of countries, the electoral success of these parties has relied on an "unholy alliance" between blue-collar workers who traditionally voted for the left, and small business owners who traditionally voted for the right (Kitschelt and McGann 1995: 10–11; Ivarsflaten 2005a: 465; Oesch 2008a). Though the reasons leading voters with apparently contradictory economic interests to vote for the same political parties have received extensive attention in the literature, little research has been devoted to the way party elites articulate these interests within their policy agenda. In this chapter, I explore the socioeconomic interests that characterize the electoral constituency of one of the strongest radical right parties in Western Europe, the Schweizerische Volkspartei (Swiss People's Party [SVP]), and the way its party elites seek to reconcile these interests in their immigration policy agenda. Immigration policy is considered here as a policy with different distributive consequences across socioeconomic groups, and not only as a policy guided by values and identity concerns.

Questioning the idea that the policy agenda of this party is geared only toward migration control, I argue that it seeks to reconcile a nativist rhetoric catering to its working-class clientele, on the one hand, and neoliberal policies that cater to its business clientele, on the other. Hence, while the SVP has claimed to champion immigration control to protect native workers, it has also advocated measures to maintain or open entry channels for low-wage migrant employment and cater to its clientele of small business owners who have been historically dependent on low-skilled migration. As will be shown in the light of a number of policy reforms since the 1990s, the articulation of these interests has been characterized by many paradoxes and internal conflicts between different factions within the party, and between its electoral base and its elected representatives. My analysis emphasizes the role of political salience in influencing the strategies of party elites: while issues with a low political salience allow the neoliberal strand to prevail, high salience tends to drive back the party agenda toward stricter immigration control.

The chapter is structured as follows. In the first section, I outline the challenges radical right parties face when articulating the interests of different social classes in their policy agendas. In the second section, I outline how these diverging economic interests play out in the field of immigration policy, and present a typology of immigration policy agendas taking into account these distributive dilemmas. Then, I explore these elements in the Swiss case in light of recent immigration policy reforms, namely the free movement of workers with the European Union (EU), the regulation of undeclared work, and revision of the Aliens law. In these different cases, I emphasize the conflicts within different strands in the party regarding immigration policy reform, and the strategies deployed by party elites to reconcile them.

Cross-Class Alliances and Radical Right Party Agendas

In general, it seems fairly reasonable to assume that the policies advocated by parties are closely connected to the interests of their core constituencies, because party leaders are dependent on votes to stay in office. Anthony Downs was among the first to argue "parties formulate policies in order to win elections, rather than win elections in order to formulate policies" (1957: 28). Even if this assumption is certainly too one-dimensional because party elites may pursue different, and sometimes contradictory, objectives (Strom 1990: 566–570), it nevertheless points out that public policies cannot be analyzed in isolation from the electoral interests of the parties that enforce them. In this chapter, I am interested in how right-wing populist parties articulate the sometimes contradictory interests of their electorate. Interests are analyzed here essentially as economic preferences determined by the position of socioeconomic groups in the political economy and labor market (Gourevitch 1986; Swenson 2002). I draw on the assumption that party policies are essentially the reflection of the power balance between different electoral interests within a party. If this somewhat materialist focus may be too simplistic, as it relegates questions of identity and culture to the background, it nevertheless highlights the specific problems of reconciling the divergent economic interests characterizing the clientele of national populist parties, as well as the redistributive implications of immigration policy.

In many ways, the articulation of these heterogeneous economic interests in unified party policy agendas is an exercise in contortionism for political parties. If party platforms have to display a certain degree of internal coherence, the interests of voters are much more heterogeneous because the electoral base of political parties is also heterogeneous; different social groups may vote for the same parties for different reasons, and socioeconomic groups with similar standards of living may have radically opposed preferences. For instance, some relatively privileged segments of new middle classes vote for left parties, while substantial segments of the working-class vote for the national conservative right (Oesch 2008a, 2008b). As their social base becomes more heterogeneous, political parties have to represent possibly contradicting interests, thereby making it more difficult to formulate policy agendas without alienating part of the electorate. Moreover, this heterogeneous electoral base may also translate into different factions within party elites, generating potential conflicts between them.

Party leaderships can be assumed to be aware of these divergent interests and use different strategies to solve them. For instance, they may seek to stay ambiguous or "blur" their agenda on certain issues to maximize their vote share and avoid the issues on which different sections of their voters disagree, or on which the party elites differ from their voters. Rovny (2012: 1) argues that "parties emphasize their stance on some issue dimensions, while strategically evading positioning on others, in order to mask the distance between themselves and their voters." Hence, a party may want to adopt clear ideological positions on an aspect that federates different segments of the electorate, and stay vague or conceal its positions on aspects susceptible to create disagreements. However, if "blurring" strategies are common in electoral politics, they may be more problematic when it comes to actual policymaking. The ability of parties to blur or conceal their position is more difficult once they are elected in parliament, and even more so when they hold office, when concrete policy choices have to be made. In these contexts, the contradictions and problems of reconciling the interests of different social classes in a common policy agenda may become more visible and potentially damaging electorally, depending on the salience of these issues with voters.

Radical right parties are particularly exposed to these kinds of dilemmas because of the cross-class composition of their electorate (Ivarsflaten 2005a; Oesch 2008a; Rovny 2012). In general, radical right parties have made substantial electoral advances in countries in which they managed to source votes from two specific socioeconomic groups, namely—and primarily—the blue-collar working class who traditionally voted for the left and—to a lesser extent—the *petite bourgeoisie* (shopkeepers, artisans, and independents) who traditionally voted for the right, even if the respective balance of these two groups varies across countries. Hence, production workers, service workers, and clerks taken together represented 68 percent of the electorate of the Austrian FPÖ in 2002, and 67 percent of the Flemish *Vlaams Blok* in 2002, while they only represented 39 percent of SVP voters in Switzerland (Oesch 2008a: 358). In Switzerland, salaried middle classes, big employers, and small business holders still constituted the largest part of the electorate of the populist right. What is particularly interesting is that these two groups have historically advocated different agendas in terms of economic policy, the former championing redistribution and the expansion of the welfare state, and the latter opposing state interventionism and taxation. The objective alliance of these socioeconomic groups with a priori contradictory interests has been observed in a number of national populist parties in Europe (Ivarsflaten 2005a: 465–466), and has been analyzed by a now relatively vast literature (ibid.; Kitschelt and McGann 1995; Lubbers et al. 2002; Mayer 2002; McGann and Kitschelt 2005).

There have been different approaches to explain the emergence of this cross-class alliance. The first approach, initially formulated by Kitschelt and McGann, assumed that socioeconomic change had induced a realignment of preferences of previously opposed social groups, thereby allowing radical right parties to use a "winning formula" combining authoritarianism and neoliberalism (1995). This combination allegedly allowed radical right parties to appeal to the antistatist *petite bourgeoisie*, whereas the anti-immigration agenda appealed to a growing fringe of the working class that felt threatened by immigration and globalization. The second approach argues that neoliberalism does not play such a prominent role in the first place in the success of populist radical right parties. De Lange (2007) and Mudde (2007) notably showed that populist radical right parties do not advocate similar economic policies everywhere, and populist parties in France, Belgium, and the Netherlands have adopted more centrist positions in economic terms.

While earlier analyses emphasized the neoliberal ideology of radical right parties in the 1980s, this picture no longer seems accurate to describe a large part of these parties today. Based on data on party placement in 17 countries, Rovny shows that radical right parties "emphasize and take clear ideological stances on the authoritarian fringe of the non-economic dimension, while deliberately avoiding precise economic placement" (2012: 19). In short, they are particularly prone to use the "blurring" strategy outlined above to please their electorate with different economic preferences. However, once again, this strategy is more difficult to pursue when radical right parties are engaged in actual policymaking, and even more so when they take part in government. The blurring strategy is less of an option, and their actual economic policy agenda becomes more salient for voters.

If these parties have to vote on legislative proposals in which the interests of their different constituencies cannot be reconciled, a central question is *whose interests* they will ultimately support, and when they will favor one specific segment of the electorate over another. Indeed, even if economic issues have been said not to be a central element for the working-class electorate of the radical right (Ivarsflaten 2005b; Oesch 2008a), supporting economic policies that are perceived to go against the interests of their voters can still be risky for the elites. Parties can appear as "betraying" part of their constituency, as shown by the electoral misfortunes of some parties after they accessed public office. The Austrian Freedom Party, for instance, implemented a series of neoliberal policies in alliance with the conservative ÖVP (*Österreichische Volkspartei*) that proved highly unpopular with its electorate, and underwent an electoral collapse just after it assumed office (Heinisch 2003). In the 2012 Dutch general election, Geert Wilders's PVV (Partij voor de Vrijheid) similarly underwent a major electoral setback after it had committed itself to support a right-wing government determined to implement tough austerity measures.

As a working hypothesis, one can assume that the political salience of issues plays a prominent role because salience has asymmetric consequences for the influence of different socioeconomic groups in politics. As Culpepper convincingly shows in the case of corporate governance reforms, business interests tend to prevail when issues have low salience or highly technical (2010: 5ff.). When issues become politically salient, however, policymakers are spurred to pay more attention to the preferences of the median voter, and they may be less willing to favor business interests if chances of reelection are at stake. Transposing this logic to radical right parties, one can assume that party elites will support the interests of the business segments when issues are weakly salient. By contrast, when issues are very salient, party elites will avoid advocating policies that are perceived to go against the interests of their working-class voters, because this constituency is more interesting in terms of votes. Small businessmen will be more aware of issues that relate to their special preferences even if they are not much debated, while the blue-collar electorate has more diffuse interests and will pay attention only when issues become prominent in the media. While the blue-collar electorate is much bigger—the one with the biggest growth potential—the "business" faction can entail other benefits, such as funding or other forms of financial support. In short, "betraying" the working-class electorate is easier when issues keep a low profile. This proposition will be explored in the case of immigration policy, which can also be considered as a policy with redistributive implications for different constituencies, and across cases displaying different degrees of salience as measured by their coverage in the media.

Migration Policy and Socioeconomic Interests

In this section, I argue that migration policy can be understood as a policy with different distributional consequences across different socioeconomic groups, which makes it difficult for radical right parties to advocate policies that satisfy both their working class and their small business clientele. My approach draws on two assumptions. The first is that immigration policy is a policy guided not only by values or identities but also by economic interests, entails different socioeconomic implications for different economic groups, and is influenced by the power balance between different socioeconomic interests (Freeman 1995; Tichenor 2002: 23–26). The second is that populist radical right parties do not only make a rhetoric use of anti-immigration sentiments for electoral purposes, but also pursue political-economic objectives in their immigration policy agenda, reflecting the interests of the social constituencies they represent. In order to explore the economic objectives that can be pursued through immigration policy, I draw upon a typology of immigration policy agendas differentiating positions over the admission of immigrants and immigrant rights.

In his analysis of immigration policy in the United States, Tichenor outlines a two-dimensional typology of immigration preferences that he applies to US interest groups and political parties (2002: 50). Immigration policy preferences can be classified along two dimensions, namely the admission of immigrants (the restrictiveness of conditions regarding access to a country and its labor market) and the rights granted to them once in the country (the requirements regarding permanent stay, access to social security, mobility on the labor market, access to citizenship) (Ruhs and Martin 2008). First, *classic exclusionists* advocate both tight immigration control and restrictive immigrant rights. Immigration should be tightly restricted and rights for foreigners should be limited to reduce incentives for immigrants to enter the country. This is the archetypal stance assumed to be endorsed by populist radical right parties. Second, *national egalitarians* advocate tight immigration control and tend to oppose temporary migrant worker programs, but support equal rights for immigrants once they have been admitted in the country and tight control of labor standards. The leading idea of this stance is to defend the interests of national workers and, therefore, not to allow the creation of a secondary labor market of immigrants paid at lower rates. Within the category of immigrant rights, one could also classify measures of labor market regulation such as labor inspection or fight against illegal employment, drawing on the idea that these measures—at least in principle—prevent the exploitation of migrant workers. Third, *free-market expansionists* advocate rather open immigration policies but oppose the expansion of immigrant rights to maintain a source of cheap foreign labor for businesses. Groups within this category would favor temporary worker programs but would oppose sanctions against employers employing illegal immigrants, which de facto fosters the creation of dual labor markets, or an "industrial reserve army" (Castles and Kosack 1972; Piore 1979). Finally, *cosmopolitans* advocate both open door policies and expansive immigrant rights.

In light of the cross-class socioeconomic base of populist radical right parties, this typology can help outline the conflicts faced by these parties in articulating immigration policy agendas that can rally both working-class voters and small business owners. Hence, whereas native working-class voters may favor either a "classic exclusionist" or an "egalitarian nationalist" stance either to keep immigrants out or at least prevent them from undercutting wages by granting them the same rights as indigenous workers, small business owners may rather favor a free-market expansionist stance to access a pool of low-wage workers with limited rights. This is, for instance, particularly important in the hospitality sector, which is dependent to a large extent on migrant workers. Small business owners and smallholders have an interest in the availability of cheap immigrant labor, contrary to native blue-collar workers. If they want to reconcile the two social groups that they claim to represent, national populist parties face a dilemma between different agendas, notably between a classic exclusionist, national-egalitarian, and free-market expansionist stance. In connection with the role of political salience outlined in the previous section, one can assume that radical right parties will be more prone to advocate a free-market expansionist position in line with the preferences of their business clientele on issues that are weakly salient, while they may adopt a national-egalitarian or classic exclusionist position, believed to be more in line with the preferences of their working-class voters, on issues that are highly salient. This idea will be explored in the case of the SVP in the next section.

The SVP and Immigration Policy in Switzerland

Switzerland is an interesting case for the exploration of the immigration policy agenda of radical right parties. On the one hand, it houses one of the most powerful radical right parties in Europe. On the other hand, immigration has played a central role in its political economy. Immigration policy reforms have regularly featured high on the agenda, and the electoral strength of the SVP has allowed it to influence those reforms quite substantially, even if they have also regularly revealed the conflicts and paradoxes between different factions within the party.

The SVP is now by far the biggest Swiss party in electoral terms with 26.6 percent, far above the Social Democrats with 18.7 percent in the 2011 national elections. Reputational analyses indicate that it has even become the single most important actor in the Swiss decision-making system (Fischer et al. 2009: 45). The party doubled its representation in the lower chamber over the past 20 years, from 25 seats (out of 200) in 1991 to 54 in 2011 (Kriesi and Trechsel 2008: 93). As noted by McGann and Kitschelt, the SVP, together with the Austrian FPÖ, has been the only radical right party in Western Europe to outvote its center-right counterparts (2005: 147). The SVP first outvoted the liberal FDP by 3 percent in 1999, and the gap in subsequent elections has been constantly increasing, reaching 13.1 percent at the 2007 elections. In many respects, this evolution can be put in relation with a fundamental change in party elites from the late 1980s onward (Kriesi and Trechsel 2008: 94–95). While the party traditionally represented farmers, self-employed workers, and artisans with strongholds in rural areas, a new elite within the party emerged around the emblematic figure of businessman Christoph Blocher in the late 1980s, making the opposition to European integration and uncontrolled immigration the central themes of the party agenda. The SVP takes part in the seven-member government with two ministers, increasing its representation at the expense of the Christian Democrats in 2003.

In many respects, the SVP has sought to present itself as the "party of the economy" and champion business interests, with less state interventionism, less social protection, and less bureaucracy. At the same time, it has been using an anti-immigration rhetoric supposed to appeal to the working class and advocated measures of protection for its traditional clientele of farmers and small shopkeepers in agricultural and competition policy. The SVP embodies fairly well the conflicts between the core electoral groups of radical right parties emphasized above, even if it has kept a more neoliberal profile than some of its counterparts in other countries. This can be put in relation with the somewhat different power balance within its electorate. The salaried middle classes and the "small traditional bourgeoisie" still account for a bigger share of the SVP electorate than the "extended working class," who constitute the highest share of voters of the radical right in Belgium or Austria (Oesch and Rennwald 2010; Oesch 2008a: 358).

Also, in contrast to developments in other countries, this apparently contradictory combination of neoliberalism and anti-immigration discourse has not translated into major electoral setbacks. In a system of grand coalition, the SVP can always claim that its preferences are ignored by other parties even if it takes part in government, and regularly uses the tools of direct democracy (initiatives and referendums) to challenge government decisions. In Switzerland, any law passed in parliament can be challenged in a referendum if 50,000 citizens request so by way of signature. The SVP has been the keenest user of this institutional tool to challenge government policies. This set of institutions has enabled the party to avoid electoral sanctions until now, even if its electoral share has declined somewhat in the 2011 national elections (down to 2.3 percent). However, this combination has also fostered divisions within the party between an "economic-liberal" wing interested in limiting state intervention and a "xenophobic-authoritarian" wing keen on law and order, traditional values, and immigration control.

Immigration has played an especially important role in the labor market in Switzerland, one of the European countries with the highest share of immigrants in its workforce. In 2009, 22.9 percent of the Swiss population did not have Swiss citizenship (Swiss Statistics Office 20012). The proportion of immigrants was even greater in some economic sectors such as hotels and restaurants (42.5 percent), or construction (32.6 percent) (ibid.). The dependence of the Swiss economy on foreign labor has been underpinned by policies of immigration control of the free-market expansionist type in the typology proposed above. This model, however, has eroded since the 1980s as migrants could access a wider range of rights with a longer stay status (Piguet 2004). Although admission policy in Switzerland after World War II has been fairly liberal—despite a system of immigration quotas—the rights granted to migrants, in contrast, have been restrictive (ibid.). In particular, precarious stay statuses and temporary work permits introduced in the 1960s were especially designed to provide low-skilled labor to domestic, partly sheltered sectors of the economy, such as agriculture, construction, hotels and restaurants, and crafts, without allowing migrants to stay if they lost their jobs (Dhima 1991). In many ways, the economic sectors benefitting from these kinds of work permits also represented the traditional clientele of the SVP (Kriesi and Trechsel 2008: 95), which makes it particularly interesting to analyze its migration policy agenda in the light of the socioeconomic interests of its voters. While its anti-immigration discourse has been a major trigger of its success among blue-collar workers, its electorate of farmers and small businessmen has traditionally been very dependent on sources of cheap foreign labor.

Methodsa ndC ases

In order to explore the discourse and actions of the SVP in the field of immigration policy, I analyze its positions and the parliamentary interventions of its MPs over three legislative reforms in the mid-2000s: the ratification of the bilateral agreement on the free movement of workers between Switzerland and the EU (2005), the revision of the Aliens Act (2005), and the law on undeclared work (2005). These three reforms touched upon the regulation of immigration and had a strong economic component at the same time. Moreover, they vary in terms of their political salience. As proposed by Epstein and Segal (2000), a fairly reliable proxy to assess the salience of issues among political actors, as well as voters, is the coverage they receive in the media (2000). Hence, the case selection provides for different degrees of salience as measured by media coverage. I use the number of articles devoted to a topic in the biggest quality newspaper in Switzerland, the *Neue Zürcher Zeitung* during the years 2004 and 2005 as an indicator of salience. The search was carried out on November 5, 2012, on the archive server of the NZZ (http://nzz.gbi.de/NZZ.ein) with the timespan January 1, 2004–December 31, 2005, thereby allowing for some time before and after the issues were debated in Parliament.

The first case, the free movement of workers with the EU, was probably one of the most debated issues in Swiss politics in recent years. As it involved the overall relationship between Switzerland and the EU, the referendums on these issues have been considered among the most important votes in recent history, and this issue has been voted on four times since 2000: once on labor market opening for the EU15 in 2000, once on the extension to ten accession states in 2005, once on the extension to Bulgaria and Romania in 2007, and once on the confirmation of the initial agreement in 2009 (Afonso 2010; Fischer et al. 2002; Sciarini 2002). Hence, a search with the words *Personenfreizügigkeit* (free movement of persons) and "European Union" returned 531 hits in the period under scrutiny. The second case, the revision of the Aliens law, which regulated the entry of non-EU migrants, was also voted on in a referendum, but can certainly be considered less salient than the free movement of workers. Accordingly, a search with the words *Ausländergesetz* (Aliens law) returns 145 hits, showing a clearly lower degree of salience. Finally, the law on undeclared work was even less discussed, and was not challenged in a referendum. A search with the words *Schwarzarbeit* (undeclared work) and *Gesetz* (law) returned 47 hits.

I have left aside another prominent area of immigration regulation, asylum laws, because it does not contain such an important distributive-redistributive dimension in economic terms, and does not generate substantial distributional conflicts. The "business" strand of the party basically supports a restrictive stance in this domain because asylum policy is only considered as a net cost for the Swiss economy, while labor migration policies are perceived as a major asset. The case studies are based upon the analysis of parliamentary debates (*Amtliches Bulletin*), official documents from the Swiss federal administration, as well as an analysis of the coverage of the policy reforms in the major Swiss quality newspapers (*Le Temps*, *Neue Zürcher Zeitung*, *Tages Anzeiger*). In each case, I show the stance of the party with respect to the economic aspect of these reforms, and provide quotations mainly from parliamentary debates to substantiate the case study analysis (Moravcsik 2010).

Economic Interests and Migration Policy Reforms

Agreements on the Free Movement of Workers with the EU

The establishment of the free movement of workers with the EU after the EU enlargement of 2004 was probably the case in which the conflicts between the different interests represented by the SVP were the most visible. Switzerland, which is not a member of the EU, concluded a series of bilateral agreements with the EU on specific domains, including the free movement of workers (Afonso 2010; Fischer et al. 2002). To replace the system of quotas that was hitherto in force, EU citizens— including those of the accession states that joined in 2004—would be entitled to freely move and seek employment on the Swiss labor market after a transitional period. This agreement was part of a wider series of agreement that would allow Swiss companies to access a single market on a reciprocity basis, and—after a relatively long transitional period— source labor from EU countries in an unrestricted manner. As the Swiss labor market would become fully open to EU migration, trade unions asked for regulation measures to protect local wage standards, notably through the creation of minimum wages, the universal applicability of collective bargaining, or the reinforcement of labor inspection (ibid.).

The SVP showed a divided stance between its "neoliberal" and "xenophobic" wings both during parliamentary debates and the referendum campaign related to this agreement. While the economic wing was ready to support the bilateral agreement to access new markets, ensure the continuity of exports to the EU, and access a large pool of labor in EU countries, the xenophobic wing refused the agreement and pleaded for the maintenance of mechanisms of immigration control on a unilateral basis. It also strongly criticized employer associations, accused of collusion with trade unions in agreeing measures to regulate the labor market against downward wage pressures. As a newspaper editorial stated, "the SVP is playing a double game: on the one hand, business circles [within the party] are looking toward markets in the East. On the other hand, the party spreads fears of mass immigration and opposes binding collective labor agreements to protect local workers" (*Neue Zürcher Zeitung* 2004: 13).

If the party was divided as to the "admission policy" side of this reform, it was united as to the "rights" side, in its sharp opposition to measures to protect the Swiss labor market from downward wage competition. The following citations, one from a member of the xenophobic wing and the other from a prominent representative of the economic wing, illustrate these different positions:

> "Flanking measures" will never be enough, because the movement of downward leveling is inevitable! The [president of the Swiss Trade Union Federation] says that it is "suicidal" not to implement protection measures for the labor market in one way or another. My reply is that there is no way we will be able to implement these measures successfully, because the free movement of workers itself is suicidal! The employers are always playing the same tune and say that we would have equal access to the emerging markets. For this I have to say: This association is giving millions [to the probilateral agreements] campaign with a false argument, because the markets are already open. It is not about opening markets, but it is a question of free immigration. (Luzi Stamm [SVP], *Amtliches Bulletin* 2004: 2006)
>
> It is clear that we need the markets in Central and Eastern Europe in order to generate some much needed economic growth in Switzerland. The price, however, must not be that we have to set up "flanking measures" that undermine our competitiveness here in Switzerland. This cannot be so! There is something that continues to be a big advantage for Switzerland in international competition: our liberal economic order. We need to preserve this economic system, especially the labor law. We may lose this advantage with these flanking measures. (Peter Spuhler [SVP], *Amtliches Bulletin* 2004: 1990)

While the first citation may represent the classic exclusionist stance outlined in the previous section, the second is more in line with the free-market expansionist stance. In the final parliamentary vote, in which both labor market opening and measures of labor market protection were bundled together, the SVP was split: 15 MPs accepted the bilateral agreement whereas 36 voted against it (Nominal Vote on Bilateral Agreement on Free Movement of Workers 2004). After a referendum was launched against the bilateral agreement by a small extreme right party, the Swiss Democrats, the party direction hesitated as to which position to adopt, but then decided to oppose the agreement, while some prominent party members closer to business circles supported it (*Tages Anzeiger* 2011). It must be noted that an overwhelming majority of the electoral base of the party voted against the agreement, showing that the xenophobic wing is clearly the one that SVP voters tend to follow. When it came to voting on the continuation of the bilateral agreement in February 2009, dissensions appeared again. Twenty-four SVP MPs supported the continuation of the agreement, while the overwhelming majority opposed it (*Neue Zürcher Zeitung* 2008; *Tages Anzeiger* 2011). The party direction first refused to challenge the agreement, which caused significant resistance from many cantonal sections. Some of them launched their own campaign of signatures against the agreement. When the referendum challenge resulted in a popular vote, the party delegates' assembly decided to support a "no" by 432 against 45 votes, showing that the party base was strongly against the agreement while the elites had tried to prevent the party from engaging in a political campaign that would reveal its internal dissensions. The party direction and its leader, Christoph Blocher, having to negotiate the positions of both the business and the xenophobic strand were accused of confusing the party's electoral base (ibid.). The vast majority of SVP voters opposed opening the Swiss labor market to EU workers, even if this was less clear than in previous referendums (Hirter and Linder 2009).

Revision of the Aliens Act

The revision of *Ausländergesetz* (the Swiss Aliens Act) provided for an update of the existing legislation on immigration that dated back to 1931. Set against the fact that intra-EU migration would be regulated exclusively by the bilateral agreement on the free movement of workers analyzed above, the Aliens Act would exclusively regulate the admission and employment rights of non-EU citizens (Afonso 2007: 27; Conseil Fédéral 2002b). In line with reforms carried out elsewhere, the initial focus of the legislative revision was to restrict the entry of non-EU immigrants to high-skilled personnel, while low-skilled workers should be sourced exclusively from EU countries. In the face of higher unemployment rates of low-skilled immigrants throughout the 1990s, this measure was thought to prevent low-skilled immigrants from imposing a further burden on the welfare system (Afonso 2005). On the other hand, as admission was becoming more selective, a certain number of improvements in terms of rights, such as family reunification, were provided. The initial version of the piece of legislation provided for a strict closure of the labor market for non-EU unskilled migrants.

When the project was examined by parliament, a proposal mainly supported by the SVP proposed to introduce a new type of short-term permits for low-skilled non-EU migrants, thereby watering down the limitation of admission to high-skilled migration. These permits would not be renewable and would not allow for family reunification. In many respects, this new status shared many similarities with the seasonal guest-worker schemes that Switzerland had run between the 1950s and 1990s (Afonso 2007: 10). These permits were geared to provide unskilled labor to the domestic sectors of the economy such as agriculture, tourism, or catering, and were progressively phased out on both humanitarian and economic grounds, as they fostered the survival of obsolete economic structures based on low wages (Sheldon 2001). Eventually, this proposal was refused in the plenary session of parliament despite the support of the SVP group. However, another proposal by a SVP MP relaxing the skills criteria for admission, thereby allowing low-skill non-EU migrants to enter the Swiss labor market, was accepted by a short majority (*Le Temps* 2004). This was explicitly justified by the need to provide low-skilled personnel for some economic branches that could not find workers on the Swiss or EU labor market:

> Economic sectors and regions that rely on the recruitment of low skilled workers—such as hospitality, health care, construction, agriculture and horticulture—also have a right to a sustainable future, to a sustainable economy. These branches fulfill to a large extent a general interest for the economy, especially in rural regions. [...] What is qualification? For me it is still also hard work—and not only the distinction between manual labor and office labor. [...] I therefore ask you to agree to the request of the minority here, because it is important that the allocation of permits is not made alone according to qualifications. (Hansjörg Walter [SVP], *Amtliches Bulletin, Nationalrat* 2004: 686)

After this proposal was accepted with the support of other right-wing parties, it came in for extensive criticism from the Social Democrats and Greens, who would eventually vote against the law in the final vote after supplementary measures to limit migrant rights were introduced by the right-wing majority in Parliament:

> A bit discriminatory, but relentlessly advantageous economically, that is the motto of the migration policy of the SVP [...]: cheap labor in agriculture, cheap labor via short-term permits, with no clear or strict controls on wages and working conditions through collective bargaining agreements, universal applicability and minimum wages. (André Daguet [SP], *Amtliches Bulletin* Nationalrat 2004: 656)

Along similar lines, the newspaper *Le Temps* (2004) emphasized "the ambiguous position of the party, strongly opposed to the extension of free movement of people, a majority of SVP MPs support nevertheless the arrival of unskilled workers who are undemanding in terms of wages."

A referendum led by left-wing parties challenged the act in a popular vote, but it was accepted by 68 percent of voters on September 24, 2006 (Results Referendum on Swiss Aliens Law 2006). In this case, in slight contrast to the bilateral agreement on the free movement of workers, the free-market expansionist stance seems to have prevailed, and did not give rise to substantial conflicts within the party. This case, also, was clearly less politically salient than the free movement of workers, thereby allowing a more business-friendly stance to prevail without generating much resistance from the electoral base of the party.

Undeclared Work

The regulation of undeclared work can be considered an important policy element that touches closely upon the regulation of immigrant employment. Undeclared work is "a form of social dumping that introduces unfair competition between firms on the basis of low wages and the non-payment of social security benefits" (Labor Administration and Inspection Program 2010: 5). A lax regulation of undeclared work de facto creates incentives to employ low-wage immigrant workers and an increase in inequalities. Interestingly, the SVP was the most vehement opponent of a reinforcement of labor market inspection and sanctions against employers making use of undeclared work. The revision of this piece of legislation, however, was certainly the least politically salient of the three analyzed here, as it was protracted for a long time and ultimately voted on in haste just before one of the referendums on the free movement of workers.

The project of a federal law against undeclared work was presented to parliament in 2002 and adopted only in June 2006 (Conseil Fédéral 2002a). On the one hand, a series of administrative adaptations would make it easier for companies to declare workers and collect social security contributions through a new, allegedly less bureaucratic, system of work declaration. This would be done through modifications in the legislation on unemployment, pension, and accidents insurance (3423–3425). On the other hand, labor market control would be enhanced, the transfer of information between different administrative entities would be facilitated, and sanctions against contravening companies would be strengthened (3423). The last change would involve above all tougher sanctions for employers, with higher fines, the exclusion of companies from public tenders, or possibly the suppression of public subsidies for companies employing workers illegally.

Whereas all parties acknowledged in principle the importance of fighting undeclared work, there were substantial conflicts as to how to achieve it. Social Democrats and Greens advocated a strengthening of sanctions for contravening employers, while right-wing parties emphasized the lightening of the bureaucratic burden on companies and reductions in payroll taxes. For its part, the SVP opposed the most vehemently the strengthening of sanctions against companies, arguing that the main problem was the bureaucratic burden and payroll taxes. As a member of the economic wing of the SVP argued,

> We have here a proposal from the Federal Council on a new law against undeclared work. Here in Switzerland, when we want to introduce a new law, we have to achieve an effect on a specific goal and not simply have another law that wants other laws to achieve their goal. My question is: what can we do here? There are two ways. The first is to reduce payroll taxes, which are a big incentive for undeclared work. The second is to reduce the bureaucratic hurdles to help entrepreneurs and small businesses. (Peter Spuhler [SVP], *Amtliches Bulletin* Nationalrat 2005: 697)

Moreover, the party strongly opposed the possibility to withdraw public subsidies to companies using undeclared work, as well as the list of contravening companies being made public (Parliament 2006; Travail Suisse 2005). On the eve of the final vote in the lower chamber, the Swiss Employers' Union issued a recommendation to right-wing parties to refuse the law in the final vote, on the grounds that it would introduce an unnecessary burden on companies (*Tages Anzeiger* 2005: 3). Whereas all major parties on the left and right agreed to support the legislation, the SVP was the only party to follow the Employers' Union's recommendation and refuse the law:

> Undeclared work is already illegal. Undeclared work is already fought. Workplace inspections are already carried out efficiently, and evildoers and criminals are punished. [...] what we have done is a "cleaning lady" law, accompanied by an intensification of repression and an increase of the control apparatus on companies. [...] We, the SVP are against undeclared work, but we are also against inefficient laws. Therefore, we will reject it. (MP Hansrudi Wandfluh [SVP]. *Amtliches Bulletin* Nationalrat 2005: 970)

In the final vote, 42 SVP MPs refused the law, 6 abstained, and 1 accepted it. Social Democrats, Liberals and Christian Democrats accepted the law with a majority of 121 out of 200 MPs (Nominal Vote on Law on Undeclared Work 2005). The stance of the SVP was criticized by other parties, a Christian Democratic MP arguing, for instance, that they "protected foreign employees and discriminated the Swiss" by opposing tougher sanctions on companies using the very practices that they continuously criticized (*Tages Anzeiger* 2005: 3). In this case as well, the relatively low salience of the issue allowed for the probusiness stance within the SVP to prevail.

Conclusion

The stance of the SVP over migration policy reforms has been characterized by the problematic articulation of the interests of small businessmen who have traditionally relied on cheap foreign labor, and the anti-immigration agenda that has underpinned the electoral success of the party. The empirical analysis has shown that the former has tended to prevail over the latter particularly on issues of low political salience (undeclared work and to a lesser extent the Aliens law), while internal conflicts have been specifically prominent on issues of high salience (the free movement of workers). In terms of the immigration policy typology outlined above, its position oscillates between a free-market expansionist stance tolerating open borders but restricting rights for migrants, and a classic exclusionist stance advocating both closure and weak rights for migrants. The latter stance, in line with the preferences of the working-class base of the party, prevails when issues are of high political salience. When issues are salient, party elites find it hard to openly advocate policies that go against the interests of their electorate, and it is difficult to contain internal conflict so as to hide the contradictions implied by a heterogeneous electoral base. When issues are less salient, however, the "neoliberal" faction within the party tends to prevail.

The prevalence of the interests of small business holders over the working class within the party can be explained by a series of factors. The first has to do with historical patterns of political recruitment within the party. Hence, if the electoral base of the SVP has become increasingly working class, this has not been the case of the party elite, with a clear prominence of business owners among SVP MPs. This is not only a feature of the SVP but of all Swiss political parties, as the "militia" (nonprofessional) system of parliamentary representation makes it difficult for working-class citizens to gain parliamentary office. This is also accentuated by the second factor, the fact that Swiss political parties are highly dependent on private donations, particularly by companies, as there is no system of public funding of political parties. This induces a strong "double dependence": parties need votes but also money from business circles to support their activities, making even a party that claims to represent the "man on the street" very dependent on corporate donations. Hence, "to satisfy its electoral base and not to worry business circles, the SVP is constantly forced to contorted maneuvers" (Feuz 2011).

The third is that, as emphasized by previous research, the economic dimension is still of relatively low salience for working-class SVP voters, unless issues receive significant media attention, as was the case for the free movement of workers in the EU. Hence, the fact that the SVP advocates policies that go against the interests of part of their electoral clientele in the economic domain may not be that damageable electorally, because it is primarily the cultural and authoritarian agenda of the SVP that appeals to them. However, the ability of the SVP to advocate neoliberal policies while expanding its working-class base may not be pursued indefinitely, and it may have to adopt the economic reorientation toward the center observed in other radical right parties (De Lange 2007). The national elections in 2011 already marked a slowdown in its electoral success story and a stabilization of its electorate, as the party lost a number of seats in the lower Chamber as compared to 2007. In the future, the SVP may have to choose between the neoliberal agenda of its elites and the votes of its working-class base.

CHAPTER 2

Domestic Work, Gender, and Migration in Turkey: Legal Framework Enabling Social Reality

*Hande Eslen-Ziya and
Umut Korkut*

Introduction

This chapter demonstrates that the composition of the labor market in a host country, the labor demands of the economy, and the related official indifference to migration can foster a gendered composition of migrants. Moreover, the gender and labor dynamics in a host country can illegalize immigration even if the legal infrastructure as well as political discourse does not condone such illegality. In this context, there arises an inevitable conflict across the legal framework, political discourse, and social reality as immigrants find work in the gendered and informal labor market despite the restrictive legal procedures regulating migration. In order to determine the validity of our assumption, we debate the immigration regime in Turkey, bearing in mind its politico-legal environment, the prevalent social preconceptions about the role of women in the job market, and the eventual rights and position of women migrants in the Turkish labor market mostly as caretakers of children, the elderly, or the sick. Our argument is that despite the strict legal system that sets harsh rules handling migration and the anti-immigration political discourse and public sentiment, there remain loopholes for clandestine migrants to enter the Turkish labor market through informal channels. Dominant ideas regarding women and employment enhance the pervasiveness of such channels. We debate how these loopholes prevail, looking into the conflict between socioeconomic interests and political discourse.

In order to respond to this research question, we refer to the clash between the underlying interests of the public and the politicians regarding the employment process, both with respect to gender and informality, and the political discourse and public philosophy that contribute to the generation of restrictive migration regime in Turkey. To be more specific, we come across conflicting interests and discourse that affect the functioning of the Turkish migration regime. Thus, we trace the process of emergence and expression of conflicting interests and discourses considering the economic, legal, social, and political composition of the migration regime in Turkey. In effect, our theoretical assumption is as follows. While the vulnerability of women migrants has featured extensively in the migration literature (Anderson 2000; Engle 2004; Hochschild 2000; Yeates 2005), we foreground the study of such vulnerability in the context of socioeconomic interests and the functioning of informal economy. Thereby, we explore how vulnerabilities emerge and affect women migrants not only because of the actual politics and political discourse, but also due to the galvanized socioeconomic interests that operate both at the expense of the social rights of the immigrants as well as the actual politics of immigration. Below, we introduce our empirical case study in relevance to our theoretical assumption.

Why Turkey?

Since the end of 1980s Turkey has become a destination country in the international migration process. The erection of Fortress Europe, in a way, has diverted immigrants to new destinations and, in this case, Turkey became one of the main receiving countries in its region due to its relative economic prosperity and stability (İçduygu 2004: 88). This relates mostly to the sociopolitical changes in the neighboring region especially after the dissolution of the Soviet Union and the Eastern Bloc as well as the restriction of immigration to the European Union in the 1990s (Apap et al. 2005; Corliss 2003). Certainly, the remarkable economic growth in Turkey for the past decade and accompanying scale of informal economy also waged an impact on the number of migrants entering under employment. This context gave birth to a plethora of immigration firms that find employers for foreign domestic workers as caretakers in private homes, despite the fact that such workers are on tourist visas or are at times illegal (Akpınar 2010). The most recent figure from 2011 of illegal migrant workers in Turkey put the estimate at almost 200,000 according to the report by the Istanbul Chamber of Independent Accountants and Financial Advisors (ISMMMO 2012).

Turkey is a case where the informal labor market is massive, open to migrants, and provides ample opportunities simply to drop out of sight once you are in. This is largely a consequence of nonagricultural economic activity carried out in very large cities at a global scale, not merely in Istanbul, Ankara or Izmir, but also in certain central Anatolian cities that have witnessed unprecedented economic performances in recent years. We argue that the needs of the labor market in such places benefit out of clandestineness and, hence, economic activity profits out of informality. This assumption is also in line with the empirical observation that for all newcomers cities frequently perform as an entrance to the social network. They act as an identified geographical reference point, a meeting place where people and information circulate (Ribas-Mateos 2004: 1049) in labor submarkets within metropolitan areas (Sassen 1998: 96). Without doubt, this works to the benefit of the locals, but it also mitigates the hardships of the newcomers to enter the labor market. Especially, since the 1960s, Istanbul has been a showcase for the ease of settling down and finding work for domestic immigrants from Turkey's expansive inland. We find it plausible to argue that foreigners use similar means to enter the labor market even if they could merely arrange insecure work arrangements.

At the same time, the dynamics and the nature of the Turkish labor market produce a niche for migrant women who can only work informally and are willing to accept the vulnerability that comes with such informality. The predominant patriarchal norms accustomed in the employment process, despite gender-neutral labor legislation, at times favor migrant women landing on jobs. On this basis, we highlight the gendered and informal nature of immigration to Turkey, and document two mechanisms that are at play. On the one hand, the patriarchal composition of employment relations generates a demand for immigrant women as domestic workers. This rests on the enduring male breadwinner model, engrained in public philosophy, and the expressively patriarchal business culture and informal economy, aligned with economic interests. Thereby, the female migrant workers enter into the labor market and contribute both to informality and gendered labor market (Akalın 2007: 223; Akpınar 2010; Parla 2007). On the other hand, there is evident indifference to informal economy and migrants employment therein (Parla 2007) despite the politico-legal context that we will later outline. To an extent, such official indifference profits out of the practice of soft law, that is, "only moderately explicit, mostly non-obligatory, and not clearly enforceable by a single body" (Kollman 2009: 42), in the Turkish legal system. This, in return, as Buzogány argues, causes polices to be ambiguous and opens up the possibilities for different interpretations, both political and discursive during the implementation of laws (2011).

In order to shed light on overlapping informality, illegality, and gender in the constitution of migration to Turkey, we employ both an interests-oriented logic and a discursive logic. Our argument is as follows. It is apparent that the Turkish politico-legal system pursues an underlying interest in keeping immigrants illegal as long as they fulfill a prescribed function while in employment relations. This function also serves to the prevailing gender bias in the labor market. At the same time, their illegal status deprives immigrants of access to their basic rights and perpetuates vulnerability. That is how illegality, gender bias, and informality pertain to and overlap with prevailing socioeconomic interests. This is despite an anti-immigration political discourse and public sentiment. We qualify such discourse and sentiments as public philosophy. The result is that while socioeconomic interests and public philosophy clash over deliberations of immigration, they converge in ridding the migrants of protection, stability, and necessary rights to endure their vulnerable status. Therefore, we argue that the Turkish case presents a noteworthy example of a context where socioeconomic interests prevail over discourse whereby illegal migrants are tolerated and visible. The conditions of domestic work, illegal migration as well as laws and policies regarding illegal domestic work in Turkey substantiate our conviction. Thereby, we offer an account of how gender and labor dynamics in a host country can illegalize migration. In order to investigate how such dynamics prevail despite the politico-legal context, in the next section let us shortly illustrate the legal framework of the migration regime in Turkey.

The Background and Legal Aspects of Illegal Migration

Turkey has been facing a significant level of migration of foreigners since the end of 1980s for the first time in its history. Its difficulties are acute in the regulation of this new environment with outdated migration legislation, policies, and public understanding of issues central to migration. Increasing irregularity deserves our interest. İçduygu and Köser-Akçapar classify illegal migration in Turkey into four stages: fertilization; maturation; saturation; and degeneration (2005). The first period named fertilization is composed of irregular migrants coming from Iran in 1979 while the second period called maturation includes refugees coming from Bulgaria and Iraq between 1988 and 1993. The third period titled saturation saw illegal refugees increasing in number, due to the Turkish Asylum Arrangements that took place in 1992 and 2001–2002 (2005). The last period titled degeneration includes refugees from 2001 onward whereby illegal migration continued amidst institutionalized trafficking. We concentrate on those migrants entering Turkey to seek jobs predominantly as domestic workers and nannies. We qualify them as irregular migrants based on an empirical observation that they come to Turkey as tourists or with a tourist visa and continue to stay after their visas expire or commute between Turkey and their home countries. Most of these immigrants are women, employed in the domestic sector in private households catering for the increased need for caretakers.

Given the illegal and undocumented nature of migration, it is not possible to estimate exactly the number of foreign immigrants residing in Turkey. There is widespread discrepancy between the official and the scholarly data, and this is significant insomuch as it depicts common misperceptions of migration within Turkey (İçduygu 2003; İçduygu and Keyman 2000: 390; Parla 2007: 158). An International Organization for Migration (IOM) study, entitled "Irregular Migration in Turkey," in this respect, demonstrated the variety of legal and illegal migration to Turkey (Erder and Kaşka 2003). Most of the migrants are rejected asylum seekers reluctant to return to their countries of origin, transit migrants primarily arriving from the Middle East and various Asian countries, and migrants from Eastern European countries in search of work (İçduygu 2003: 17–18). Regardless of the number and the composition of migrants. Turkey is clearly faced with an increasing number of illegal migrants and the accompanying challenge of developing effective and sustainable policy options.

There are multiple laws that regulate the entry and deportation as well as the work and resident permits of the foreign migrants in Turkey, namely the Passport Law, the Labor Law, the Law on the Stay and Movement of Aliens, and the Social Security Law. Given the plethora of laws in effect, the existing legal framework is short of a coherent framework. According to İçduygu, the reasons behind this negligence and failure of regulation of irregular migration have been due to the lack of organized immigration policies and unfamiliarity with illegal immigration (2003). İçduygu states that Turkey's "experience with irregular migration is of relatively recent origin and partly because of the lack of established immigration policies and practice" (5). Nevertheless, there have been, recently, legislative amendments in the Turkish legal system in effect to immigration, residence, and work permit requirements for migrants, along with repealing the article that a list of occupations where immigrants could not receive employment—among many, domestic work was one (ibid.). Yet, our point is that inadequate regulation should not mean that migrants cannot acquire residency in Turkey. Let us explain below how.

Acquisition of work permit is a difficult process in Turkey. The work permit law, introduced in February 27, 2003, gives authority to the Ministry of Labor and Social Security to regulate work permits and determines occupations in which foreigners are not allowed to work. Starting from February 2012, a new law to regulate migrants who live and travel is in action. It is designed to allow the possibility for gaining a work permit and staying legally. Such work permits will be granted upon their application to the Ministry of Labor and Social Security. However, Şefika Gürbüz, the head of the Organization for Assistance and Solidarity with Migrants (Göç Edenler Yardımlaşma ve Dayanışma Derneği), stated that this law was insincere and primarily designed as a "threat and intimidation for the Armenians" (http://bianet.org/bianet/dunya/135667-yasa-cikti-ermenistanlilar-gonderiliyor). In this respect, a major inconvenience of the restrictive migration regime is the long duration that the issuance of work permits may take. Only in obscure "rare occasions" such as "in cases where the country's benefits require or depend on *force majeure*, the work permits maybe given after starting work, provided that information is provided to the relevant authority beforehand, on condition that the working period will not exceed one month and Ministerial approval has been obtained" (Kaşka 2006: 30). Certainly, such occasions do not apply to the case of domestic workers and, in the end, the interests of the employers and employees prevail over the tedious legal regulations for obtaining a work permit. Hence entering Turkey as a tourist and finding work appeal to the majority of migrants. Generous visa waiver agreements with a plethora of countries assist this process. Currently, visa waiver policies apply to all of Turkey's neighbors (with the exception of Iraq), Russia and Ukraine included, along with citizens of Turkic countries, and wider Middle East and North Africa. It is rather straightforward that the Turkish politico-legal system pursues an underlying interest in keeping immigrants illegal as long as they fulfill a prescribed function in the labor market tolerating illegality and extensive informality. In the next section, we discuss what type of gendered and informal arrangements this framework pertains to the nature of migration to Turkey.

The Gendered and Informal Nature of Migration to Turkey

Nonoperational regulation with respect to the legal employment of foreigners as caretakers is evident in Turkey, despite prevailing socioeconomic interests. That is why a large informal labor market persists in Turkey whereby migrants without permits find work. The definition of informal market, in this case, pertains to the permanent professional activities undertaken outside legal, regulatory, or contractual obligations (Quassoli 1999: 213). Erder and Kaşka argue that informality is due to a dynamic process shaped by the interaction of characteristics of migrants and the features of the receiving societies. As the Turkish case also illustrates, liberal border policies, geographical location, and the large and strong informal economy can trigger informal immigration. At the same time, the lack of formal social service institutions necessitates caretakers even if communal solidarity networks are widespread (2003: 70) in Turkey. Thereby, migrant caretakers enter as tourists and engage in employment illegally. Such informal employment enhances vulnerabilities of migrant women: informal and unregulated work imply a lack of fixed working hours and being perpetually on duty with rare holidays (Weyland 1994: 85). Furthermore, as Suter asserts, "their stay is not free of problems: on the one hand, the police is reported to harass irregular migrants on the streets, and on the other hand, East European women suffer from negative stereotypes that the Turkish society has towards them, by stigmatizing them as *Natashas*" (2008: 4)—a term indiscriminately used for East European implying that they are sex workers. This is an issue that we will tackle further while deliberating the public philosophy in effect to the reception of migrants to Turkey.

It is very common that informality and illegality have a gendered character in the Turkish labor market (Çelik 2005; Ege 2002; İçduygu 2004; Kaşka 2006; Kümbetoğlu 2005). The gendered aspect of the labor market becomes most evident when we look at the involvement of the Filipino (Weyland 1997) and the Gagauz (Keough 2003) communities in domestic work—both of which are almost all composed of women. There are various descriptions of the work that caretaker migrants are involved in. Engle describes these jobs as the three Ds, namely, dirty, demanding, and dangerous (2004) whereas Anderson calls these jobs the three Cs, namely, cooking, cleaning, and caring (2000). Overall, as Lutz argues, "domestic workers can be found working for dual earners, middle class families and single people, for double or single parents, for young urban professionals as well as for the elderly and invalid" (2004: 2). Likewise, in Turkey women constitute the majority of immigrants generating a feminization of migration serving for the needs for a gendered labor market. Similar to Lutz, Cindoğlu and Özçürümez presented that in Turkey immigrant women work in the service industries as domestic workers (caretakers for children, elderly, and the sick), entertainers (sex workers and dancers) as well as traders (*bavul ticareti* or suitcase trade became the Turkish qualifier for such trade in the 1990s) (2008: 5). Furthermore, Akalın explores how immigrants are "hired as caregivers and demanded as housewives" (2007: 220), that is, they fulfill several functions simultaneously.

Besides the difficulty of being associated with sex workers, that is, "sexually accessible" and "eager" women, according to İçduygu and Köser, migrant women face several further difficulties when illegally employed. These are, namely, bribery, loneliness and separation, anxiety, debts they owe to mediator agencies, and visa expiration fines that they may need to pay when exiting Turkey. Furthermore, they note that in certain circumstances they have to surrender their passports to their employers, which limits their freedom to leave the country if and whenever they want, and are forced to live in perpetual fear of being caught by the police; also, the anxiety of deportation conspires to limit their already much hindered freedom of movement (2005). In these contexts, their labor power becomes an eminently disposable commodity (De Genova 2004: 161). Therefore, having crossed the globe to work in Turkey, immigrants often find themselves in an enclosed domestic space with very little chance to self-determination. Vulnerability that illegality and informality bore and the closely related gender element to such position, in the end, turn migrant women into prisoners with increasing anxieties about their well-being (Weyland 1994: 85) often with little or no recourse to any semblance of protection from the law (De Genova 2004: 168).

The migration literature indicates that the increasing migration of women from the periphery to core countries to work as domestic workers demonstrates a "crisis of care" (Zimmerman, Litt, and Bose 2006). Hochschild views the global care chain as a demand created by the working women in rich countries in need of help in domestic chores or child care. The help is provided from a poorer household either locally or abroad (2000). As Yeates explains, the woman from the poorer household can be married with dependent children and has migrated to take up paid domestic labor. By doing this the poor migrant woman finds herself unable to discharge her own domestic duties because she is geographically distant from her children, creating a need for another woman to substitute for her (2005: 2). Thereby, the vulnerabilities of migrant women are enhanced even further given their predicament at both homes in their native and receiving countries alike. Hereby, a type of "care drain" emerges in these contexts as women who normally take care of the domestic responsibilities in their own countries move to richer countries to take care for the young, the old, and the sick. This concept is noteworthy since it reflects a general trend in migration: globalization of migration and love as well as the "importation of care and love from poor to wealthier countries," a mechanism for extracting "emotional surplus value" (Hochschild 2003: 17).

Alongside these debates in the migration literature, what reveals itself in the Turkish case is significant. Bearing in mind the low levels of participation of women in employment relations, we can surmise that it is not necessarily the crisis of care that asks for immigrants, but it is the patriarchal organization of family lives alongside increasing household incomes that brings the need for migrant caretakers. Thereby, with the help provided by the maid, an upper-middle-class woman transfers her household and child-care responsibilities to other women (Ehrenreich and Hochschild 2002) and migrant caretakers assume the responsibilities of domestic duties that used to be attributed to the upper-middle-class women earlier. Therefore, as Akalın argues, the "invisibility of domestic work that has long been suggested by feminist scholars is now projected onto the new migrant actors of domestic work in Turkey" (2007: 217). As the migrant domestic is a live-in caretaker and as her workplace is her employer's home, the "boundaries between her private life and that of the employers can easily become blurred" (Akalın 2007: 220). This, according to Akalın, creates a fictive relationship between the employer and the employee that makes her professional work seen as her natural responsibility, very similar to the responsibility that once (before the arrival of the migrant domestic caretaker) was attributed to her employer (ibid.). In a case where informality is rife, such as in Turkey, the migrants are even more vulnerable as they are "neither incorporated as an employee in the public sphere with social and legal rights under the jurisdiction of the state nor a member of the familial where relations are governed by non-market factors" (Huang and Yeoh 1996: 488). Elaborating on diverging roles in households that host immigrants, Akalın asserts that the migrant domestic then becomes a housewife for all (2007: 221).

Public Philosophy and Political Discourse

As our discussion above illustrates, gendered and informal immigration serves a certain type of socioeconomic interest in Turkey. In other words, the gender and labor dynamics in Turkey illegalize migration. This section will demonstrate that the socioeconomic demand for migrants is operative despite the predominant public philosophy and political discourse in effect to migration. Therefore, our contention is such that there is an anti-immigration sentiment and political discourse in Turkey despite the prevalent socioeconomic interest in favor. Why is this the case? Irregular migration to Turkey, especially since the collapse of the Soviet Bloc, contributed to a feeling of threat by foreigners. The collapse of communist regimes, the easing of travel restrictions, opportunities in the sprawling informal market economy in Turkey for foreigners enhanced both tourism and illegal entry to Turkey. Parallel to this, nationals of ex-communist countries have been observed to be working informally in Turkey, in sectors such as domestic services, entertainment and sex, textile, agriculture, and construction (Mirekoç Policy Briefing 2009/1) and were looked down upon.

Thereby, while widespread informal employment is a direct result of ad hoc solutions generated by the immigration regime and serves various economic benefits, it also promotes an image of foreigners who are in such despair to assume abysmal work and living conditions. In this respect, Yahya Arıkan, the president of the ISMMMO (Istanbul Chamber of Certified Public Accountants), states, foreign illegal workers have been made one of the significant pillars of the unrecorded economy and unfair competition. He further added that inspection has failed to prevent wrongdoings in this field (ISMMMO 2012). Moreover, the media reporting of the circumstances of migrants coming from certain Asian and African countries who are in transit through Turkey to cross to Western Europe or other developed countries confirmed the adverse image around immigrants. The repercussion of this picture on public philosophy with respect to migrants and immigration is negative.

Yet, this perception has deeper roots and cannot merely be explained by the conditions that migrants, either employed informally or in transit, find themselves in. A 2011 Ipsos survey showed that 81 percent of Turkish respondents stated that the number of immigrants increased in Turkey during the past five years; 45 percent conceded that immigration was bad for the country; only 6 percent believed that this was a positive phenomenon. Strikingly, 61 percent of the Turkish respondents claimed that the number of immigrants in Turkey was excessive. Similarly, 61 percent thought that immigration makes job opportunities for the natives difficult. This is partly a reflection of the increasing exposure of Turkish citizens to immigrants either in public or in private spheres, but mostly due to the general perception in the Turkish society that people with different ethnic, linguistic, and sexual orientation are nonnative. Similar discourse was apparent among the Justice and Development Party (AKP) leaders who held a nationalist/conservative view (Küçük 2010).

EUROSPHERE Project Turkey 2010 Country Report provides ample data regarding the position of public actors toward immigrants. In this report, Küçük looked at the appreciation of diversity in the Turkish public sphere and argued that the claims of equal treatment to migrants seem to disappear based on their nationalities (2010: 11). For instance, the Turkish respondents in Küçük's survey seemed to favor immigrants with coethnic backgrounds. This was apparent in the response of one of the participants mentioned in the report: "if one accepts everyone like migrants coming from Bangladesh, Sri Lanka, India or China, that would bring chaos to Turkey... it is normal that the Turkish state makes its own decisions as to whom it accepts or rejects" (11). Such view was also evident among some of the respondents who associated themselves with the main opposition party—Republican People's Party (CHP)—when discussing whether or not migrants should have political rights. For example, one of the respondents stated that "every state has to protect its physical, economic and social life and its future and giving such political rights to non-citizens could jeopardize the social life and future of the country" (11). The education level of the immigrants was found to be another factor that resulted in favoring certain immigrant groups over others (ibid.). For instance, one respondent from Women's Centre called KAMER, mainly active in Eastern Turkey, believed that "due to existing unemployment problems, only highly educated immigrants should be accepted to the country" (42).

We believe that an aversion of migrants as long as they represent a deviation from "what is common" is rather prevalent in Turkey. In order to substantiate why deviation is considered aversely in Turkey, we refer to the results of a 2010 survey entitled "We, Others, Othering and Discrimination in Turkey" by Hakan Yılmaz. The results demonstrated that 66 percent of the respondents did not believe that they had any linguistic or cultural ethnicity and they stated that they fully live in

Turkish language and culture. Only 2 percent of the respondents stated that they have no linguistic or ethnic link whatsoever with Turkish language and culture. Almost 40 percent stated that linguistic and religious rights—other than for those who speak Turkish and practice Islam—could be fully curtailed. Almost three-quarters of the respondents stated that homosexuals could not express their identities in Turkey. As such, it is not only foreigners who threaten the Turkish society, but any general deviation from what is commonly perceived as the linguistic, religious, and sexual traits of "Turkishness." We surmise that such aversion of nonnativeness mostly accounts for negative perception of immigrants in Turkey.

Socioeconomic Interests in Support of
Illegal Immigration
Despite such aversion both in private and public, how come there prevail socioeconomic interests in support of migration in Turkey? According to Akpınar there are several reasons why the employers give preference to illegal immigrants in employment decisions. One of them is the search for cheap labor from the employer's side and the other is the government's unofficial tolerance to such informality (2010). Plausibly, it was the political economy in the late 1980s and the desire to lower the labor expenses that opened its way to informal employment (Koç 1999). The availability of migrants who are willing to work for less turned this desire into a reality availing the employers with a workforce willing to work cheap and informally (TUIK 2009 cited in Akpınar 2010: 7). Refik Baydur, the general manager of the Turkish Confederation of Employers' Unions (TISK), expressed very clearly the underlying interests in maintaining informal arrangements in handling migration to Turkey. Baydur stated that "if needed we can bring workers from former Soviet block countries who are willing to work for less than 80 dollars per month. In Russia workers are willing to work even for less than 50 dollars per month" (Koç 1999: 39). The political interest also has been in line with the socioeconomic interest, that is, tolerant of illegal immigration. Prime Minister Erdoğan's expressed awareness and tolerance of the illegal migrants of Armenian origin, mostly domestic workers residing in Turkey, is noteworthy. In an interview with BBC on March 10, 2010, Erdoğan stated:

> In my country there are 170 thousand Armenians; 70 thousand of these are my citizens. We are covering up the other 100 thousand. So, what am

I going to do tomorrow, if necessary I will tell this 100 thousand, "Come on, you go back to your homeland"; I am going to do this. Why? They are not my citizens. I do not have to keep them in my country.

Yet, despite showing his awareness of illegal migrants in the labor market, the prime minister did not initiate any policies to expel such migrants in order to fully regulate the informal economy. Both Baydur's and prime minister's statements exhibit what Parla described as "official indifference/tolerance" to illegal migration (2007).

As we discussed above, the gendered aspect of such prevailing informality and indifference serves social interests. Beyond the advantages that it provides to informal sector and economy, a further function of employing such vulnerable women workforce in informal economy is the preservation of the politically conservative and patriarchal culture that puts nuclear family with male breadwinner and female housewife at the core. This has been the system that increasingly kept Turkish women out from formal employment. In other words, an instrumental function of the production of such illegality is the preservation of the traditional family. How does this emerge?

Turkey has a patriarchal culture where its social policy reflects a patriarchal value system with its traditional gender division of labor evident in the family (Buğra and Yakut-Cakar 2010). Though female labor participation is increasing worldwide, Turkey seems to be one of the countries lagging behind. In fact, as Buğra and Yakut-Cakar put, "Turkey represents a rare exception to the worldwide increase in female employment in that during the last two decades, the overall female employment rate has declined in the country as a whole, from 33 per cent in 1988 to 23 percent in 2007" (2010: 518). Most certainly, the actual level of women's participation in the labor market is much higher when we consider how expansive the informal market is in Turkey. Elsewhere we argued that women's low-level participation in the Turkish work force is due to the impact of "conservative ideas on gender relations and the ensuing conventional interpretations of gender roles" (Korkut and Eslen-Ziya 2011: 408). Furthermore, the socially conservative discourse along with the strong tradition of honor, shame, and the nature of control of female sexuality all have an impact on women's low levels of labor participation (ibid.). The desire to preserve a conservative culture and the traditional family structure with a male breadwinner and female stay-in-housewife is visibly one of the reasons that stimulate socioeconomic interest in maintaining informality.

In fact, as Sev'er and Gökçeçicek pointed out, Turkish customs "explicitly emphasize the family roles of women and deem secondary any work or career aspirations women may have" (2001: 969).[1] There is certainly a class element at play here as such pressure is more evident on women from lower classes. As Akalın's elaborations on the patriarchal control demonstrates,

> [e]ven under severe economic hardship, many male relatives have been resistant to allowing the women in their families to work outside. Those who did, at least initially, allowed their wives or sisters to work only for employers who either lived close by or whom they personally knew; such as doormen letting their wives work for the residents of the flats who lived in the same building. Due to this bounded availability, Turkish domestic workers chose to work predominantly as live-out workers, doing mostly cleaning, thus structuring the sector in a special way. (2007: 213)

This in turn creates a demand for the migrant domestic over the live-out Turkish domestic caretakers who are both from lower classes and are not encouraged to engage in formal employment.

Changing family structures in Turkey also relate to the need for such workers. Similar to other Southern European countries, in later years, the family structure witnessed a shift from extended family to nuclear family in Turkey. As a result, while the unpaid women members of the family who used to perform domestic works disappeared, the shift enabled the commercialization of domestic work (Kaşka 2006). At the same time, employing a domestic helper became an important status symbol even if the rate of women participation in the labor force remained low in Turkey (Momsen 1999: 4). Other factors that contributed to this demand, according to Kaşka, were the demographics, the trend of an aging population, and the changing role of women (2006). Thereby, the changes in both the global economy and the rise of the service sector with the shrinking of the welfare state created a demand for women's labor and became a push factor in women's migration. In the end, there came an ever-increasing demand for paid domestic labor in the migrant-receiving countries such as Turkey.

While a major discussion in the literature on welfare state and immigration relates to high unemployment and the crisis of welfare state and a perception of foreign immigrants as a "problem" (Ribas-Mateos 2004: 1060), the counterargument has been that the welfare state is inward looking and constructs a kind of safe house in which to shelter its members from the outside world (Freeman 1986: 52–53, 55). In the Turkish case, however, the nonexistent welfare state with regard to caretaking and child-care facilities promote informal solutions for these activities such as the employment of foreign domestic workers. Lack of state support in child care (as well as elderly care) created a demand for domestic help (Korkut and Eslen-Ziya 2011) and the upper-middle-class women receive domestic help to ease their gendered responsibilities. Public child-care facilities and preschool education are almost absent in Turkey while child care is considered primarily as the main responsibility of women and the state plays a limited role in providing such services. Thereby, women with children either drop out from the labor market or solve their problems via their individual networks and capacities (ibid.). While local domestic workers also participate in the domestic care market, the entrance of more trained women migrants in the labor market shifts the demand to illegal migrants.

Conclusion
This chapter depicted the use of interest-based and discursive accounts in examining the politics of migration in Turkey. We demonstrated that the gender and labor dynamics in a host country could illegalize immigration amidst political tolerance. As the Turkish case presents, this is despite the migration averse public philosophy and political discourse. In a highly patriarchal country like Turkey, where gender role ascriptions are quite rigid, dependence on foreign domestic workers has become a necessity to maintain the existing gender balance in the workforce. Employing foreign caretakers is a status symbol and the prevalent informal labor market conditions maintain the networks that migrants need to hold of jobs. Hence, the Turkish case demonstrates the link among the economic, legal, and the cultural environment of immigration. In other words, the specificities of Turkish immigration regime make immigrants visible but vulnerable. The result is that socioeconomic interests prevail at the expense of discourse in the making up of migration politics.

In order to reach this conclusion, this chapter offered a review of the politico-legal environment in Turkey, the prevalent social conditions about the role of women in the labor market, and the eventual rights and positions of women migrants in Turkish labor market. In this respect, we consider it highly remarkable that labor market, economic, societal, and political factors simply wage a compound impact on the gendered composition of migrants that are stuck in the informal market. At the same time, despite the increasing prevalence of the migration phenomenon, the Turkish society and politics is reluctant to come to grips with their need for migrants. We explained this with aversion of nonnativeness in the Turkish public philosophy. However, further studies should aspire to underline what specific factors within these sentiments trigger rejection of migrants.

Note

1. Women's group like KAGIDER (Women Entrepreneurs Association of Turkey) challenges such patriarchal control by developing entrepreneurship among women to strengthen their status economically and socially.

CHAPTER 3

Struggling with EU Safe Country Practicesi nA sylum

Sarah Craig

Introduction

This chapter considers how the struggle to promote the protection of refugees has played out in relation to European Union (EU) and member state procedures that limit and restrict the consideration of asylum claims. The measures under consideration form part of the Common European Asylum System (CEAS) that includes the Asylum Procedures Directive (APD) (Council of the European Union 2005) and its Recast Proposal (European Parliament and Council 2011a), the Reception Conditions Directive and its Recast (Council of the European Union 2003a), the Qualification Directive (European Parliament and Council 2011b), and the Dublin Regulation (Council of the European Union 2003b) and its Recast Proposal (European Parliament and Council 2008). Of greatest relevance in this instance is the APD that established minimum standards on procedures for granting and withdrawing refugee status.

One of the original aims of the CEAS was to protect refugees and maintain the principle that refugees would not be returned to persecution. In practice, however, its measures are often aimed at deflection of refugees, rather than at their protection, and the APD has come in for criticism because of the ways in which it deflects refugees. Three of those criticisms are mentioned here.

1. The inadequacy of its standards and the extensive exceptions and qualifications from basic safeguards that it provides. Here, the APD promotes the deflection of refugees by sanctioning member

states' use of procedures that curtail or exclude the consideration of asylum claims.
2. The wide margin of discretion afforded to member states. Rather than stating the ways in which member states should ensure that individual asylum seekers can access the process effectively, the APD contains crucial gaps that reveal the weakness of cooperation among member states. This weakness is demonstrated in the limited protections provided for in its procedures that leave essential aspects to be filled by state discretion. Even where protection duties should constrain state discretion, the APD fails to spell out those constraints. The consequence is that protection is not given and exclusionary practices prevail. So while the APD aimed to articulate a lowest common denominator set of standards for the treatment of asylum claims, below which member states would not go, this chapter explores how the struggle to maintain even that lowest common denominator of protection has played out. Stark evidence of that struggle is provided when those procedures fail and asylum seekers are not able to access procedures at all. This chapter also explores how the European Court of Human Rights and the Court of Justice of the European Union (CJEU) have addressed the presumption that all EU countries meet basic procedural standards.
3. The impossibility of accessing procedures at all. The adoption of common standards for asylum procedures is actually far from reality. This can be proved from just one example: since all EU member states had adopted, in theory, legal measures that complied with the terms of the APD, the presumption that those standards would be applied in practice was proved false by the experience of asylum seekers in EU "entry points" such as Greece, where procedural and substantive protections were completely denied. (Amnesty International 2008; Commissioner for Human Rights 2009; UNHCR 2008a)

Given this background, it is not surprising that research into EU asylum procedures has focused on their shortcomings, and this chapter draws on research comparing the application of the APD in selected member states, which highlighted the need to reform the APD in order to strengthen its potential to protect (UNHCR 2010). The absence of agreement on the recast APD as in October 2012, some four years after the European Commission acknowledged critical flaws in the current CEAS (European Commission 2008), illustrates the strength of the deflection tendencies at play in EU discussions on asylum and the weakness of its protection aspects.

Delineating the CEAS framework, the chapter highlights the extent to which member states require to take a protection-oriented approach rather than a deflection-oriented approach if the Refugee Convention (United Nations 1951) is to be implemented in accordance with its underlying intentions. Aspects of the APD that promote protection include its measures on linguistic assistance and recognize that unless they understand how to do so, asylum applicants cannot begin to communicate their claim. Interpretation and other linguistic assistance can, therefore, promote the protection of refugees, but procedures must also provide a context that prioritizes the full and inclusive consideration of asylum claims. The protection aspects of the CEAS are weak, and as a result, member states are given discretionary space that, encouraged by other CEAS measures, they are tempted to populate with practices aimed at deflecting refugees into abbreviated and fast-tracked procedures. Such practices include the presumptions about safe countries contained in the APD itself. In this context, language can be used as a deflection tool. Where linguistic analysis is used as a means of testing an asylum applicant's claim to be from a particular country of origin and such analysis questions the credibility of that claim, consideration of the claim may be curtailed. The risks associated with relying on such tools as a means of diverting claims into curtailed procedures is also discussed. In addition, the connection between the exclusionary politics of asylum and the introduction and use of such tools of deflection is observed.

The next section explores in more detail the deflection tools used by member states, with particular focus on the Dublin regime for the transfer of asylum seekers between member states. It shows how the disparities in the asylum decision-making systems across the EU became so stark, and the presumption that asylum seekers could expect basic protections against *refoulement* anywhere in the EU so impossible to maintain, that the European Court of Human Rights (*MSS v Belgium and Greece*) and the CJEU (*C-411/10 NS and C-493/10 ME*) each concluded that it could no longer be automatically presumed that it was acceptable to transfer asylum seekers to the member state through which they entered the EU for the consideration of their claims. The individual case, and the situation in the destination country, should be considered.

The chapter concludes by considering the position of individual decision makers and applicants for asylum. The framework for decision making leaves so many possibilities for deflection of claims that the task of connecting the individual applicant to the protection principles expressed by the Refugee Convention lies with individual decision makers within determining authorities. In this context the challenge is to create an environment in which applicants have the means to communicate their narrative, decision makers can decide to protect, and both parties are able to overcome the exclusionary politics of asylum.

The CEAS: Protection or Deflection?

The CEAS was conceived in 1999, when the Tampere Conclusions mandated the EU to establish a system "based on the full and inclusive application of the [1951] Geneva Convention, whereby the principle of *non-refoulement* would be maintained" (European Presidency 1999: paragraph 13). The first phase would lay down minimum standards on accommodation and reception of asylum applicants, as well as on decision-making procedures and criteria for identifying those who qualify for international protection, ahead of establishing a common procedure and uniform status valid throughout the EU. Although the first phase instruments have been implemented, negotiations toward improving the standards reflected in those instruments, and negotiations aimed at addressing "the situation of Member States whose asylum systems face particular pressures" (European Presidency 2012) have frequently stalled. As a result, negotiations over a recast Dublin Regulation and a recast APD have been tortuous and inconclusive and, in the meantime, refugees arriving in the EU are met with efforts to deflect rather than protect them.

An example of the "deflection" side of the CEAS can be seen in the establishment of the Dublin regime, which was said to contain "clear and workable" rules for the determination of the state responsible for the examination of an asylum application (Treaty on the Functioning of the European Union [TFEU] Article 78(2) (e)) (European Union 2008). Member states wanted to ensure that asylum could be claimed in only one EU state and, implicitly, wanted to deflect asylum seekers away from their own state. The establishment of the Dublin regime, some years before the CEAS, reflects this desire to deflect. From its inception, therefore, the CEAS has had both a protection aspect and a deflection aspect. The protection aspect arises from the fact that all EU member states are signatories to the Refugee Convention and to the European Convention on Human Rights (ECHR) (Council of Europe 1950). They all profess adherence to democratic principles, including adherence to international obligations. Commitment to human rights principles is also a fundamental aspect of EU law (TFEU Article 78) (European Union 2008).

The deflection aspect of the CEAS reflects the fact that the motivations for states to sign up to instruments like the Refugee Convention are not solely (or even mainly) humanitarian, but arise from their recognition that, in the world that they inhabit, an individual state's sovereignty has limits. Without entering into a discussion of its nature, a tentative definition of sovereignty would be to describe it as the power to act without constraint and to control the outcomes of that action (Dauvergne 2004: 593). Motives for states to sign up to the Refugee Convention can, therefore, be prompted by self-interest, from states' recognition of the limits of their own sovereignty and of their need to participate in markets and systems of governance beyond the state (including the EU) and globalized markets.

As a result, the growth and development of the CEAS has been hindered by the struggle between actors that promote protection and others that promote deflection. Measures that promote deflection include the Dublin regime, as already mentioned, but also the EURODAC Regulations governing the common system across the EU for fingerprinting "irregular" migrants on entry to member states (Council of the European Union 2000, 2002, and 2012), safe third country procedures, which develop the Dublin regime's principles but apply them to non-EU countries that are considered similarly "safe" for the consideration of asylum claims (APD Articles 27 and 31), and admissibility and abbreviated procedures, which are aimed at curtailing the consideration of asylum claims on a number of grounds (APD Articles 24 and 25).

The reasons behind deflection-oriented measures in the CEAS are complex and include, as proven in the public discourse, looking at asylum seekers as a type of "undeserving" migrants. Although such depictions do not arise from the Refugee Convention itself, that Convention has a gap that such perspectives can, and do, exploit. The gap is that the Refugee Convention does not specify a right to enter a state to claim asylum, but instead relies on the state's duty not to *refoule* (return) a refugee to persecution (Refugee Convention, Article 33(1)). As a result, most people seeking refugee status enter illegally.

The development of the EURODAC regime to identify people who have applied for asylum or who have entered or stayed illegally in a state reflects this conflation of asylum seekers with "irregular" migration. So while the Refugee Convention requires that refugees are not penalized for entering illegally (Refugee Convention, Article 31(1)), this provision cannot protect asylum seekers from being described, along with so-called illegal or irregular migrants, as "undeserving" (Dauvergne 2004: 601).

Protection-oriented measures in the CEAS have relied on the efforts of proprotection bodies to press for the basic requirements of the Refugee Convention and related instruments, such as the Handbook on Procedures and Criteria for Determining Refugee Status (UNHCR 1979) to be reflected in the development of measures, but these efforts have often involved trying to ensure that lowest common denominator standards are protected. In crucial areas, the measures that have been developed fail to spell out in clear terms what is required of states, even where principles of refugee law state that protection should be given. An example of such failure can be found in Article 39 of the APD, which deals with the provision of an effective remedy for the determination of asylum claims, but does not spell out the obvious point that a refused asylum seeker cannot challenge a decision to return them to their home country after they have been sent back there (Craig and Fletcher 2005). In order to be effective, appeals against the refusal of asylum claims must suspend removal (Reneman 2010).

In these circumstances, it falls to decision makers to fill in the blanks. Protection-oriented measures rely on the ability of decision makers and judicial bodies within individual states to make decisions in ways that are in compliance not only with the CEAS measures themselves, but also with the principles and precedents of refugee law that should underpin those measures. So, for example, the Qualification Directive, also a CEAS measure, defines international protection in a manner that can be interpreted inclusively (European Parliament and Council 2011b: Chapters II, III, and V), and the APD requires that linguistic assistance and information rights be made available to ensure that individuals can access the process (Article 10), but it is up to the decision maker to determine whether to grant refugee status or subsidiary protection, or whether to refuse the claim. In similar vein, the proposed amendments to the Dublin regime would also require that applicants be given linguistic assistance to ensure that the applicant knows that they might be removed to a different country to have their claim considered (European Parliament and Council 2008, Articles 4 and 5), but it is up to the decision maker to decide if such a transfer should take place. Furthermore, it is up to the member state to use its discretion to ensure that there is an opportunity to challenge the asylum decisions of its officials before removal. The role of the decision maker in resolving the tensions between the deflection and protection aspects of the CEAS in a protection-oriented manner is, therefore, crucial, but the potential for decision makers to take such an approach also depends on the member state providing the appropriate decision making and appeal structures that enable a protection-oriented approach to be taken.

Safe Country Practices as Deflection Techniques

The discussion in this chapter now turns to certain aspects of the APD and the Dublin regime that reflect the struggle between deflection and protection that has played out in the CEAS thus far. It also focuses on decisions of the European Court Human Rights (ECtHR) and of the CJEU, as the topmost asylum decision-making institutions in Europe that reflect that struggle.

The struggle between these two sides of EU cooperation, the protection side and the deflection side, can be seen in the provisions of the APD, but the deflection side is stronger. The strength of the deflection side is also seen in the fact that proposals for a recast APD, aspects of which would improve protection for refugees, for example, by spelling out the right of an asylum applicant to remain on the territory pending an appeal, have been in train for several years without final agreement and, in the UK's case, in its decision to opt out of the recast APD (European Parliament and Council 2011a).

The motivations for the proposed recast of the APD arose from the inadequacies of the original version. As already noted, the APD is a controversial measure because its detailed provisions include many possibilities for member states to deflect applicants away from full and fair decision-making procedures, and such deflection mechanisms include "safe country" practices. Safe country practices have a number of different forms, but they can be divided into two main types.

The first type involves practices that accept that an asylum seeker may have a well-founded fear of persecution, but these practices aim to divert asylum seekers away from the country in which they have sought refuge on the basis that the responsibility for determining whether or not to *refoule* them to their home country belongs to a third country. These are known as safe third country practices. Although the legal basis of safe third country practices has been authoritatively questioned (Costello 2005), the mechanisms are so well established in the EU that, as mentioned above, the Dublin regime, crystallizing those practices, was established many years before the CEAS itself. The Dublin regime has been criticized on a number of grounds, including that its implementation can lead to the indirect *refoulement* of refugees back to the country where they fear persecution (*TI v UK*). Further, the notions prompted by expressions like "asylum shopping" that suggested that asylum seekers chose destination countries somewhat like consumers, on the basis of the generosity of their asylum systems, and that had been used to justify the introduction of the Dublin regime in the first place, were shown not to have empirical support (Crawley 2010; Zetter et al. 2003). It also transpired that the Dublin regime did not prevent asylum seekers from being sent back and forth from one EU member state to another, as discussed below. The fact that the justifications for operating the Dublin regime lacked legitimacy did not prevent safe third country mechanisms from being included in the APD, thus sanctioning member states to establish mechanisms for the transfer of asylum seekers to non-EU countries for the consideration of their claims. The continuing popularity with governments of safe third country mechanisms is, of course, connected to the exclusionary politics of asylum. In the case of the UK, Squire has noted that EU and UK levels of governance both expressly associate asylum with illegal immigration and terrorism as an issue to be "tackled" (2009). They construct asylum seekers as "threatening" or "culpable" in ways that cover over the tensions in their diverging articulations of political community, while at the same time allowing both levels of government to work together to exclude them from the community (57–58). As they deflect asylum seekers away from member states, safe third country mechanisms express cooperation within the EU in avoiding the "asylum burden," not in sharing it.

The second type of safe country practice sanctioned by the APD is the safe country of origin concept, a concept that has also been associated with the categorization of claims as "manifestly" or "clearly" unfounded. The APD sanctions the designation of claims from safe countries of origin as "manifestly unfounded" (Article 23(4) (c) (i)) and, in the UK, an asylum claim can be certified as "clearly unfounded" for a number of reasons, including that the applicant is a national of one of the countries listed in the relevant legislation as "generally safe" (UK Government, Nationality Immigration and Asylum Act 2002 Section 94). Treating countries of origin as generally safe denies many applicants from those countries the opportunity for a full and individual determination of their claim for asylum since it requires the individual to overcome the presumption that their claim is unfounded. The purpose of categorizing claims as unfounded is to allow their consideration to be curtailed. Thus, where a claim is treated as clearly unfounded, there is scant opportunity for applicants to put across their claims, and nonsuspensive appeal provisions remove the right to appeal a refusal prior to removal (ibid.). In these circumstances, though access to the process is given, substantive protection is denied.

Language is relevant here because of the practice, among some countries, of using forms of linguistic analysis to test whether applicants are really nationals of their claimed country of origin, or whether they originate in a neighboring (and usually safer) country (UK Government, Home Office 2010). Such tests can lead to claims being treated as manifestly or clearly unfounded, particularly where the neighboring country is deemed safe or the linguistic analysis questions the applicant's credibility on the basis that they appear to have concealed their true nationality. The use of such tests to facilitate the fast-tracking of claims into procedures that provide minimal opportunity for challenge is particularly detrimental given that live concerns exist as to the reliability of some of the methods used to assess the links between the language and origin of applicants (Craig 2012; Zwaan et al. 2010). Here, again, applicants are denied the opportunity to have their claim fully considered. Although access to the procedure is given, substantive protection is effectively blocked. Given this background we can see why Steve Peers commented that the legitimacy of EU asylum law depended on finding key provisions of the APD invalid or radically reinterpreting them (Peers 2006: 335–342).

Discrediting the Applicant

This is not the end of the depressing picture from the protection perspective. Building on evidence gathered by nongovernmental organizations and others in civic society, UNHCR conducted research into the application in practice of the APD in 2009–2010 that showed that even its low standards were not being met. For example, there were instances when an applicant's basic entitlement to an individually motivated decision was denied and obstacles were created: for example, an interpreter told an applicant to say in an asylum application that they had come to the host country to seek a better life (UNHCR 2010). Such an intervention can destroy the credibility of an asylum claim. Neither the definition of a refugee in Article 1A nor the non-*refoulement* provision in Article 33 of the Refugee Convention mentions credibility, and yet credibility is said to be at the core of the asylum process (Thomas 2006). The obstacles that asylum seekers face in their efforts to persuade decision makers of their credibility are so immense that the existence of a "culture of disbelief" among asylum decision makers has frequently been cited (Sweeney 2009).

Institutionally and individually, asylum decision makers in the UK appear preoccupied with credibility, and criticisms of UK Border Agency (UKBA) decision making have focused consistently on their approach to credibility (Asylum Aid 2012; UNHCR 2007, 2008b). Baillot, Cowan, and Munro have commented on the ways in which the institutional actors involved in the asylum process approach the credibility of asylum-seeking women's narratives of rape and sexual assault, and how their approaches can have the effect of silencing those claims (2012). Campbell's study of the application of UKBA policies on the use of language analysis to determine country of origin led him to argue that language analysis is used as an inherently political tool to determine the nationality of asylum applicants and, essentially, to discredit their claims (2012). Sweeney has argued that the UKBA's institutional approach to credibility in asylum decision making is confused because its advice to decision makers does not distinguish between the use of the term "credibility" in the broader sense of whether the decision maker finds the applicant credible overall, on the one hand, and the use of the term in the narrower sense of the reliability or admissibility of individual items of evidence, on the other (2009: 708–714).

Given their legislative context, it should, perhaps, be no surprise to find that UK government policy on decision making, and the approach taken by individual decision makers, both seem to be preoccupied with credibility. Legislation that shares the same preoccupation can also be found. At the EU level, Article 23(4) of the APD allows claims that are found to be inconsistent, misleading or lacking in credibility on a number of grounds to be considered, on that basis, in abbreviated and/or fast-tracked procedures that minimize and sometimes exclude the possibilities for asylum seekers to communicate their claims, and the UK's Asylum and Immigration (Treatment of Claimants Etc.) Act 2004 Section 8 instructs decision makers to regard credibility as damaged where applicants have "behaved" in certain ways, including where they have failed to claim asylum at the earliest opportunity, or have failed to produce identity documents. These instructions prevail despite the fact that the behaviors that they identify, although they may distinguish compliant or cooperative asylum seekers from ones who are less so, have nothing to do with the credibility in the broader sense of the strength of an asylum claim (Sweeney 2009).

In this context, therefore, it is a commonplace to say that credibility can be treated as damaged for spurious reasons. As already noted, some member state practices treat claims to originate in certain (often war-torn) countries with suspicion, and where such practices involve the routine use of linguistic analysis to test those claims, the aim is to discredit them. Where such linguistic analysis is practiced according to controversial methods, then credibility is damaged for spurious reasons. Where such practices combine with curtailed procedures for so-called manifestly unfounded claims (Craig 2012: 259), substantive protection is denied.

Deflection Techniques Once More

In this way, the protection-oriented approach, whose aim is to ensure that persons with a well-founded fear of persecution should be protected from *refoulement,* is weakened, and the deflection-oriented approach gains strength. The success of the deflection-oriented approach can be seen as flowing from the discretion given to states to establish procedures. When we look at this from the procedural perspective, we find that deflection happens because states have been encouraged to exploit their discretion in ways that divert refugees away from substantive protection. EU measures, such as the APD and Dublin arrangements, encourage that approach because they sanction and facilitate practices aimed at the deflection of refugees through the "mainstreaming" of safe country practices across the EU.

The deflection approach can be seen on a daily basis in the treatment of asylum seekers across the EU. But from the courts' perspective, a low point in protection was reached when the use of Dublin safe country practices worked together with the existence of common procedural standards to defeat a claim that transferring an applicant from the UK to Greece would run the risk of exposing him to inhuman or degrading treatment and of indirect *refoulement* back to his home country. This case concerned an Iranian national who claimed asylum in the UK having previously traveled through and been fingerprinted in Greece. The UK authorities ordered that he be removed to Greece to have his asylum claim considered there, and the applicant took his challenge to this Dublin transfer to the European Court of Human Rights on the basis that he ran a serious risk of inhuman or degrading treatment contrary to Article 3 of the ECHR if he were returned to Greece. His challenge failed (*KRS v UK*). The court found that although the conditions in which asylum seekers were held in Greece had been poor, and access to the process severely limited, Greece did not send people back to Iran.

Most disappointingly, it appeared that the very existence of common EU standards on procedures, in the form of the APD's provisions, led the court to look no further than the legislative framework that applied in Greece. The presumption that asylum seekers could safely be transferred to other member states for the consideration of their asylum claim appeared, in this case, to be practically irrefutable. This seems clear from the manner in which the court took account of the fact that Greece had obliged itself under the APD to adhere to minimum standards in asylum procedures and in the reception conditions for asylum seekers:

> The presumption must be that Greece will abide by its obligations under those Directives. In this connection, note must also be taken of the new legislative framework for asylum applicants introduced in Greece. (*KRS v UK*: paragraphs 16–17)

The legislative framework referred to was the one that implemented the terms of the APD into Greek law. In this way, the implementation of common procedural standards for the treatment of asylum claims was allowed to mask the reality of what was happening to asylum seekers. The court also said that an asylum seeker who faced the possibility of *refoulement* back to his home country, or who faced inhuman or degrading conditions in detention in Greece, could take a complaint about Greece to the ECtHR. In other words, lack of access to asylum procedures in Greece and poor conditions experienced by asylum seekers there did not overcome the presumption in law that Greece, and not the UK, was the appropriate country to deal with KRS' asylum claim. This ECtHR judgment was relied on in subsequent cases (*Secretary of State for the Home Dept. v Nasseri*): to support the *refoulement* of asylum seekers from the UK and elsewhere to Greece, where that country had been the person's entry point to the EU. This occurred notwithstanding the live concerns that continued to exist about the unfairness of the asylum "burden" experienced by Greece, which was the country of arrival for 88 percent of the foreign nationals who entered the EU in 2009 (*MSS v Belgium and Greece*: paragraph 125), and about the treatment of asylum seekers and other migrants in Greece.

Some Protection Ground Regained

In (*MSS v Belgium and Greece*), some of the protection ground lost in (*KRS v UK*) was regained. *MSS v Belgium and Greece* concerned an Afghani applicant. He arrived in Greece in December 2008, where he was detained and had his fingerprints taken, before being ordered to leave Greece. He applied for asylum in Belgium in February 2009, and in April 2009 the UNHCR wrote to the Belgian authorities asking them to stop transferring asylum seekers to Greece because of deficiencies in its procedures and in the reception conditions of asylum seekers (*MSS v Belgium and Greece*: paragraph 194). In spite of this, *MSS* was returned to Greece in June 2009, and he subsequently complained to the European Court of Human Rights. In their decision of January 2011, the court criticized the detention conditions in which the applicant and others were held, but the court also referred to the fact that asylum seekers required information about how to claim, as well as linguistic assistance, before the non-*refoulement* provision in the Refugee Convention could have practical effect.

Some Basic Principles Reiterated

The basic procedural requirements of the Refugee Convention are found in Article 1A, which defines the refugee, and in Article 33, which mentions ways of preventing their expulsion. In practice, the protection against *refoulement* in Article 33 can come into play only when the asylum applicant has managed to persuade the decision maker, through the telling of their narrative, that their fear of persecution is well founded. Language is relevant here because measures that allow for linguistic assistance can ensure that appropriate communication of the asylum narrative takes place.

To explore the protection potential of asylum procedures, the role played by language in the asylum process is important. Linguistic assistance can help asylum procedures ensure the communication of the asylum narrative and address difficulties that may arise because of differences in language, for example, by providing for interpretation and translation. Here the UNHCR Handbook on Procedures and Criteria for Determining Refugee Status is helpful because it recognizes that asylum seekers are unlikely to speak the language of the host state, and that access to the services of a competent interpreter is, therefore, a basic procedural requirement (UNHCR 1992: paragraph 192(iv)). The relevant provisions of the APD are those requiring that information and linguistic assistance be provided (Article 10). In a pattern already familiar in this instrument, those provisions scarcely meet even the basic requirements set out in the UNHCR Handbook, because they fail to protect the right to interpretation in the applicant's first language, and simply state that information about how to make a claim should be available in a language that the applicant may reasonably be supposed to understand, and that interpretation should be available when appropriate communication cannot be ensured without it (APD Article 10(1) (a) and (b)). Nonetheless, the very existence of the right to information and to an interpreter in the APD, and their transposition into the legislation of member states, proved helpful. In the European Court of Human Rights (*MSS v Belgium and Greece*), in addition to finding that the detention conditions and the situation of destitution in which the applicant found himself were intolerable, it was found that there was clearly insufficient provision for interpreters, that the first asylum interview was often held in a language the asylum seeker did not understand, that the interviews were superficial and did not involve questions about the situation in their country of origin, and that applicants were very seldom accompanied by a lawyer (*MSS v Belgium and Greece*: paragraph 181). The court referred to an earlier case that had held, in relation to the version of the Dublin regime that operated at that time, that an asylum seeker could not be diverted to another country if that country applied asylum law in such a way that the applicant ran the risk of indirect *refoulement* to inhuman or degrading treatment. The state had an obligation to ensure that the intermediary country's asylum procedures afforded sufficient guarantees to avoid an asylum seeker being removed, directly or indirectly, to his country of origin without any evaluation of the risks he faced from the standpoint of Article 3 of the ECHR (*TI v UK*). Although *KRS v UK* had considered the same case, on this occasion, the court looked not just at whether asylum decision-making procedures existed in law, but also at whether they were available in practice (*MSS v Belgium and Greece*: paragraphs 343–344).

Evidence about the Greek Situation

Significantly, the court took into account evidence of asylum seekers' experience in Greece. There was evidence from a range of sources about the dire accommodation conditions for asylum seekers and about lack of access to asylum procedures in Greece. The situation was such that the European Commission had instituted proposals to suspend temporarily the application of the Dublin Regulation (Council of the European Union 2003b) that allowed transfers to Greece to take place, and the court accepted that analysis of the obstacles facing asylum seekers in Greece clearly showed that the prospects of them being able to access the ECtHR through Greek procedures were illusory. The opportunity to take a case to the ECtHR had been significant in *KRS v UK*. However, on this occasion, the court reached a different conclusion. Lack of access to justice, even for an applicant as resourceful as this one, was demonstrated by the fact that *MSS* himself was represented by his

Belgian lawyer in the court process (*MSS v Belgium and Greece*: paragraph 357). The absence of information comprehensible to the applicant and the nonavailability of interpretation laid bare the systemic deficiencies in Greek procedure. While much less significant in human terms than the detention conditions and situation of destitution that *MSS* found himself in, the findings on the lack of linguistic assistance contributed to the conclusion that justice was inaccessible in Greece, and, therefore, the presumption that Greece was a safe third country was no longer automatic. It could be refuted.

Gaps in CEAS Measures and State Discretion

In a similar vein, the CJEU, addressing another Dublin safe third country case, has emphasized that, when deciding how to use their discretion about whether to transfer an asylum seeker to another EU country, member states are obliged to act in accordance with relevant parts of the EU Charter of Fundamental Rights (European Union 2010). Where they could not be unaware that systemic deficiencies in the asylum procedure and in the reception conditions for asylum seekers in another member state amounted to a real risk of a breach of those fundamental rights, then the transferring member state, and its courts, had to interpret that discretion as meaning that transfer was prohibited (*C-411/10 NS and C-493/10 ME*). This is a welcome reiteration of member states' obligations to respect the prohibition on torture and inhuman or degrading treatment and the right to asylum as guaranteed with due respect for the principles of the Refugee Convention. These obligations are reflected in Articles 4 and 18 of the Charter of Fundamental Rights (European Union 2010), and the CJEU decided that member states have to consider whether these fundamental rights would be infringed before transferring an asylum seeker to another EU country for consideration of his or her asylum claim. The CJEU was, however, at pains to say that, as far as it was concerned, its judgment should not be seen as undermining the Dublin system for transferring asylum seekers within the EU. With this in mind, perhaps, the CJEU emphasized that where minor infringements of the APD occur in the handling of an asylum claim, or where asylum seekers' living conditions fall below the standards in the Reception Conditions Directive but do not infringe the Charter of Fundamental Rights, the transfer of the asylum seeker to another member state could still go ahead (*C-411/10 NS and C-493/10 ME*: paragraphs 84–85). Once more, it is left to member states to work out the tipping point at which minor infringements accumulate to form inhuman or degrading treatment, or frustration of the right to asylum.

In these decisions, the topmost courts dealing with European asylum cases have recognized that deficiencies in asylum procedures may be so systemic that it can no longer be rigidly presumed that transfers of asylum seekers to another EU country can occur if that country's asylum procedures are so poor that the fundamental rights of asylum seekers are at substantial risk. Though this is a welcome recognition, and some previously lost protection ground has been regained now, given the situation pertaining in Greece both at the time these cases were heard and subsequently, this is no great step forward in protection.

Member states are still said to have discretion and EU measures still fail to spell out their duties at crucial points. For example, even in the Dublin Recast Proposal, the opportunity to state explicitly the circumstances in which transfer to another member state is prohibited is not utilized. Instead, the measure is framed in such a way that although procedural protections, such as the opportunity for an interview, and linguistic assistance, are said to be mandatory, the decision as to whether another member state is safe is still stated to be discretionary. Also, there is no explicit regulation of how and when the presumption of safety should be considered rebutted and what the implications of a rebuttal would be in specific cases. As Moreno-Lax has noted,

> the sovereignty clause continues to be drafted in discretionary terms, creating the impression that there may be no obligation to have recourse to it (in the situation where) refusing responsibility for the examination of an asylum claim would lead to a violation of non-*refoulement* obligations... Nothing is said regarding the necessity to establish the safety of the removal at the Dublin interview. (2012: 30)

The Dublin Recast Proposal thus places responsibility on the member state to use its discretion in accordance with the non-*refoulement* principle, and it does not specify to member states that their duty is to establish the safety of a Dublin removal. Hence, member states appear to have the right to decide whether or not to transfer, even where adherence to the non-*refoulement* principle means that their discretion can be used properly only by not transferring the asylum seeker to another state. This measure is in similar vein to the effective remedy provisions in the APD, where the member states appeared to have the freedom to decide whether an appeal right should suspend removal, even though the legal position was clear, and obliged them to suspend removal (see also [Craig and Fletcher 2005]).

Conclusion

This chapter outlines the struggle between approaches to the consideration of asylum claims that promote protection and those that promote the deflection of asylum seekers. Deflection usually wins. When tragic scenes of migrants' boats in the Mediterranean cross our consciousness, we see evidence of another level of deflection—the level that deflects asylum seekers before they arrive in the EU. For those who make landfall, EU measures continue to encourage deflection. In this context, protection-oriented approaches can be hard to see, and the prospects for the kind of radical interpretation of the APD that Steve Peers advocated also look slim (2006).

Recent cases indicate that Europe's topmost courts are willing to step in where the context in which an asylum claim is considered is so poor that it frustrates the fundamental right to asylum. However, these topmost courts are accessible only to the most exceptional asylum applicants, and questions about how to encourage all decision makers to consider individual asylum applications in a protection-oriented manner will, for the most part, continue to be left to member states, as the non-*refoulement* duty lies with them. In individual cases this means that the responsibility lies with decision makers within member states, and there is, therefore, scope for those decision makers to take a protection-oriented approach to the asylum seeker's narrative. But as we have seen, the possibilities that the APD and similar CEAS measures provide for curtailing the consideration of claims limit the decision maker's scope for taking a protection-oriented approach, and such procedures work alongside the exclusionary politics of asylum to underscore a culture of disbelief. In this situation, the biggest challenge involves creating an environment in which asylum applicants are sufficiently informed and empowered to be able to communicate their case in a way that reconnects them to the protection principles talked about at the institutional level, but all too often ignored on the ground. In recent years the European Courts, both the ECtHR and the CJEU, have shown that they are willing to follow-up on member states' implementation of CEAS measures, observe the operation in practice of mechanisms designed to deflect refugees, and remind member states of their duties to individual asylum seekers. These duties include the basic procedural requirement that linguistic assistance be provided to ensure that applicants are aware of how to make their claims. From that point, applicants can begin to communicate their claim and address the task of persuading the decision maker to give their narrative full consideration, as is required of all decision makers, not just those located in Europe's topmost courts. In order to avoid reaching the conclusion that for most asylum seekers such high-level intervention will continue to be too little, and to come too late, it still falls to individual decision makers to recognize their role in overcoming the exclusionary politics and the deflection techniques that stand in their way and to make decisions that reconnect the asylum applicant with the principles underpinning the Refugee Convention.

PART II

HostNations

CHAPTER 4

The Politicization of Roma as an Ethnic "Other": Security Discourse in France and the Politics of Belonging

Aidan McGarry and Helen Drake

Introduction

Since the accession of Romania and Bulgaria to the European Union (EU) in 2007, the situation of the Roma community has taken on a much higher profile, forcing the EU to take action on its most marginalized and discriminated minority group. The increased attention on Roma issues has been caused by regressive policies that have targeted Roma in a number of EU member states leading to calls by Roma activists and human rights groups for the EU to intervene. This chapter focuses on the political discourse elaborated by French authorities during the summer of 2010 when Roma migrants were explicitly targeted, marked as security threats, and returned to their home states, notably Romania. The security discourse elaborated by French authorities transformed Roma into an ethnic "other" who did not belong in France and facilitated a context in which their expulsion could be understood. However, this initiative by and large backfired politically, and France found itself the subject of intense opprobrium from the European Commission, as well as numerous domestic actors. At the same time, this "French exception" created a crisis in the EU that hastened the elaboration of the EU Framework for National Strategies on Roma Inclusion in 2011 (hereafter "EU Framework"), effectively making Roma a member state responsibility. On the basis of this single country case study, and with reference to Romania, the chapter explores issues of exclusion and belonging, legal status and responsibility vis-à-vis Roma in national and transnational contexts.

This chapter begins, first, by examining the politics of Romani ethnicity. It does so through an initial focus on Romania, where Roma are frequently excluded from society. Second, the chapter outlines the French Roma crisis that peaked in 2010, but had been building for several years beforehand, and argues that Roma were targeted for expulsion because of their ethnicity, a claim initially denied by French authorities. Subjected to securitization as a group, Roma were constructed as a deviant population who did not belong in France, facilitating a context where they could be expelled. This is despite the fact that subsequently, the government argued that this was not the case, and denied that they had been targeted. Yet while France consistently maintained that the expulsions were legitimate according to laws governing migration, the policy, we argue, was motivated by a populist legitimation that itself was part of a broader discourse linking law and order with immigration and integration. Moreover, responsibility for Roma migrants volleyed between France and Romania in a manner that undermined the freedom of movement principle, while stopping short of breaking it. Ultimately the EU intervened when it became clear that Roma were being targeted as an ethnic group that violates the Race Equality Directive. Accordingly, the chapter explores whether the EU Framework should be seen as a clear signal from the EU that national governments, including France, hold the sole responsibility for Roma communities, and that they should elaborate national policies, monitored by the EU to ensure that Roma can be integrated into the social fabric of member states. The chapter concludes by considering the significance of this for issues of belonging and responsibility.

The Roma community number 10–12 million across the EU and are the most marginalized community in Europe, suffering from discrimination, exclusion, extreme poverty, and an inability to access basic socioeconomic provisions such as health, education, and employment (CoE 2012 and European Commission 2004). Amnesty notes that Roma have "lower incomes, worse health, poorer housing, lower literacy rates and higher levels of unemployment than the rest of the population" that are "the result of prejudice—centuries of societal, institutional and individual acts of discrimination that have pushed the great majority of Roma to society's margins" (2010: 4). The EU has gradually acknowledged the importance of addressing these interconnected problems by elaborating programs and policies that attempt to foster the inclusion of Roma

(McGarry 2012). At the EU level, commitments to inclusion, equality, and rights have informed the debate on how to improve the lives of Roma. If Roma are to be equal citizens then their dire socioeconomic and political situation requires serious attention and must be matched with concrete policies. Roma are a transnational minority community without a kin state and maintain that they are a "nation without a territory" (Acton and Klímová 2001: 216). Indeed, the absence of a kin state to lobby and advocate on their behalf creates a context where governments do not fear the intervention of third party governments concerning their treatment of Roma communities within their territories. Due to a hostile sociopolitical climate toward Roma communities, witnessed recently in a string of repressive measures by member state governments, the EU has emerged as a vocal and powerful ally (McGarry 2010), particularly the Parliament and the Commission.

The issue of responsibility toward EU citizens in the context of migration is nothing new (Bader 2001; Bauböck 1994; Crowley 1999) with the issue centering on how member states address migrants within their territories. However, unlike most other EU migrants, Roma are attempting to escape extreme poverty, widespread societal marginalization, and persecution. Academic discussions on transnational migration have thus far failed to capture the specific dilemma of Roma migration, as they are a transnational minority without a kin state. Debates within the Roma activist community have focused on issues of belonging and responsibility with some advocating a member state responsibility (Gheorghe 2010), while others emphasize the importance of the EU (Daróczi 2011). The case of France reveals the precarious situation of Roma that are seen by the majority society as belonging neither in their home states nor in the host states to which they migrate. This begs the question, who is responsible for the inclusion and integration of Roma communities? The transnational dimension to the situation of Roma is at once the cause of the problems they endure, as they are constructed as a "European problem," as well as the potential solution to these problems, through the intervention of EU institutions.

Roma migrations have resulted in struggles over discourse including how Roma are constructed, defined, and understood. However, Roma themselves have little or no impact on this political discourse, with the voice of Roma in national and transnational debates often silenced or ignored. Roma migration highlights the dilemma Roma face: by migrating from their home countries, they escape problems of poverty, unemployment, and discrimination, but encounter similar problems of marginalization in Western Europe. On the whole, EU member states have thus far proven themselves unwilling or unable to address the integration and inclusion of Roma. Given this situation, the EU has intervened, creating a policy that, not without irony, places the responsibility of Roma firmly back in the hands of member states governments. The EU has come to realize that it cannot ignore the dire socioeconomic and political marginalization of Roma; yet, at the same time, it is wary of Roma becoming a "European" issue, which member states can ignore by passing the responsibility to Brussels.

Roma Belonging in Romania: The Construction of an Ethnic "Other"

Before examining how identity politics and ethnicity are relevant for Roma, it is first necessary to establish the context of Roma migration, and ask why Roma leave their homes in Central and Eastern Europe even when opportunities and quality of life are often no better in Western Europe. The state with the largest Roma population is Romania, and it is to this country that the vast majority of Roma were repatriated from France, as we discuss below. In Romania, both *Rom* and *Țigan* are still used in everyday speech to describe the Romani community, but the *Rom* endonym is regarded as problematic by mainstream society because of its similarity to "Romania" (Rughiniş 2010: 345). "Roma" and "Romanian" are used interchangeably in everyday speech, and due to the negative perception of Roma across Europe Romanian migrants endure prejudice and discrimination. The public debate in Romania reflects an ongoing debate on ethnic boundaries and belonging. Even today, the use of "Roma" is controversial, with the moniker sometimes spelled "Rrom" by those hostile to Roma communities to denote a distinction between Roma and Romania. In Romania, Roma are frequently discriminated against and signify a marginalized community that faces challenges in accessing basic social services, particularly health, education, and employment (Fleck and Rughiniş 2008). Pejorative associations and racial discrimination of Roma are rife, and increasingly Roma are the main targets of far-right extremists (Mudde 2005: 174). During the negotiations for EU accession, Romania demonstrated a willingness to elaborate policies to address the marginalization of its Roma communities, including the establishment in 2001 of a National Strategy for the Improvement of the Situation of Roma and the creation of a National Agency for Roma. However, it has been argued that these initiatives lack teeth and have not adequately addressed the problems the Roma face (McGarry 2008). Exclusion and stereotypes of Roma permeate all levels of society and have created a context where public discourse regarding Roma is almost always pejorative, and remains so despite the creation of the aforementioned Strategy and Agency.

In 2007, journalist Andreea Pana interviewed President Băsescu, after which the president made a comment to his wife, not realizing the microphone was still on: "how aggressive that stinky Gypsy was" (Romani CRISS 2007: 2). Romani CRISS, an NGO, wrote a public letter of protest to Băsescu highlighting the racist manifestations of his comment by citing the ethnic origin of the journalist and the negative associations, respectively "aggressive" and "stinky," to the term "Gypsy," the latter an exonym seen as derogatory for many Roma. Romani CRISS argues that Băsescu, "through his behavior, not only violates the law, but gives a signal of high tolerance towards acts of discrimination" and that this is made worse because of the constitutional provision that states that "the President of Romania represents the Romanian State" (Article 80, paragraph 1) whose role is to guarantee national unity (2). Because Roma are on the margins of society in Romania and elsewhere, they migrate westward, hoping for better prospects. It is the negative ascription of Romani ethnicity that underpins their dire socioeconomic and political situation as the group is stigmatized collectively.

Identity Politics

Identity politics is driven by a desire for emancipation and social justice for members of a given group, yet group identity is constructed and challenged by internal and external forces. Group identity is exploited by ethnic entrepreneurs within the community who articulate claims informed by injustices, discrimination, and marginalization. Yet in the case of the French Roma crisis, the voice of Roma is conspicuously absent. This is typical of the situation in Europe more broadly, where Roma are unable to adequately participate in public life due to structural disadvantage and widespread societal discrimination. The debate in the media and elsewhere was dominated by elites in national political contexts, particularly in France and Romania, as well as in the EU. Across Europe, Roma communities suffer oppression and exclusion, which means that the negative ascription of Romani ethnicity informs their interests. Put another way, in the case of Roma, their identity and interests are insoluble because one informs the other (McGarry 2010). Of course, Romani identity is simultaneously constructed by non-Roma, for example, the discursive intervention by Băsescu reveals the negative ascription of Romani identity. Roma are frequently seen and treated in categorical terms, that is, their identity is distorted by inaccurate and negative associations that are constructed by the majority, many of whom have not met Roma (Hammarberg 2012: 39–40). Due to existing relations and structures of power, Roma are constructed as ethnic "others" who do not belong.

But politicized identity is problematic as it becomes attached to its own exclusion, "because it is premised on this exclusion for its own existence as identity" (Brown 1995: 73). Roma become trapped in a cycle of exclusion; thus their existence as a group is predicated on their marginalization and they in turn become a "stigmatized other" (Calhoun 2003: 532). In so far as Roma as a social group exist, negative ascription of group identity matters because Roma are treated as a marginalized group with policymakers and activists ontologizing them as a "problem" community, elaborating policy interventions and articulating interests, respectively, which reinforce the status quo. Calhoun argues that "treating ethnicity as essentially a choice of identifications [...] neglect(s) the omnipresence of ascription (and discrimination) as determination of social identities" (536). Thus Romani identity, like all identities, is relational and requires recognition from others in order to exist and have meaning.

Roma Migration and Migrants in France

Roma or *gens de voyage* have been present in France for several hundred years and currently number approximately 400,000. Around 10–12,000 of these are estimated to be migrants, 80 percent of whom are thought to come from Romania or Bulgaria (CoE 2010: 4). More recent Roma migration to France began in the 1990s from Central and Eastern European states and accelerated after the removal of the Schengen visa requirement for Romania and Bulgaria in 2001, which paved the way for a three-month stay as a tourist. The fact that citizens of Romania and Bulgaria no longer needed visas in order to travel to France did not mean that the status of these migrants was automatically legal; many would, indeed, shift between a legal and illegal status, regularly returning to Romania to "clean" their passport (Nacu 2011: 136). If a Romanian Roma migrant outstayed his/her three-month period of grace, returning home could be problematic, as home country authorities could confiscate passports or issue an interdiction on leaving the country for several months or years (137). France, particularly concerned about inward migration from Romania, pushed for a bilateral agreement between France and Romania in 2004 for the return and reintegration of Roma migrants. For its part, the EU frequently highlighted the discrimination and exclusion endured by Roma preaccession, particularly in Romania, yet simultaneously sought to restrict the Westward migration of Roma both pre- and postaccession (Guglielmo and William Waters 2005). Indeed, restrictions on the movement of EU citizens from 2004 onward for accession countries (Romania and Bulgaria remain outside of the Schengen Agreement, meaning that work restrictions apply) that had not been put in place for previous enlargements, created a context post-2007 accession where the EU sought to intervene more readily on matters relating to Roma; and we are arguing here that the French crisis accelerated such interventionism.

EU accession means that Roma from Romania and Bulgaria and their fellow citizens have the right to travel and reside for a limited period in France. France introduced work regulations in January 2007 that conspired to inhibit the ability of Roma and other Romanians and Bulgarians to access the labor market. Amid criticism of its continued practice of dismantling camps, the newly elected left-wing government announced in August 2012 that it would expand the number of sectors where Roma can gain employment. A French governmental regulation (Circulaire INT/D/06/000115/C) from 2006 states that "Romanians and Bulgarians are liable to receive notification to leave France ('Obligation de Quitter le Territoire Français' or OQTF) in case they become 'an unreasonable burden for the French social assistance system,' a somewhat unclear notion that makes Roma liable to be fined if they are caught begging in the streets" (Nacu 2011: 138). Such restrictions are to be seen in the broader context, moreover, whereby the 2004 EU enlargement was unprecedently unpopular in France, and included the all-too fictional figure of the "Polish plumber" stealing French jobs and, crucially, undermining France's model of workers' rights; and where France exercised its EU right to implement transitional—restrictive—measures in response to this enlargement. Accordingly, and from 2007, Roma migrants living in camps were collectively given OQTFs, followed by collective "voluntary returns" by plane or bus, organized by the International Organization for Migration; yet many continued to return to France after a short time in their home country. Moreover, the repatriation of Romanians and Bulgarians is still an ongoing practice monitored by the European Roma Rights Centre, that notes that some Roma are being served expulsion orders and placed in detention centers even before their 30-days notice period is up (ERRC 2012). Nacu argues that post-EU accession integration means that the management of Roma migration was increasingly passed down to local authorities; in particular to *les prefets* (the state's representatives) in the regions and *départements* (2011). However, events that occurred in France in the summer of 2010 demonstrate that the Roma issue was chiefly a national rather than a local one, incorporating discussions of exclusion and belonging of Roma as well as political-legal responsibility for Romani communities. Political elites made Roma a national issue whereby the debate on Roma migration and belonging was initiated and pursued for political gain. Roma were an easy target, lacking an effective voice nationally to challenge the hostile discourse.

Indeed, and first, Roma migrants were targeted as an ethnic group by exclusionary policies that served to at once marginalize Roma and question their belonging in France. Through security discourses elaborated by the French authorities, the Roma community was, and still is, constructed as a threat—a body that is not constitutive of the French nation. In short, Romani ethnicity was politicized, meaning that the status and future of Roma in France were deliberated by national and supranational policymakers, and was the object of political competition. The fact that many Roma migrants reside in semipermanent camps in France, including in Marseilles and Grenoble, reinforces the idea that they are outsiders, and strangers whose expulsion can be justified on the grounds that they are different, living by norms and practices that place them outside the majority community, and which, moreover, are deemed to endanger themselves: big brother—or the French state—apparently knows best. In summer 2012, for example, in a notable mirror image of events two years earlier, interior minister in the newly -elected left-wing French government, Manuel Valls, declared that "as Interior Minister, citizen and 'man of the left,' he could not tolerate 'shantytowns' in which 'men' live in intolerable conditions" (Europe 1: 2012). Moreover, living in such camps means that Roma are perceived to be nomadic, that they will move on eventually, although Roma migrate for the same reasons as anyone else, particularly economic necessity and to search for a better standard for living. As EU citizens, Roma are entitled to avail themselves of the freedom of movement principle, and move to France for economic necessity as well as to escape discrimination and marginalization at home. Second, the French Roma crisis has revealed a contentious debate in France, and beyond, regarding the responsibility for Roma, a transnational minority without a kin state. This debate has for the most part been contained within the parameters of legal duty and responsibility and cuts across several political contexts. This includes the supranational level in terms of EU rules governing migration and work; bilateral relations between national governments, notably France and Romania; and the international level, as France has endured widespread criticism from international organizations such as the Council of Europe and the EU.

Yet the politicization of Roma in France reveals a process of "othering" where Roma individuals become members of a culturally defined category. Nationality, gender, class, and sexual orientation are significant categorical identities in contemporary Europe that serve to represent a group, the members of which are somehow equivalent, the same, in terms of the needs and interests. Calhoun maintains that ethnicity can be understood this way, "especially when it is made an object of bureaucratic administration or large-scale media and political attention" (2003: 548). Elite discourse targeting Roma in France demonstrates "a social process of reification that is central to the practice of politicized ethnicity" (Brubaker 2003: 554) in which Roma as a group "become" a security threat. Furthermore, "state and societal discrimination and violent incidents have the potential to politicize Roma ethnicity to explosive heights at worst or to perpetuate unacceptable socio-political and economic inequality at a minimum" (Nancheva 2007: 372). Elites in France ascribe negative associations to Roma ethnicity, creating a context where Roma are seen and treated in categorical terms. This reinforces the claim that they do not belong, because the only projections of Romani ethnicity in political discourse that receives publicity tend to be those "carrying the scandalous, criminal or abnormal" (384).

The Construction of Roma as a Security Threat

President Sarkozy initiated what we conceptualize as the security discourse with the *Déclaration sur la sécurité* (Déclaration de M. le Président de la République sur la sécurité, Conseil des ministres, Palais de l'Elysée) on July 21, 2010, in reaction to events that had conspired to diminish the popularity of the government including a faltering economy, scandal, unpopular pension reform, societal unrest and violence in the suburbs, as well as clashes between police and *les gens du voyage*. Romania and Bulgaria house two of the largest Romani populations in 2007 and their accession to the EU had already marked an immediate change in France in terms of security and immigration policy on Roma, and, crucially, had coincided with the election in May 2007 of Nicolas Sarkozy to the French presidency. Sarkozy, as minister of the interior from 2002 to 2004, and again from 2005 to 2007, had become notorious for his tough talking on immigration, and had lent his name to a succession of bills seeking to tighten the rules of immigration and integration. Upon election as president, Sarkozy fueled an already highly politicized debate on ethnicity and identity. In 2007, for example, Sarkozy had overseen the creation of a controversially named Ministry of Immigration, Integration, National Identity and Co-Development in his first government. Intellectual disgust at the collocation of the terms immigration and national identity was vociferous, and very public—such as the protest petition signed by over two hundred intellectuals from France and abroad, and the resignation of prominent historians and other figures from the board of the *la Cité nationale de l'histoire de l'immigration* (History of Immigration museum) in Paris (L'Express 2007)—and the ministry was disbanded before the end of Sarkozy's five-year presidential term. In a similar vein, in October 2009, the then minister of the interior, Eric Besson, launched a nationwide "Great Debate" on French identity. This was a top-down, state-heavy initiative that fizzled out less than a year later, with no memorable achievements or results to its name but, as with the ministry discussed above, plenty of opprobrium and scorn.

A campaign targeting Roma migrants followed Sarkozy's security declaration in July 2010 that constructed Roma as a security threat and provided a context in which deportations of Roma (primarily to Romania) could be executed. Bearing in mind that they (deportations) were ongoing, and not only of Romanians, on July 29 Sarkozy issued a communiqué declaring the lawlessness that characterized the situation of the Roma population coming from Eastern Europe to France as unacceptable (CoE 2010: 5). He announced that the government was going to dismantle 200 illegal Roma sites that he described as being a source of illegal trafficking and the exploitation of children for the purposes of begging, prostitution, or crime (5). In a now infamous speech at Grenoble the following day, Sarkozy lumped together "*gens de voyage*, Roma immigrants and French citizens 'of foreign origin' and linked, at the same time, crime and migration" (Nacu 2011: 148). This was not the first time that Sarkozy had drawn such an explicit line between immigration on the one hand, and law and order—and thus, crime—on the other. His response, as interior minister, to the large-scale riots of late 2005 had provided a golden opportunity for him to make this connection (misguidedly, as it turned out); and his election itself, in 2007, had followed a campaign that largely aped *Front National* discourse on this terrain. By 2010, members of the government, led by Interior Minister Brice Hortefeux, were referring explicitly to Roma as beggars and law-breakers; by 2012, Interior Minister Manuel Valls was, on the face of it, somewhat more specific in his references to "Romanian delinquancy", although he was also adamant that the illegal camps whose clearance he ordered in August 2012 (Europe 1: 2012) were inhabited by Roma—*les Roms*.

Not surprisingly, Hortefeux's 2010 discourse provoked condemnation of the actions of the French authorities by international organizations, including the EU and the Council of Europe, transnational human rights advocacy networks and Roma activists both within and outside France. These included the national association La Voix des Rroms (The Voice of the R[r]oma, http://la-voix-des-rroms.agence-presse.net), as well as the well-known organization Réseau Éducation Sans Frontières (Education Without Borders) (RESF, http://www.educationsansfrontieres.org/?page=sommaire), whose mission is to protest against and influence policy on all deportations affecting children, and who were vocal in 2010 against the expulsion of "Roma families from Romania," and continue to raise awareness; and local groups such as Solidarité Roms (Roma Solidarity) (http://www.collectifromslille.org), based in Lille in northern France; in 2010, public outrage was directed at the support lent by Lille's Socialist mayor, Martine Aubry, to the expulsion of Roma from the area. Indeed, "observers pointed out that it was the first time in decades that the French authorities had adopted an extreme right-wing position on immigration—using the rhetoric of xenophobia—in line with a supposedly menaced French identity" (Nacu 2011: 149); we saw above how a new ministry was established precisely to institutionalize this connection between immigration, on the one hand, and a supposedly threatened national identity, on the other—and that it was unpopular and short-lived.

Sarkozy made sweeping announcements on the need for future legislative reforms relating to internal security, migration, and citizenship rules, and underlined as a political priority the fight against criminality and his intention to launch an "authentic war on traffickers and delinquents" (Carrera and Atger 2010: 4). He subsequently declared that the behavior of certain travelers and Roma was a particular source of problems in this context and proposed the adoption of a set of measures for dismantling irregular Roma settlements and expelling their inhabitants from France (4). As a follow-up to these presidential declarations, a ministerial meeting "on the situation of travellers and Roma in France" (*Communiqué de presse, Communiqué faisant suite à la réunion ministérielle de ce jour sur la situation des gens du voyage et des Roms*, available at www.elysee.fr) formulated ministerial guidelines deciding to (1) dismantle "irregular settlements" that were referred to as lawless and the source of "illicit trafficking, child exploitation for the purposes of begging, prostitution as well as crime"; (2) return irregularly staying EU citizens accused of "abusing" EU citizenship and freedom of movement law and widening the possibilities for invoking expulsion on the grounds of threats to public order and public security (Statewatch 2010); and (3) increase cooperation with Romanian authorities to facilitate the return of their nationals as well as the socioeconomic inclusion of Romanian Roma.

At a press conference on August 30, Interior Minister Hortefeux said there had been a 259 percent increase in the number of crimes committed by Romanians in 18 months. He stated that "today in Paris, the reality is that nearly one in five thefts is carried out by a Romanian. There is no question of stigmatizing this or that population... but nor is there a question of closing our eyes to a reality" (*Le Monde*, August 31, 2010). According to the French Ministry for Foreign and European Affairs, between July 28 and August 27, 2010, 98 Bulgarians and 881 Romanians were returned to their countries of origin. It should be noted that this practice is nothing new. In 2009, 10,777 Romanians and 863 Bulgarians were returned and prior to the presidential statement in July, 7,439 had already been returned. Those who returned did so "voluntarily" accepting 300 euros per adult and 100 euros per child to facilitate reintegration. In defense of denunciations from abroad, the French government asserted that its policy operated within the confines of the law, namely the Freedom of Movement Directive, because states are allowed to impose restrictions of the movement of persons in the interests of public policy or security (Directive 2004/38/EC, no. 16). They are also able to restrict movement if the individual does not have the financial resources to support themselves and have to depend on social welfare services. In one significant ruling, an administrative court in Lille overturned deportation orders issued against seven Roma on the grounds that the authorities had failed to prove that they were a threat to public order simply for residing in an illegal settlement (CoE 2010: 5).

The French Roma crisis generated significant media attention and international political scrutiny because Roma were targeted as an ethnic group, bringing the legality of the French authorities' actions under the spotlight. To compound matters, several *circulaires* (administrative guidelines) were issued to give instructions as to the ways in which the ministerial guidelines needed to be interpreted and applied. They remained confidential until their disclosure by the media in the beginning of September 2010 (http://www.lecanardsocial.com/Article.aspx?i=193). In fact, until their publication, their existence had been openly denied by representatives of the French government. While it transpires from their reading that the order to evacuate illicit settlements was already given in June 2010, the *circulaire* of August 5, 2010 instructed the authorities to target Roma when implementing the dismantling and expulsions measures (Carrera and Atger 2010: 6). This specifically contravenes a raft of international law including the Racial Equality Directive (2000) that expressly forbids policies that target groups on the basis of ethnicity. In addition to the setting of target numbers of settlements to be dismantled (at least 100 a month so as to reach 300 within 3 months) explicit command was stressed to give priority to those settlements occupied by Roma (Circulaire IOC/K/1017881/J du 5 Aout 2010, Paris, Objet: Evacuation des campements illicits). The *circulaire* even regretted that the implementation of previous governmental instructions had so far resulted in "too few" expulsions of Roma. The operational instructions of August 5 thus provided for the evacuation of irregular settlements and for the immediate return of those Roma irregularly staying in France. When the details of the *circulaire* became known, the French authorities drew widespread condemnation particularly from EU commissioner Viviane Reding. A new *circulaire* was hurriedly adopted by the Ministry of Interior on September 13, 2010, reasserting the overall objective of the original instructions but avoiding any explicit mention of Roma.

The fallout of the French Roma crisis has focused on the fractured diplomatic relationship between, and the legal arguments deployed by, the French authorities and the European Commission, as well as a swathe of public criticism of the French authorities by international organizations and human rights groups. Indeed, it led to a diplomatic row between France and Romania, with President Băsescu asking Sarkozy to stop the expulsions (*Daily Telegraph*, November 1, 2010). However, less is known about the impact of security discourse and the politicization of Roma in terms of belonging and responsibility. While we are careful not to draw a causal arrow from the French Roma crisis to the intervention of the EU, it would appear that the EU Framework places a clearer responsibility on member state governments to integrate Roma. The French Roma crisis is part of a wider postaccession EU context where Roma are the victims of discrimination, racism, and even violence (ERRC 2012), meaning that the EU's intervention should be read as a wake-up call to member states to address the needs and interests of their Roma populations.

EU Intervention and Responsibility: The Impact of Security Discourse

In order to justify its actions, French authorities deployed the language of security, a language that, as seen above, came to typify the Sarkozy presidency. The French argued that the destruction of illegal Roma camps and the deportation of Roma to Romania and Bulgaria were necessary, and this interconnection between labels and policy has emerged as one of the key aspects affecting the relationship between Roma and the French authorities. The pace at which the new security agenda was adopted and implemented was startling but, in retrospect, can be seen as one further illustration of Sarkozy's uniquely "fast presidency" (Cole 2012). However, events themselves, in the summer of 2010, did have a precedent: in France as well as in Italy, from 2007 to 2008 (McGarry 2011). While the protests concerning the deportation of Roma generated media and international political attention in 2010, the fact was that Roma had been evicted from their camps and their residents sent back to their respective home countries for several years. As indicated above, these evictions and deportations did not unleash a wave of protest at that time for several reasons. First, there was no proof that Roma were being targeted specifically as an ethnic group, evicted and deported simply because they were Roma. Second, public discourse had on the whole remained ambivalent about Roma; but when French authorities began to construct Roma as a security threat, it meant Roma were increasingly seen as an unwelcome group that did not belong in France. In short, the public discourse created a situation in which the eviction and deportation of a group of people was possible and could be understood.

The Roma issue, viewed from the perspective of French authorities and citizens, was presented chiefly as an issue of public order and security, and only to a lesser extent was linked to values such as identity and belonging. That secondary message, however, was ever present as bedrock for the language of securitization. Sigona argues that "the citizens' demand for security can be seen as 'legitimate' because citizens, being full members of the social fabric, are bearers of rights and entitlements" (2005: 752). As political elites construct Roma as a threat, they do not belong in France, that is, their entitlement to stay is trumped by the security of French citizens and annulled. But Roma experience a dual process of rejection, from their home and host state, that is, they become symbolically, if not legally, stateless, as governments shirk their responsibility to protect and integrate Roma. In addition, Roma do not possess an effective voice in either Romania or France to lobby on their behalf and articulate their interests. In the absence of any other viable candidate with the requisite legal, technical, normative, and financial authority, the EU has emerged a powerful ally albeit reluctantly. For this reason, the EU Framework was created to send a message that the responsibility for Roma integration lies with member state governments.

Security discourse has taken an increasingly prominent place in national political debates as a consequence of the economic crisis, rising unemployment, and perceptions of rising levels of crime. The security discourse in general is frequently used in conjunction with discriminatory language that tends to "link insecurity with ethnic minorities, including migrants, using them as scapegoats, as has been the case recently with Roma" (CoE 2010: 2). For example, the Parliamentary Assembly of the Council of Europe calls on its member state governments to ensure that a clear distinction be made "in political discourse between individuals who have committed crimes and entire groups of people such as Roma" and highlights the responsibility of political elite to eliminate negative stereotyping or stigmatizing of any minority or migrant group from political discourse (1). France is not the only state in which Roma have been constructed as a security threat with politicians in Italy, Denmark, Sweden, Hungary, and Czech Republic coming under the spotlight for anti-Roma rhetoric.

The Council of Europe's commissioner for human rights, Thomas Hammarberg, condemned the security discourse deployed by French political elite and warned of the responsibility of politicians in the language they use: "During the on-going government campaign in France against crime, Roma from other European Union countries has been targeted as a 'threat against public security.' I am afraid French Government spokespersons have failed to make a clear distinction between the few who have committed crimes and the whole group of Roma immigrants" (Press Release, September 9, 2010). He concludes that sustained efforts are needed to eliminate negative stereotyping of Roma from political discourse and notes that a sense of responsibility toward Roma is missing from Europe's political leadership. In the absence of EU member state governments addressing the needs of Roma and in the case of France, exacerbating marginalization, it fell to EU institutions to take a more critical stance. EU institutions, particularly the Parliament and the Commission, have been vocal in their condemnation of the French authorities. The European Parliament (EP) adopted a resolution on September 9 highlighting the "stigmatization of Roma and general anti-Gypsyism in political discourse" and conveyed its deep concern "at the inflammatory and openly discriminatory rhetoric that has characterized political discourse during the repatriations of Roma, lending credibility to racist statements and the actions of extreme right-wing groups [and] therefore reminds policy-makers of their responsibilities and rejects any statements which link minorities and immigration with criminality and creates discriminatory stereotypes" (EP 2010: 3–4).

Significantly, the EP emphasizes that, in line with the Race Equality Directive (2000), restrictions on freedom of movement and residence on grounds of public policy, public security, and public health can be imposed solely on the basis of personal conduct, and not on the base of ethnic or national origin (4).

The most vocal and senior denunciation of France came from Viviane Reding, the commissioner for justice and fundamental rights. Initially she was concerned that "some of the rhetoric that has been used in some member states... has been openly discriminatory and partly inflammatory" (*EU Observer*, August 31, 2010). However, once the *circulaire* of August 5 was leaked, identifying Roma for specific treatment, the EU adopted a much more threatening tone criticizing France for its targeting of Roma and comparing the current situation of Roma to that of Jews during World War II. Moreover, Reding confirmed "France would be in violation of EU law if the measures taken by French authorities in applying the Freedom of Movement Directive had targeted a certain group on the basis of nationality, race or ethnic origin" (European Commission 2010a). In a press release on September 29, the Commission announced that it would present an EU Framework in 2011 that would assess the use of national and European funds to tackle Roma exclusion in policy areas including poverty reduction, employment, and education. On October 19, Reding confirmed that the Commission would not pursue infringement proceedings, following official commitments made by France to ensure that Roma were not being targeted as an ethnic group (European Commission 2010b). Reding further outlined future EU policy on Roma based on the conviction that integration of Roma requires the active participation of multiple actors at different levels and thus "policies on education, housing, access to health and employment are in the hands of local, regional and national authorities" (European Commission 2010c). Tellingly, Reding notes that "today, in Europe, Roma are discriminated against on the basis of the ethnic origin" (ibid.), which would appear to confirm that racial discrimination is the reason why Roma are targeted, that is, she points that the EU must take into account the "groupness" of Roma and should not treat Roma merely as a socially disadvantaged community. However, what is revealed in the subsequent EU Framework appears to ignore the motivations of the French authorities, the elaboration of security discourse on Roma and the resultant politicized ethnicity.

Prior to the French Roma crisis, the EU had been relatively quiet on Roma issues, regarding it as principally a member state issue; and as scholars such as Boswell and Geddes demonstrate, the EU's contribution to the politics of "immigrant integration" lag far behind those of control over entry to national territories, although a body of EU law is gradually developing in this domain (2010). The EU has been reluctant to treat Roma as a specific ethnic group with particular interests and instead relies on mainstreaming the interests of Roma into existing community policy. The success of such an approach depends on the ability of the EU to coordinate diverse departments and funds. Such an approach is wary of ghettoizing Roma further by creating specific instruments to address the interests of Roma such as a targeted Roma Strategy. The EU announced the EU Framework in April 2011 that will help guide national Roma policies and mobilize funds available at the EU level to support inclusion efforts (European Commission 2011). The EU Framework intends to develop a targeted approach for Roma inclusion by focusing on education, housing, health, and employment. Significantly, the EU is keen to develop 27 national strategies rather than one European strategy; national governments are primarily responsible for developing and implementing policies to protect fundamental rights, tackle discrimination, and promote social inclusion.

For its part, the French government produced a national strategy that rejects an ethnic approach to inclusion, favoring general domestic social inclusion policies in strategic areas (employment, education, health, housing, antidiscrimination) in line with the Republican approach to universal citizenship. Roma advocacy groups have criticized the resultant responses for failing to address how the strategies will be monitored, the lack of attention to discrimination, and for the failure to empower Roma communities to participate in public life (ERPC 2012). However, the EU Framework is silent on the issue of racial discrimination and the politicization of Roma ethnicity through security discourse. If policy does not address the explicit and implicit anti-Gypsyism that pervades political discourse and tackle embedded negative associations of Roma then any integration efforts are bound to fail. The EU Framework affirms the conviction that Roma are a social group with fundamental social problems such as accessing employment and adequate health care but does not recognize that racial discrimination informs their needs and interests. Indeed, "while the Framework recognizes the need to fight discrimination against Roma and ensure their equal access to all fundamental rights, it fails to specify measures to combat discrimination, intimidation, anti-Gypsyism, hate speech or violence against Roma" (ERRC/ERPC 2011).

Conclusion

The French Roma crisis highlights the importance of political discourse regarding the construction of ethnic groups, and demonstrates how hostile policies can be enacted to exclude certain groups. The Roma community are one of the most vilified minority groups in Europe, and face discrimination and exclusion in home states and in those they migrate to. The security discourse elaborated by the French authorities has categorized Roma as a threat, a "problem" group that is not welcome. The Council of Europe notes that high levels of unemployment can lead to increased levels of crime and feelings of insecurity among the general population (2010: 10). What is clear is that the construction of Roma migrants as a security threat by political elite is easy, self-serving, and shortsighted. Dismantling Roma camps and expelling EU citizens of Roma origin because of alleged criminal activity will not address the integration of Roma in the long term. Moreover, "the failure to integrate immigrants into society aggravates social tensions and growing feelings of insecurity and discontent among other inhabitants" (CoE 2010: 10). Security discourse can result in the conviction that Roma are the source of diverse social problems and become blamed for crime but it also suggests "their 'lifestyles' at home or abroad cause troubles to their 'decent neighbors'" (van Baar 2011: 321). Either category means that Roma occupy a nexus of illegality, criminality, belonging, and responsibility.

Roma group identity is ascribed negative associations that serve to reinforce pejorative stereotypes held by society and create a context in which the expulsion of Roma collectively can be tolerated. While the French government maintained that they acted within the parameters of the law, the leaked *circulaire* of August 5 revealed what many had suspected, that Roma were targeted as an ethnic group, which contravenes international norms on human rights. Whether or not the *circulaire* was drafted in part out of ignorance, of the difference between Roma and Romanians; and/or of EU law itself, French authorities were in breach of EU law in targeting a group based on ethnicity, and discussing this group—Roma—as a community that engages in criminality. It is questionable whether the intervention of the EU will work and will surely depend on how willing member state governments are to address the needs of Roma within their territories; the French case studied here rather suggests that, left to their own devices, national governments are unlikely to facilitate their integration, or seek to improve their socioeconomic and political marginalization. Roma in the EU require the same rights and duties as other EU citizens; a crucial aspect of citizenship is belonging. Perhaps because Roma are a transnational minority, member state governments treat Roma as a population who are not their responsibility, but if not member states, then whose? Increasingly, in media and political discourse we hear that Roma are a "European problem," which would suggest a European, that is, EU, solution, but only national governments have the tools and instruments to respond to the needs of EU citizens, including Roma. The commitment to Roma from the EU is important, and certainly the EU can put pressure on national governments, but the ultimate responsibility lies in the hands of member states, even if member states are unwilling to acknowledge and act upon this responsibility or as in the French case, deliberately flout it.

CHAPTER 5

"Good" and "Bad" Immigrants: The Economic Nationalism of the True Finns' Immigration Discourse

Mikko Kuisma

Introduction

The populist radical right parties (PRRP) have received a considerable amount of interest in European politics during the past ten years. Their increasing popularity and electoral success has been debated both in the academic literature and in the wider society. While many PRRPs are now actively engaged in an anti-immigration discourse, many of them arguing against multiculturalism and the difficulties of integrating immigrant communities into native cultures (Eatwell 2004: 2), one central theme in the current debates has been the relationship between cultural and economic motivations in the PRRP social and political discourse. Economic motivations have been emphasized by some (Betz 1994; Kitschelt and McGann 1995) while others have argued that the cultural motivations are primary (Rydgren 2004, 2006; Mudde 2007).

This chapter follows authors such as Zaslove (2009: 314) in arguing that despite the importance of the cultural explanations, we should not disregard the economic motivations or the link between the economic grievances of voters and the electoral success of the PRRPs. The case study here is the True Finns[1] (Perussuomalaiset [PS]), still a relatively understudied party that has often been included in the PRRP cluster, and especially their immigration discourse and policy. True Finns is an openly populist and nationalist party and currently one of the two main opposition parties in Finland after gaining a "big bang" victory in the Finnish parliamentary elections in 2011. The central puzzle about the True Finns is that it seems to be difficult to locate it along the left-right continuum. Further, specifically on immigration, the party seems to have an internal tension between the rather moderate old populism of the mainstream party and the more radical politics of the nationalist anti-immigration wing of the party. Instead of arguing that the party is a chameleon or some kind of a continuous compromise, I argue that it is more coherent than appears at the outset. The glue that ties the party together is nationalism, more specifically economic nationalism. The contrast here is Mudde's "nativist nationalism" (2007: 19) that, as I will argue below, does not fit in with the True Finn approach to immigration. Economic nationalism could be seen as a useful compromise between nativist nationalism and "welfare chauvinism" (Andersen and Bjørklund 1990; Andersen 1992; Kitschelt and McGann 1995) as the core of the PRRP ideology, especially in the case of the True Finns.

The argument in the chapter proceeds in three steps. First, the chapter begins by discussing the immigration discourse and policy of the True Finns and points at the interesting tensions between cultural and economic arguments that arise from their distinction of immigrants into two normatively opposing categories, "good and bad immigrants." Second, in order to analyze this further, as a way of reconciling some of these tensions, I propose that economic nationalism is adopted as an approach that problematizes this wider debate on PRRPs and immigration. It has hitherto been a rather underutilized approach within the literature. Concentrating on the nationalist ontology instead of the policy content of economic nationalism can provide a useful insight into the PRRPs. Indeed, this could be seen as particularly pertinent in the Nordic context where immigration could be seen as a catalyst for "welfare chauvinism" (Andersen and Bjørklund 1990; Andersen 1992; Kitschelt and McGann 1995).

However, I argue that welfare chauvinism goes only some way in explaining the True Finns' ideology and that economic nationalism could offer a more rounded and balanced view of what they stand for and what their discourse is centered on. Their economic nationalism is not only an approach to protectionist economic policies but also one that is essentially built on a nationalist ontology and, as such, fits as a coherent part of their overall ideology. As such, it reconciles some of the apparent tension between the mainstream party and its more extreme anti-immigration wing. Furthermore, approaching immigration primarily through economic justifications can also be a sound strategic choice, as this serves to depoliticize and deradicalize their immigration policy, hence doing away with the more sensitive ethno-cultural arguments and accusations of racism and xenophobia.

Methodologically, the chapter relies on discourse analysis of True Finns' party programs and manifestos. They are also triangulated with speeches and blog entries from various key political actors within the party. As Mudde (2007: 256–276) argues, while the explanations concentrating on structural transformations and social upheavals are of value, the PRRPs also possess political agency and, as such, the parties themselves should be considered as a major factor explaining their success. Thus, the chapter concentrates on an internal supply-side analysis and aims to understand how the party at the central level combines economic and cultural arguments founded upon a nationalist ontology.

From Thin Multiculturalism to "Good and Bad Immigrants"

The True Finns emerged as a major player in the Finnish political scene in the 2009 EU elections and consolidated its position by gaining a "big bang" election victory in the 2011 parliamentary election. They more than quadrupled their share of the national vote from the parliamentary election of 2007 and became one of the two main opposition parties after refusing to enter the coalition government due to fundamental disagreements on the Euro bailout packages.

The True Finns have their foundations in "old" agrarian populism of the 1950s and 1960s when Veikko Vennamo founded the Finnish Rural Party (Suomen maaseudun puolue [SMP]). While not often recognized as such, SMP fits quite nicely in the second phase of radical populist parties as described by von Beyme in his seminal article (1988, see also Andersen and Bjørklund 2000: 193–194). The central role of the charismatic leader Veikko Vennamo has also led some to classify SMP as a "new populist" party (Taggart 1996: 37).

The True Finns had a slow start after they were founded on the ruins of the SMP but found their success through a combination of old Vennamo-style populism and immigration-criticizing statements. This has meant that they have quite readily, especially outside Finland, been clustered in the PRR party family. However, there is not a clear consensus on what a PRRP looks like and, most importantly, if the True Finns actually fit that model.[2] Indeed, some commentators have argued that they are not a radical right party (Andersen and Bjørklund 2000: 193–194; Ignazi 2003: 60). Some, especially the Finnish commentators (see useful discussion in Arter 2010: 500), have also placed them to the left of center due to their support of the universal welfare state, taxation, and the role of the state in general. However, in one of the most recent additions to this debate it is claimed that certain aspects of nativism in their politics and the way in which "Finnishness" has been put on a pedestal does, indeed, make them a PRR party (502). However, it seems from this that Arter is conflating the concepts of nativist nationalism and radical right. While he is correct in suggesting that national culture and national values are the "basic *geist*" of the party, these features alone do not make them into a radical right party. Indeed, pride in national culture and national values are not exclusive property of radical or, indeed, any right-wing parties.

The debate on the role of national culture and nationalism as the centerpiece of True Finn ideology is obviously linked to the popular discourse on immigration. The party has had its fair share of racist anti-immigrant controversy both before and after the 2011 election through statements made in blog entries and interviews by its members. One of the most documented examples is the court case of Jussi Halla-aho, an unappointed leader of the anti-immigration faction of the party and one of its most visible parliamentarians. He was convicted in 2009 of disturbing religious worship after making offensive comments about Prophet Mohammad and Islam in his blog. After appeals, the case was heard by the Supreme Court, which found Halla-aho guilty of both disturbing religious worship and ethnic agitation and increased the original fine given by the District Court (Helsingin Sanomat 2012). It is notable that at the time of the Supreme Court's decision, Halla-aho was already a True Finn MP and the chair of the Parliamentary Administration Committee that deals with immigration affairs and matters pertaining to the Church. He was forced to leave his position as the chair of the Committee following the Supreme Court's verdict.

This and many other scandals relating to the conduct of some individuals within the party have led to rather widespread accusations of the party being racist and xenophobic. A major argument was propelled by an opinion poll that demonstrated that a quarter of True Finn voters recognized racist characteristics in themselves. The then president Halonen also publicly noted this and commented that "people who recognize racism in themselves have ended up voting for the True Finns" (Mykkänen 2011). However, a close reading of the party documents demonstrates that the True Finn discourse and policy on immigration is less extremely nativist or hostile to foreigners in principle than one could assume based on both the popular understandings and the dominant academic, strongly cultural, explanations behind PRRPs.

The True Finn approach to immigration adopted in the first party program was that migrants are welcome and are treated as equals as long as they treat Finnish society with respect.

> We also welcome foreigners to build our country and to live here but we won't allow any of them to come here to harm our people's home. They have to accept our social and justice system and we will in turn accept their different cultural point of departure and worldview and give them the right to live as equal individuals with us. (Perussuomalaiset 1995)

Notable here is the last statement about respecting the cultural differences, which could go as far as to advocate a thin form of multiculturalism (Baumeister 2000: 35–37, 2003).

In the following four-party programs and manifestos there were no statements about immigration (Perussuomalaiset 1999, 2000, 2001, 2003b). It seemed to be largely a nonissue for the party. However, immigration resurfaced again in the 2003 general election manifesto. In the manifesto, one paragraph under the section on population and family policy was devoted to immigration, and the tone was much harder than in the 1995 program. The paragraph begins by stating that Finland's remote location has thus far shielded it from "the population and racial problems" that have emerged in the wider world (Perussuomalaiset 2003a). In other words, here the party began making noise about its skepticism toward multiculturalism. The party conditioned everything again by saying that foreigners should be welcomed but the condition for this is wholesale assimilation. This follows Eatwell's (2000: 413) "holistic nationalism" where assimilation into the "home" culture is acceptable. Here also they were much less understanding of cultural difference. Basically, all immigrants should have adopted a Finnish way of life and, more or less, become Finnish. They also made strong cultural hints about more specific cultural differences that might clash with their worldview:

> In Finland we should not tolerate practices that are alien to our culture and traditions that insult human dignity, such as female circumcision, child marriage and cruel honour-based practices. (Perussuomalaiset 2003a)

Most interestingly, however, the 2003 election manifesto is the first place where the party made a clear statement about the desirability of labor migration by claiming that "immigrants should give their professional work effort into creating our common welfare" (ibid.). While it is not said aloud, the implication obviously is that refugees and asylum seekers, whose legal rights and possibilities for employment are more limited in any case, have become the unwanted group for the party.

The 2003 election campaign in general was a turning point for the True Finns, as Timo Soini was able to persuade the former wrestler, boxer, and actor Tony Halme to stand in the election. Halme was a popular, though a controversial, figure who stood as an independent candidate on the True Finns list and ran his own campaign that was only loosely connected to the party (Soini 2008: 106). This strategy must have suited the party rather well, as they received his votes but had a "get out of jail" card in case his statements became too extreme for the party to handle. However, some argue it was through Halme that the True Finns were able to reach to a new constituency and to claim ownership of the immigration debate (Hannula 2011: 72–80; see also Kestilä 2006; Arter 2010). His political career was, in the end, very short due to a number of personal issues, but his role for the party was undeniably important.

After the 2003 manifesto it took another four years before immigration resurfaced on the True Finns agenda in the 2007 election manifesto. This time the party devoted much more significant sections of the manifesto to immigration and it also clearly began consolidating its views on the issue. Between the 2007 and 2011 elections, a more radical anti-immigration wing joined the party and this is when immigration really became a key issue for the True Finns. The main statement on immigration in the 2011 election manifesto was that Finland should remain strict "with regard to immigration that has negative consequences to Finnish society" (Perussuomalaiset 2011: 40). This was followed up by stating that "Finland should be open to immigration that has neutral or positive impact" (40). Negative and positive impact could be, of course, interpreted in a number of ways. This could easily relate to both economic efforts from the wider society on immigrants and the cultural impact of immigration. However, in the manifesto, this is primarily qualified by saying that "an immigrant who is able to sustain her/himself is welcome" (40). This would mean that the party *tolerates* the very least those immigrants who have a job and who pay their taxes even if they represented a different ethnic or religious group. This, it could be argued, is a step away from the thin multiculturalism in the previous programs. As such, Mudde's nativist nationalism does not necessarily fit in with the True Finn immigration discourse.

However, the distinction between good and bad immigrants is an important one. It is suggested by the party that most asylum seekers are simply fleeing poverty and have no grounds to begin with for their asylum cases. The debate has its roots in the late 1980s and 1990s when groups of Somali migrants came to Finland from the disintegrating Soviet Union and when the first groups of refugees entered Finland from the former Yugoslavia. These groups were quite widely labeled as "life standard refugees" (Hannula 2011: 18). This debate has continued since, and in the anti-immigration discourse there is a constant suspicion of groups of migrants coming to Finland simply to abuse the system. And here the party has recommended a change in the processing of asylum claims and a 24-hour system for extraditing ungrounded asylum applications from applicants who have, for example, already been declined by another EU country (Perussuomalaiset 2011: 41).

The party is also very strict about the policy of reuniting family members and would want to include a work-based criterion to these processes. They advocate a policy by which also family members who join their husbands, wives, parents, and so on should be able to sustain themselves. One way in which this is to be done is through adopting the so-called Danish model according to which the person who applies for family reunification must not have been in receipt of income assistance for the past two years (43). The process of family reunification is one key item that has been fought by the more radical anti-immigration wing of the party, and obviously there is a link here to the "life standard refugee" discourse as well (Hannula 2011: 18).

While the immigration policy of the True Finns at the mainstream party level is relatively moderate and often argued through economic discourse, there is also a more radical anti-immigration wing within the party. After Tony Halme, the wider anti-immigration movement emerged outside of the party and was then very much a movement in search of a political party (74–76). Some True Finn members from this radical wing of the party belong to an organization called Finnish Sisu (Suomen sisu[3]), originally a youth organization of the Association of Finnish Culture and Identity (Suomalaisuuden liitto) (ibid.). Finnish Sisu had to then leave the main organization, as claims about members of the organization having national socialist sympathies emerged. Recently, anti-immigration groups have organized through the Internet an online discussion forum "Homma."[4] This was founded after the guestbook of Jussi Halla-aho's Internet blog *Scripta* was not able to handle the increased flow of messages (ibid.). The cofounder of the forum, Matias Turkkila, was appointed as the editor of the True Finn party newspaper *Perussuomalainen* and webmaster of the True Finn Party website (www.perussuomalaiset.fi) in May 2012 (Perussuomalaiset 2012).

In the run up to the 2011 election, 13 True Finn candidates came together and published their own election manifesto, the Sour Election Manifesto (Nuiva vaalimanifesti), which was specifically profiled to address views critical of immigration and multiculturalism (Nuiva vaalimanifesti 2011). Six of the candidates who signed the manifesto got elected to the Eduskunta. Their unappointed leader Jussi Halla-aho received over 15,000 personal votes, the sixth highest vote share by a candidate in the whole election. The signatories to the Sour Election Manifesto received a total of around 60,000 votes, which is significantly more than the whole party received in, for example, the 2003 election. The 43,816 votes received by True Finns in 2003 were enough for the party to return three MPs to the Eduskunta. As such, based on the above, it could be said that this current anti-immigration faction of the party represents a "party within a party."

However, while the signatories to the Sour Election Manifesto emphasize the ethno-cultural more, they also use more economic arguments in putting their case forward. This is done especially toward the end of the manifesto, after the strong claims against multiculturalism. In the final paragraphs of the manifesto, the signatories duplicate almost word for word the claims of the party election manifesto about not being against immigration but being against immigration that is neither neutral nor positive for the Finnish society (ibid.). Similar views were voiced by Jussi Halla-aho, the leading anti-immigration voice of the party already a couple of years before the Sour Election Manifesto:

> My supporters and I do not, of course, oppose immigration per se but only bad immigration. There is no problem at all with people migrating because of work. If a person has a sensible reason to come to Finland, then welcome to Finland. (Ajankohtainen kakkonen 2009)

So, after seemingly departing from the official relatively moderate party line, they return to the fold and make the good immigrants versus bad immigrants argument and do this by bringing back the more economic rather than the purely ethno-cultural claims. Hence, even here the party discourse cannot be explained purely through Mudde's nativist nationalism.

The True Finns' immigration discourse provides also a direct link to what some have labeled "welfare chauvinism" (Andersen and Bjørklund 1990; Andersen 1992; Kitschelt and McGann 1995; Banting 2000; Andersen 2007). Much of the debate is built around Alesina and Glaeser's seminal work that raises questions about the possibility of reconciling ethnically diverse society and generous welfare regime (2004). The two hypotheses related to this are that, first, ethnic diversity challenges heavy redistribution toward the poor because it is difficult to generate feelings of national solidarity across ethnic lines. Second, it has been suggested that multicultural policies designed to accommodate ethnic groups further undermine national solidarity. This has also been coined as the "progressive's dilemma" (Kymlicka and Banting 2006: 283). The ethnic heterogeneity of the United States, it has been argued, has been the reason for the reluctance to introduce generous welfare programs across America. While some argue that the American experience is unique (Banting 2000; Finseraas 2012), some have demonstrated that it could be replicated in Europe as well (Larsen 2011). Indeed, contrary to the American roots of Alesina and Glaeser's theory, Menz (2006: 393) considers welfare chauvinism to have Scandinavian origins.

Welfare chauvinism could also provide a link between the True Finn immigration discourse and the wider responsibilization of social citizenship (Rose 1996). The "no rights without responsibilities" discourse advocated by neoliberal scholars, such as Mead (1986), and New Social Democrat politicians, such as Göran Persson, Paavo Lipponen, and Tony Blair, also fits in with the True Finns discourse. Third Way Social Democrats (see, for example, Giddens 1998) singled out "unconditional" social citizenship entitlements as promoting "moral hazard," called for conditionalities and responsibilization of social citizenship on the principle of "no rights without responsibilities," and put a premium on personal pension savings and workfare policy (Giddens 1998; Kuisma and Ryner 2012; see also Putnam 2000). However, the difference between Third Way Social Democrats and True Finns is that the True Finns are advocating an ethno-national division for responsibilization of welfare and citizenship (Kuisma and Ryner 2012: 336). Obviously, their take on the responsibilization of social citizenship is obviously closely related to welfare chauvinism. Having said that, as I have argued above, welfare chauvinism alone does not explain the True Finns' immigration discourse and policy.

Economic Nationalism and the PRR in Europe

Hence, both cultural and economic explanations could be used in understanding the motivations behind the immigration discourse and policy of the True Finns. Elements of nativist nationalism and welfare chauvinism are clearly present but neither of these approaches seems to be able to fully characterize the True Finns as a party and especially their stance on immigration. More importantly, both of these approaches continue to pull into two opposite directions, not reconciling the culture versus economy tension in the current scholarship on PPRPs. The existing literature on PRR has, of course, not neglected its political economy aspects, and this is not what I argue in this chapter. On the contrary, rather a lot has been written about the political economy of the PRR (Rydgren 2004; Zaslove 2008a, 2009; Afonso: pp. 17–36 this volume). It is the *relationship* between cultural and economic arguments that I am mostly interested in exploring here, and economic nationalism can be a useful tool in that quest.

The mainstream approaches to (International) Political Economy could be divided into two broad categories. Despite representing an otherwise different worldview, both liberalism and socialism are founded upon a cosmopolitan ontology, against which prominent economic nationalists, such as Friedrich List, were arguing (Abdelal 2005: 25; Hont 2005). It could be said that economic nationalism is the alternative to liberalism and socialism in political economy because it, due to its particularist ontology, cannot accommodate the cosmopolitanism of either liberalism or socialism. In the literature on PRRPs political economy is generally rather understudied area but economic nationalism in particular is largely ignored, despite the explanatory potential it could offer to the study of the PRRPs.

Despite the mainstream International Political Economy literature viewing neoliberalism and nationalism as antithetical (Harmes 2012), neoliberalism features as a crucially important aspect of Kitschelt's "winning formula," which essentially argued that the key for electoral success for PRRPs is in combining neoliberal economics with authoritarian politics (Kitschelt and McGann 1995; see also Betz 1994). Even after Kitschelt's slight revision of his winning formula to include more centrist economic positions of the PRRPs in the 1990s (Kitschelt 2004), this strand of literature emphasizes the economic liberalism, broadly defined, within PRRPs. Hence, at least in this formulation of populist political economy, liberalism and nativism can coexist.

In addition to the liberal economics argument from Kitschelt, Betz, and others, some have, however, pointed out that some populist parties have also adopted a clearly antiliberal economic position. Zaslove argues that some parties within this party family belong to an antiglobalization movement (Zaslove 2004, 2008b). This would, of course, fit in well with their ontological critique of cosmopolitan liberalism. Hence, they reject at least the neoliberal worldview based on global capitalism. Indeed, in addition to rejecting global capitalism, True Finns could also be seen as belonging to the center-left with regard to their economic policy through which they support the welfare state, funded by heavy redistribution through progressive taxation (Perussuomalaiset 2011: 44). Therefore, it seems that within the PRRP family both liberal and socialist economic arguments could be used and appropriated through nationalism.

However, economic nationalism has often ignored its own ontological foundations and has tended to emphasize economic policy instead of the nationalism it is built on. Indeed, following Pickel (2003) and Helleiner (2002) I argue that instead of connecting economic nationalism primarily to its policy manifestations, such as protectionism or (neo)mercantilism, we should concentrate on the nationalist ontology of economic nationalism. What we can achieve through using economic nationalism as a vantage point is moving away from the more or less irreconcilable culture versus economy debate toward a more holistic understanding of the ideology of the PRR. Through using economic nationalism as a theoretical framework it is possible to incorporate the economic concerns as part of a wider nationalist ideology of PRR. Here the case in point is the True Finns but I suggest that this framework could be a more general approach to looking at the PRRPs in Europe.

What is significant here is that an approach to the political economy of the PRR focused on its nationalist ontology could incorporate liberal and socialist economic policies depending on how they are linked through discourse to the nationalist project. Indeed, as Pickel recognizes

> The economic dimensions of specific nationalisms make sense only in the context of a particular national discourse, rather than in the context of general debates on economic theory and policy. (2003: 106)

Here, economic nationalism could have a liberal flavor if advocated in, for example, the context of the British political tradition, whereas in countries where the institutions of the universal welfare state have been significant in framing the boundaries of the national logics of appropriateness, the solutions could be more redistributive in nature but equally nationalist.

While Friedrich List appreciated liberal principles more than is often acknowledged, Istvan Hont also argues that Adam Smith, the most prominent economic liberal, was, in fact, also an economic nationalist, be it a moderate liberal one (2005: 124–125). Furthermore, Levi-Faur points out that John Maynard Keynes was also an economic nationalist (1997: 367, n. 30) and even contemporary examples could be found from the group of broadly moderate liberal politicians and economists.

Therefore, it is problematic to present economic nationalism and economic liberalism as antithetical. Even for Friedrich List himself economic nationalism was a synthesis of liberalism and mercantilism rather than extreme protectionism. Other prominent economic nationalists, such as Hamilton, also supported the principles of free trade (Harlen 1999: 734).

This is also replicated by the True Finns who buy into the principles of free-market liberalism at home but see it necessary that international markets are controlled by nation-states and not turned into a playground of global corporations and footloose capitalists. The EU is an example of where this is already happening, and while the True Finns are not against cooperation between governments, they do oppose the common market and monetary union, as they go against their nationalist worldview and maintain that democratic decision making at the supranational level is not possible and so the only outcome of transnational or global capitalism is the increasing power of the global financial sector over national political institutions (Perussuomalaiset 2011: 33). As such, economic nationalism could be seen as a very helpful way in which the cultural and economic grievances and the apparent tensions between liberal and socialist economic policy solutions could be reconciled and also through which it is possible to begin appreciating the nationalist ontology that lies at the heart of the politics of many PRRPs.

Economic Nationalism of the True Finns

It is appropriate to return to the True Finns and ask how economic nationalism can be used as a framework to further understand their immigration discourse and policy and problematize the apparent tension between the mainstream of the party and its anti-immigration wing.

True Finn Leader Timo Soini's own politics has maintained a strongly traditional SMP populist line that has been revitalized for the twenty-first century through what could certainly be labeled as economic nationalism. He openly and proudly describes himself as a populist (Soini 2008: 168). His variety of populism is as much about the "how?" as it is of the "what?" of politics. He is deeply influenced by the idea of the individual and of the people. And here the people represent the third way between the state and market. Populism is also about the way in which the political message is delivered. Soini openly admits to being a political dissident and maverick and this is one part of how the message is delivered to the people (149). He comes up with buzz phrases and one-liners that simplify a complicated political message into easily accessible bite-size chunks that appeal to the average voter. However, the very meaning of the term "people" connects his populism with nationalism and, for the purposes of this chapter, economic nationalism. The people Soini and True Finns talk about are members of the Finnish nation and the lines between those who belong and those who do not are drawn on national terms. It needs to be added that Finnish language offers good grounds for being ambiguous, even intentionally so, about this, as the word *kansa* in Finnish means both people and nation. In other words, depending on the purpose and the occasion, either interpretation of the use of the term *kansa* can be appropriated. However, it is important to add here that the True Finns do not see this as an exclusively ethno-national definition. Integration of immigrants to the Finnish society and even naturalization are a part of their policy (Perussuomalaiset 2011: 43). Here they seem to represent a happy compromise between the nativist nationalism of Mudde and holistic nationalism of Eatwell.

Soini's politics is all about providing a third way between the power of capital and capitalism on one hand and the power of what he calls society, on the other. "The power of money, crude capitalism, is as dark as the power of society that neglects the individual" (2008: 155). Here his approach departs from liberal and certainly from libertarian individualism, as he still sees a need for people to work together, to express solidarity to each other and to acknowledge shared interests. "It is about politics that consists of more than individual but that would not exist without individuals" (149). Emphasizing the role of the people and the individual, he is able to demonstrate that he is in principle opposed to both the laissez faire capitalism of the political right and state centrism of the left.

> The True Finns is a nationalist and Christian social party. We do not believe in right-wing power of money or in the left-wing power of the system. We believe in and build all of our expectations primarily on the human being. (Perussuomalaiset 2011: 6)

However, it needs to be pointed out here that the True Finns are by no means advocating an illiberal economic model. They accept free-market capitalism in principle but see its global and regional variants as deleterious for Finnish society. They certainly buy into the competition state paradigm (see, for example, Cerny 1990). "The True Finns think that it is in the Finnish interest to engage in free trade and cooperate across borders but still decide what kind of structures Finnish society is built on" (Perussuomalaiset 2009: 5). In other words, liberalism is adopted as the main economic policy model but through a nationalist discourse. The adaptability of the Finnish society to changes emanating from the outer world is one of its strengths and Finnish culture is one of the key resources for the competitiveness of the Finnish economy (5). This, I argue, is very clearly an economic nationalist statement.

Crucially, many of their cultural and nativist statements are connected with their claims about socioeconomic issues. In the EU election platform 2009, the party claimed that the increasing European cooperation on immigration serves to worsen the taxation structures needed for sustaining a welfare state, as the willingness of citizens to pay taxes decreases because of immigration (3). So, here they effectively link the political economy of welfare to multiculturalism and other cultural issues and through this provide a link to the literature on the relationship between multiculturalism and the support for the welfare state.

Another issue, which is given both cultural and economic importance, is work. The duty to work is clearly considered as an economic issue, as work removes pressure from welfare but at the same time it is also linked to national traditions. Working and the will to gain employment are also seen as those national customs and traditions immigrants need to be integrated to (4). The welfare state is, in general, something the True Finns staunchly defend but they put a heavy emphasis on the duty of all citizens to work and to express solidarity toward their community. The commitment to the welfare state is certainly made very clear in the party platforms. More than a third of the 2011 True Finn platform was dedicated to issues related to the welfare state.

> The True Finns support the traditional Nordic welfare model where social and health services are guaranteed equally to all Finnish citizens. The health and welfare of the citizens is both a value in itself but also the pre-requisite for Finnish success in economic competition. (11)

Here in no unclear terms the party makes a very obvious connection between the cultural value of the welfare state and its economic importance in maintaining Finnish competitiveness. They go on to state later on that equality, both in terms of equality of opportunity and the equality of outcome, achieved through income transfers can have a positive effect on national unity (11). These issues and concepts create circles of cause and consequence in their ideology and manage to effectively integrate economic arguments with cultural narratives. They represent both nativist nationalism and welfare chauvinism, both of which could be understood and tensions between which could be reconciled through economic nationalism and the nationalist ontology it is based on.

Conclusion

To conclude, the immigration discourse policy of the True Finns can be definitely understood and navigated with the help of economic nationalism. What epitomizes this broad and at times rather complicated discourse is the classification of immigrants into good immigrants and bad immigrants. Labor migration is at least neutral to the economy but in many cases it has positive effects as long as the immigrants attempt to integrate and follow national laws and norms. Hence, the True Finns view this kind of immigration rather positively. However, the case against bad immigrants is made through both economic and cultural arguments, using nativist and welfare chauvinist arguments. Nonwork-based immigrants, refugees, and asylum seekers, for example, are seen to cost the economy, and their effect in an economic sense is negative. From a cultural perspective they also have a deleterious effect on the community by not being able to integrate into the mainstream society, increasing the ghettoization within Finnish cities.

What I have argued here is a revival and reassessment of the theory of economic nationalism as a tool for understanding the political motivations and strategic choices made by PRRPs. I have argued that the ongoing debate between cultural and economic motivations behind the PRRP ideology and policy is not always helpful. This debate has separated two broad areas of ideology and policy and has done this at the expense of the ontology of those ideologies. Here the apparent omission of economic nationalism from the debates is rather surprising. I suggest that through reviving economic nationalism as a theoretical tool by which the PRRPs can be understood, we can return to emphasizing the nationalist ontology of the PRR ideology and policy and appreciate the interconnectedness between cultural and economic arguments under this ontological premise.

My discussion of the True Finns demonstrates that the party has adopted a position that could, indeed, be labeled as economic nationalism. Crucially, their economic and cultural arguments are intertwined through a broad ideology that is founded upon nationalism. Here nativist nationalism and welfare chauvinism are able to explain only parts of the puzzle. Emphasis on Finnish culture and Finnish values is clear and the role of the welfare state in this is undeniable. However, there is also a more socioeconomic argument linked to the welfare state, which cannot be explained through nativism alone. The support of the Nordic welfare state and adoption of the competition state discourse are useful examples of this. However, as I pointed out in the final part of the chapter, the best example of the economic nationalism of the True Finns is their immigration discourse and policy.

As such, the cultural effects can also become economic. For example, it has been argued that the economic side effects of bad immigration can lead to a decreasing social cohesion and, hence, a decreased willingness to pay taxes and contribute to the economy and consequently a harming effect on Finnish competitiveness. All in all, while this demonstrates a dialectic and interrelational relationship between the cultural and economic aspects in the True Finns' immigration discourse, in the end what is shared between both of these is the ontology they share, namely that of nationalism. And the appreciation of the nationalist worldview is also a potential way of explaining why the mainstream and more moderate core of the party can rather happily tolerate the more radical anti-immigration wing.

Notes

1. In August 2011 the party introduced the Finns Party as its official English name. However, as the new name can cause potential confusion and as the original translation of the party's name has been used widely in the literature, it will also be used throughout this chapter.
2. Indeed, while it is common to cluster a certain number of new parties into one new party family, a debate about the appropriate terminology is rife. The terms "populism" (Canovan 1999; Albertazzi and McDonnell 2007; Zaslove 2008b), "radical right" (Kitschelt and McGann 1995; Rydgren 2007), "extreme right" (Hainsworth 1992, 2000, 2008; Ignazi 2003) and combinations of these, such as "populist right" (Bornschier 2010), "populist radical right" (Mudde 2007), "radical right-wing populism" (Betz 1993, 1994), and "neo-populism" (Betz and Immerfall 1998) are only a few examples of the terminology used to describe essentially the same broad group of parties that have emerged as a response to the new social cleavages that have challenged Lipset and Rokkan's (1967) claims about the "freezing" of the European party systems by the 1960s.
3. Sisu is an untranslatable concept in Finnish language denoting courage, guts, strength, integrity, and stubbornness. The term is widely used in national romantic literature and art.
4. Homma is a colloquial Finnish word that means, roughly translated, a job.

CHAPTER 6

"A Two-Way Process of Accommodation": Public Perceptions of Integration along the Migration-Mobility Continuum

Kesi Mahendran

Introduction

Despite decades of policy and academic focus, integration remains a contested and opaque concept. Yet in recent years with its promise of social cohesion and shared citizenship, it has obtained a morally privileged status in contrast to the political disenchantment now attached to multiculturalism. This chapter presents a case study on public perceptions of integration among migrants and nonmigrants in two cities within the European Union, Edinburgh and Stockholm. Despite the European Union's guidance within its Common Basic Principles for the Integration of Third-Country Nationals that "integration is a two-way process of accommodation by all migrants and residents of member states" (Council of the European Union 2004), there remains a stubborn focus on individual migrant competencies such as language attainment, employment, educational attainment, political participation, and citizenship, which is at best a partial reading of the dimensions outlined within the Brussels-led MIPEX initiative (Niessen et al. 2007). As a result, integration debates are now influenced by a proliferation of management information data, often coordinated by the EU. The emphasis on migrant's individual competencies is coupled with a paucity of evidence on public perceptions of integration and little understanding of how they are influencing policy.

In investigating the role of public perceptions in the politics of migration, the case study presented here addresses this gap. The aim is not merely to complicate understandings of integration and its ongoing construction but rather to reveal that it is perfectly possible to work with diverse conceptualizations of integration among a segmented public. The findings presented here challenge a common perception of an anti-immigration public often based on assumptions of xenophobic atavistic tendencies or secondary sources such as media representations.

It is worth stating at the outset that there is a wealth of literature on people's attitudes toward different categories of migrants and their integration such as the work of Bogardus on social distance scaling (1933) and within acculturation studies (Berry 2006). Yet there is a relative paucity of research that examines public understandings of the integration concept itself. Analysts who want to go beyond media representations of public opinion must rely on a small number of questions in public opinion surveys. There is also virtually no research into nonmigrants' understandings of their own integration. Even well-meaning actors can resort to ideal-type notions of integration that require migrants to live up to imagined ideals of integration. A notable exception is McPherson's Foucauldian discourse analysis of the normative nature of integration within the Australian context: she questions "how integrationism has come to saturate twenty-first century migration policy discourse and demonstrates how integration has become understood as the helping hand of civilisation to 'lesser' outsiders" (McPherson 2010: 551–552).

Public debate around integration plays a decisive role in the framing of policy agendas. This chapter introduces a dialogical analysis, concerned not only with the processes by which people creatively rework social knowledge to develop their positions, but also the movement of such social knowledge between the everyday communicative public sphere of reasoning and debate and the coordinative public sphere of policy actors. Social knowledge or discourse formation is understood as existing in the form of communicative social representations that exist between the self and the issue or object under discussion (Jovchelovitch 2007: 34). A two-way flow is assumed, with members of the public influenced by hegemonic representations (Moscovici 1990) and the institutions engaged in policy development equally porous to public discourse in what Schmidt terms discursive institutionalism (Schmidt 2010: 3).

Two distinct steps are taken within the chapter to understand integration in dialogical terms. The opening step provides an illustration of a dialogical approach introducing fieldwork extracts; this is followed by social psychological understandings of integration centered on fourfold acculturation accounts relating to contact between minority and majority cultures (Berry 1990, 2006). The chapter then introduces a relatively new dialogical approach that represents a departure from acculturation accounts. The public, within this approach, are understood as having the dialogical capacities to enact, reason, and debate. Further and equally public discourse, including the use of concepts such as integration, is understood as containing the voices of others and being orientated toward a segmented audience. The introduction of this new theoretical framing is followed by a brief account of the Europeanization of immigration that serves to frame the fieldwork itself within the key policy context.

It is the *10-point migration-mobility continuum* that is at the heart of the analysis presented below and this is set out in the middle of the chapter. The continuum (see figure 6.1) is not a taxonomical account of mobility, but an analytical framework taking a seemingly black-and-white oppositional binary "migrant/nonmigrant" and refracting this into a spectrum of differing, but continuous mobility positions through the prism of the

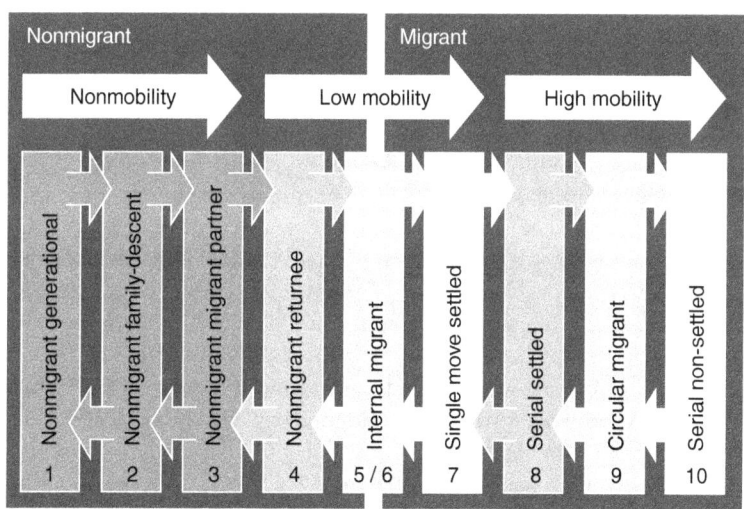

Figure 6.1 The 10-Point Migration-Mobility Continuum.
Source: Mahendran 2013.

individual's autobiographical "mobility position." This analytical device reveals a more distributed account of how integration is constructed and enacted among the public.

The empirical analysis presented in the second half of the chapter will demonstrate a variety of position on integration. An appreciation of the diversity of positions on integration within public perceptions needs to be countered by an awareness that public reasoning is socially and culturally mediated (Haste and Abrahams 2008). Social actors are collectively influenced by dominant macro narratives or hegemonic social representations—often understood as an unquestioned "common" sense—that circulate within the European public sphere. This is particularly evident in the current 'moral privileging' (Bowskill, Lyons, and Coyle 2007; McPherson 2010) of integration across Europe that often finds its concrete focus, as will be demonstrated, in an emphasis on national language acquisition.

Finally, the chapter will tackle an inherent paradox within current integration agendas that integration itself, as McPherson (2010) explains, necessarily constructs a problem migrant that is in need of integration. Such agendas do not countenance the alternative possibilities that integration is either unnecessary or occurs naturally through processes of settlement. In drawing together the findings of the analysis, this chapter will consider how the construction of a problem migrant often rests on a conflation between ethno-religious categorization and mobility.

Toward a Dialogical Analysis of Integration

There is a long tradition, particularly within social psychology, of asking individuals to make judgments about migrant groups that points to the origins of the conflation of migration with ethnic category within social research that will be returned to later in the chapter. For example, in Bogardus's seminal hierarchical 7-point social distance scale, participants were asked to judge whether they would choose, to marry into the group (1), have them as next-door neighbors (3), or bar from the nation (7) (1933). This narrow focus on decontextualized individual judgment is unable to appreciate that such judgments are culturally embedded (Weinfurt and Moghaddam 2001).

Dialogical approaches, drawing from the work of Russian ethical philosopher Mikhail Bakhtin, move away from the isolated individual making judgments and toward the notions of the relational self and "being as an event" (Bakhtin, Holquist, and Liapunov 1993: 2). Today dialogical approaches place varying degrees of emphasis on the culturally embedded self and its dialogue with social knowledge in the public sphere. A distinct line of inquiry examines the processes by which social representations in the public sphere are agentically used by individuals who are understood as having dialogical capacities termed "dialogicality" (Jovchelovitch 2007; Marková 2003). A second line of inquiry has extended Bakhtin's dialogical self into a repertoire of *I*-positions (Hermans 2001; Raggatt 2007, 2012) or works with a series of three key emotional-volitional interactions within the dialogical self "I-for myself, the other-for-me and I-for the other" (Bakhtin, Holquist, and Liapunov 1993: 54; Sullivan 2007, 2011).

The dialogical approach taken here combines the traditions above and develops a distinct route to understanding public perceptions of integration that goes further into both the public's ability to reason through a variety of positions and the public's use of social knowledge in arriving at a perception. In the next section this conceptualization of the individual's dialogical capacity is developed in more detail drawing a little from the empirical analysis that underpins this case study.

Public Perception as Dialogical Capacity

The central proposition of the analysis presented here is that dialogicality is an inherent feature of our capacities as culturally embedded individuals. Marková understands dialogicality as the "capacity to conceive, create and communicate about social realities in terms of otherness" (2003: 91). This perspective alters the framing of the understanding of public perceptions of integration. The appropriate question is no longer what the public understands by integration or thinks about the integration of certain groups of migrants. The question becomes what are the relational processes by which the public coauthors the production of discourse about integration. Key features of the dialogue to analyze are who are the others authored in the public's talk, who are the people or institutions the talk addresses, and what shared social knowledge is being used to sustain the dialogue.

Social positioning by others can be delineated from the individual's dialogical ability to take up positions. Working with Bakhtin's notion of the dialogical self and Mead's relational self, Hermans outlined the self as having a positioning repertoire. This includes internal *I*-positions such as "I as refugee" or "I as engineer," and external *I*-positions, relating to another subject position; for example, "as my father often used to say, we are all migrants." By using external *I*-positions when we talk, we effectively "author" another person often for rhetorical, polemical, or empathic purposes (Hermans and Dimaggio 2007; Hermans 2001; Hermans and Gieser 2012; Raggatt 2007, 2012).

The key delineation between different positional planes within the theoretical parameters of this case study is between the external position of where the person is placed on the *migration-mobility continuum* detailed below and the positioning inherent to a dialogical capacity to debate using the social knowledge available. Though it may seem a little early to enter the field, it is worth illustrating the interplay between subject positions on the migration-mobility continuum and how members of the public use social knowledge from the communicative public sphere in their dialogical positioning. Consider the following extract.[1]

Extract 1

KM: Would you say you feel a part of the city?
NA: Not really. I was born here, I went to school here, but I guess, I mean, like you said, I could have chosen not to come back to Edinburgh. I could have gone on from London to live somewhere else. You know, I quite like (the) city, there's a lot of things happening.
KM: So why is it that you say you don't feel part of the city?
NA[2]: (4) I don't really feel a part of anything other than living on this planet. (KM: That's interesting) (3) I've got family ties here. Memories probably, and going to work and, I suppose maybe my trip to South America I had a bit of culture (shock) going there for six months. Coming back to and during my time in South America I realized there was another equally beautifully culture somewhere else in the world, and I suppose every country has its own beauty and its own culture. I certainly felt the atmosphere in Chile and enjoyed it, enjoyed being in another culture. Someone thought I was Chilean because I lived like other people. (Edinburgh, Nonmigrant 4, "NA")

Born in Edinburgh, NA, is a nonmigrant who lived in Chile for six months and London for six years before returning to Edinburgh. OU left Chile as a child for Venezuela settling in Stockholm in 1987 as a refugee. He offers his account of integration.

Extract 2

NM[3]: If we turn then to integration (2) do you feel a part of Stockholm, do you feel integrated?
OU: Spontaneously I want to answer that I work, I can speak the language, but I notice that there exists an idea amongst Swedes that

being integrated means becoming Swedish and I think that's wrong, not that I think they can't think like that, they can think what they like, but I think it is wrong. But it's like all migrants are meant to lose their identity and being Swedish is the only way to be and acting like a Swede is the only way to be approved. I think that is like well you notice that certain people think that, you haven't integrated because you are not Swedish enough, they think being integrated is taking the Swedish side in an argument, but integration doesn't have to involve that. First thing is the language, yes, and work, but identity, that you should be able to keep, otherwise it is an oppressive society, culture if you start to get a feeling that you have to adapt and act like a Swede in order to be accepted. But unfortunately it has become that way. (Stockholm, Migrant 4, "OU")

NA and OU are in position 4 and position 8 respectively on the migration-mobility continuum. When asked whether they feel integrated, they demonstrate a dilemmatic form of thinking constructing a series of positions sometimes complementary, sometimes contradictory, enabling them to work through their conceptualizations, resist potentially stigmatizing discursive positions, and rework or employ alternative positions. They draw, in part, from discourses and social representations within the public sphere, "to work, to speak the language," combining these with imagined positions of others in relation to their differing contexts: "I notice there exists an idea amongst Swedes," leading to what Bakhtin understood as the *multivoicedness* contained within people's talk (Bakhtin and Holquist 1981).

OU's perceptions of integration reveal the social actions inherent in dialogue, for OU there is an expectation that integration is enacted as taking "the Swedish side in an argument." This then is partly a question of what can be intersubjectively agreed. Perhaps his categorization of the Swedish position is misplaced (Gillespie and Cornish 2009). However, as we will see below, where a number of people begin to utilize or resist the same social knowledge drawn from the public sphere, this suggests that a social representation is at work (Howarth 2006).

Social representations refer to the socially shared knowledge that exists to make the unfamiliar, often scientific or ideological knowledge, more familiar. Moscovici developing this approach in the 1950s wanted to emphasize that people were not entirely susceptible or irrational rather they thought rationally in ways that could be understood by scientists. Common-sense thinking becomes the "autonomous third genre of thinking," between scientific thinking and ideological thinking (Moscovici and Duveen 2000: 237–240).

OU sets up a canonical individualized form of integration, to learn the language, to get a job, and orientates himself away from this in an anticanonical direction; this rhetorical positional move works to resist a generalized call for assimilation and points to a more multicultural or cosmopolitan idea of integration. NA also resists the concept and its connotations, despite being born in Edinburgh; in an existential rhetorical move he detaches himself from city-level belonging and later draws attention to being taken as a Chilean to implicitly suggest perhaps that he is capable of adapting and assimilating into another culture. NA would be understood as a "native" or nonmigrant in the majority of public opinion surveys; here, however, in a more distributed approach to public perceptions, he is placed, as noted, in position 4 of the *migration-mobility continuum* (see figure 6.1), the returnee position. He uses his experiences in London and Chile to construct his resistant position on integration.

The dialogical capacities illustrated in the extracts above are not just the preserve of ordinary members of the public in the communicative public sphere. They are equally evident in the thinking of analysts making sense of a given public concern, or policymakers working within the ideological constraints of a more coordinative public sphere to frame up and progress policy programs. The next section considers how understanding people's dialogical capacities can inform an understanding of acculturation.

Integration: From Acculturation Theory to a Dialogical Approach

Building on Lewin's fourfold theory of acculturation that had balanced cultural chauvinism against divided loyalties, social psychological understandings of integration have focused less on migrants getting a job or learning the language and more on the extent to which individuals engage in contact with other "dominant" groups termed "acculturation" (1948). Berry's seminal and ongoing program into acculturation strategies (1990) distinguishes between "assimilation," where an individual's contact with their own group is decreased in favor of the dominant group, "integration," where the individual is able to engage in contact with the dominant group without losing cultural contact with their own group. This is contrasted with "separation" where loyalty with one's own culture leads the individual to reject contact with other more dominant groups and finally "marginalization" where the person fails to make contact with other groups but also loses contact with their original cultural group. It is hard to escape the conclusion that this is a normative account where the strategies of assimilation, separation, and marginalization are viewed as less desirable than integration.

Berry's account has been subject to a number of revisions, not least because of increasing appreciation that this was not solely a question of individual decision making but affected by the national and local political strategies and the very social knowledge discussed above. In response Berry developed acculturation to consider mutual ethnic relations (2006) as well as globalization where at the macro level the four-fold taxonomy becomes a melting pot, multiculturalism, exclusion, and segregation respectively (Berry 2008: 332). Van Oudenhoven et al. innovatively extend acculturation theory to offer a more perceptual account that included both migrant and nonmigrant perceptions of the four strategies. They notice a "discrepancy of perceptions" where Turkish and Moroccan migrants said they would favor integration when presented with each of the four strategies within a fictitious newspaper article, whereas Dutch people favored assimilation. Critically the Dutch participants believed both Moroccans and Turkish people to favor separation (1998: 1010–1011).

The parameters of acculturation theory have come under critique, particularly its lack of definitional clarity, one-dimensional focus on contact, and its current inability to understand each strategy as ipsative, that is, the possibility of being marginalized in one context and integrated in another. More trenchant criticism points to the focus on one-way cultural learning by the minority ethnic migrant (Deaux 2006; Rudmin 2003). The lack of focus on nonmigrants inherent to existing acculturation accounts risks failing to appreciate the idea that nonmigrants are also acculturating and learning from their own travels, contact with migrant groups, and other sources of social knowledge in the public sphere.

There is a growing trend among social and political psychologists to understand integration in more discursive terms. Howarth et al. have critiqued acculturation theory's treatment of culture and identity as discrete entities. They demonstrate how people use oppositional themes such as "cultural maintenance versus cultural contact" or "identity versus exclusion" that they term "acculturation in movement" from context to context (2013). Bowskill, Lyons, and Coyle, taking a critical discursive approach, explore the way integration is constructed and the function it serves in media debates about state-funded faith schools. They demonstrate that the moral privileging of integration serves to give it the "rhetorical weight of common sense" where it becomes understood as the "optimal response to diversity," that is, self-evident social reality

(2007). The maintenance of segregation within a particular context, that is, the desire to educate a child in a single-faith school, particularly when it is a Muslim school, is socially positioned, within media representations, as transgressive.

Dialogical studies into integration that are less concerned with discursive knowledge have, as noted, tended to focus on the dialogical self. Bhatia details the *I*-positional processes that migrants are engaged in when navigating transnationally between the positionings and possibilities of their new homes and their countries of origin. The strength of Bhatia's use of the dialogical self is that it allows the migrant to be capable of feeling at once assimilated, separated, and marginalized (2002). Furthermore, Buitelaar relates these strategies to Moroccan migrants within the Netherlands (2006). The approach developed here builds on social representation approaches outlined above and extends understandings of the dialogical self. Rather than focus on the subjective understandings of the migrant, the analysis outlined below understands dialogue at four levels—(1) the subjective level of the multivoiced dialogical self and its *I*-positions; (2) the face-to-face dialogue and the framings that occur; (3) the dialogics of words in use (Mahendran 2003: 240); and (4) finally, the dialogue between the individual as social actor and the social knowledge located within the public sphere in the form of social representations. Complete accounts of the four-level dialogical analysis can be found in (Mahendran 2003, 2011).

Framing the Case Study within the European Policy Context

The European Union plays an increasing role in immigration policies where progressive treaties have facilitated the movement of citizens. The EU sees itself as providing leadership and support in relation to a common agenda for the management of migration flows and the integration of migrants. This does not always sit easily with countries whose colonial histories have formed the basis of their immigration, such as UK, or have a long history of policies on immigrant integration, such as Sweden; nevertheless, such processes exert a decisive influence in what has been termed the Europeanization of immigration (Faist and Ette 2007).

Mobility as Freedom and Threat

The changing parameters of successive treaties—particularly the freedom of movement of member state citizens since the Maastricht Treaty

1992, the take-up of these freedoms by citizens of new accession countries, and the development of integration priorities in policy programs such as Lisbon, Hague, and Stockholm—have led to new terms of reference in integration debates. A tension is created between the increased opportunity for EU citizens to move between member states—mobility as freedom, and European Union policies that see only non-EU nationals as the focus of integration policies—mobility as threat. Though certain EU citizens can become the stigmatized focus of EU policy, for example, Roma people, generally EU citizens are increasingly sharply delineated from non-EU citizens, as not presenting integration concerns to member states, because they are protected by certain rights and are perceived, in social and cultural terms, as "also European." This sharp distinction between the EU and non-EU citizen risks creating a discursive frame that ignores member states own unique histories of immigration flows that are not based on such a distinction.

In what is generally termed the securitization of immigration, integration of non-EU immigrants often builds on fears around ethno-religious communitarian activities, where a tension builds between European Union aspirations around European citizenship and freedom of mobility, and ideas of integration and belonging within the European Union project (Aradau, Huysmans, and Squire 2010; Collett 2006). Though liberal accounts of integration point to its *two-way* nature, this tends to be understood as an individual's integration attempts being assisted by the efforts of residents, institutions, and agencies. The focus on civic integration relating to early settlement processes, acquisition of national language, knowledge of social norms, and a country's history and institutions has been widely commented on (Joppke 2007) and it is worth noting its parallels to the academic literature on acculturation theory.

Case Selection and Methodology

The two capital cities of Edinburgh and Stockholm provide quite different contexts for integration in debate; Scotland, though not an EU member state, since devolution in 1998, has developed a distinct discourse around immigration that found expression in an active promotion of immigration originally under its "Fresh Talent" initiative that began in 2003. Integration, settlement, and retention are devolved policies and Scotland's approach to integration is distinct within the UK, in talking of integration from day one with respect to asylum seekers. Sweden, by contrast, has a very long history in developing integration policy that originally was based around a moral compact emphasizing compassion and solidarity. Until very recently, the migrant was invariably understood as a refugee. Earlier migrations of the Finnish have slipped from collective memory, and current migration between Nordic countries because of the possibilities inherent in Nordic citizenship are not the subject of integration policy. In their seminal "paradoxes of multiculturalism," Ålund and Schierup point to an increasing emphasis on the migrant as culturally different they argue that "'the moral compact on which Swedish integration policy is built, is gradually disintegrating, giving way to a culturalist construction of new discriminatory boundaries" (1991: 10). Though national policies were not explicitly used to frame the study, such shifting political contexts undoubtedly will influence the social knowledge embedded in the two respective polities where Scotland is a relative newcomer to integration policies and Sweden has one of the longest histories of integration policy in Europe.

The Dialogues on Migration, Citizenship, and Integration (D-MIC) case study was carried out from 2007 to 2009 and used the European Union's Hague Program as its explicit frame: 32 people participated in the study, 24 interviews and 4 focus groups were conducted in Stockholm and Edinburgh. Participants were selected through advertisement in adult education colleges and through chain sampling. The basic eligibility was living in either of the two cities. There were an equal number of males and females in the interviews. The age range of participants was from 18 to 60 years: 24 participants took part in the interviews; 13 participants took part in the focus groups, among whom 7 had already participated in interviews. The aim was to have sufficient sample size to shed light on the variety of differing positions, understandings, and arguments around integration among the public and the shared social knowledge that is being utilized within these. Participants were selected to represent a variety of educational levels ranging from leaving school after primary school to postgraduate level, and including people from a range of occupations including four students and one person who was unemployed. Participants were asked to discuss their own mobility, integration, and citizenship. In the second half of the interviews and throughout the focus groups, EU stimulus materials, such as the integration priority within the Hague program and the Common Basic Principles, were used to elicit discussion on mobility within Europe, EU integration policy, and the concept of European citizenship.

The approach of giving policy stimulus materials to participants in order to elicit debate on integration was partly inspired by deliberative democracy approaches such as citizen panels and citizen juries. Participants were not required to reach an agreement; however, they were positioned, in part, as citizens rather than just asked to "tell their mobility story." As Davies, Wetherell, and Barnett explain, "to address a 'citizen' is to imagine a more active actor, integrated into a polity and participating in collective decisions about what is to be done" (2006: 2).

Analysis: Integration along the Migration-Mobility Continuum

Public perceptions of integration are segmented in the analysis below according to key positions on the 10-point migration-mobility continuum. The 10 positions along the migration-mobility continuum (figure 6.1) arose out of the first phase of analysis when participants discussing integration drew on a degree of mobility as their starting point. As the account of dialogical approaches indicates, these are dynamic relational positions, rather than static positions or bureaucratic types. The individual can move positions according to their individual circumstances, becoming more or less settled as time passes. It is also worth returning to the delineation at the start of this chapter between the *I*-positional capacity to speak from a variety of positions when in debate, and position on the migration-mobility continuum where inevitably there is a degree of fixity.

Nonmobility and Integration

The first position on the continuum is associated with generational nonmobility. Here the individual remains living in the country they were born in. It is this position that commentators or analysts often have in mind when they talk of the nonmigrant or the dominant group. Such participants may see themselves as unambiguously integrated into their communities. Consider, for example, the comment by QP.

Extract 3

NM: If we turn now to integration, do you feel integrated in Stockholm?
QP: yeh. I think so
NM: In what way?
QP: In what way do I feel at home here do you mean?
NM: yeh are you a real *08*?
QP: *yeh about as 08 as you can be* since I've lived here all my life I feel very at home here. I would say I'm absolutely a Stockholmer. I don't know what you could call me otherwise. There aren't any other alternatives for what I can be =
NM: =no. Okay
QP: I feel a part of Stockholm. (Stockholm, Nonmigrant 3, "QP")

It is worth noting that such a position does not necessarily assume a certain outlook toward the integration of migrants. It may be the position associated with an anti-immigration position, within media representations, but equally it can be the basis for an alternative public perception. Here QP takes up the issue of the "two-way process of accommodation."

Extract 4

NM: Okay if you look at number one here integration as a dynamic mutual process how do you perceive that? Do you agree with it or =

QP: = no I don't really (NM: You don't?) *no I don't think so* (NM *no*) no it depends on how you see it. I mean you have to break it up into different parts really (2) I have to always relate these things back to myself. If I was to come to another country and I was to come there then I wouldn't think that this process is a two-way process in the beginning I would just think it should (be) me that receives I think I come there I get somewhere to live maybe I get an education maybe I get help financially for example so I manage everyday life for example. (Stockholm, Nonmigrant 3, "QP")

QP's perception of integration can be understood as a "hosting position." Putting himself in the position of the migrant arriving into Sweden, he understands integration as between the individual migrant and the institutions of the host country. The dialogue continues:

Extract 5

NM: so you would think that you should be entitled to those things in the beginning?

QP: yes I would think that I *should* get those things because that is how I myself has been like so to speak raised so that's how I value wise work so if you come here as a migrant and you get a bonus start...get help with accommodation and language courses and help maybe financially. First phase I would think that I should just receive and that wouldn't be a two-way process it would just be one-way to *me*. It takes a while before you get to where you need to be to be able get your own accommodation you have a job you can speak the language and got into the society socially as well then it can become a two way process. Then you'll win both can win the individual can win and society can (get) something out of it. (Stockholm, Nonmigrant 3, "QP")

Within this hosting position, Sweden or Stockholm, is placed as the provider who will ultimately benefit. Critically QP does not articulate a position in relation to any shifts or accommodations that need to be made by him other than to support the existence of settlement processes. Another participant a former employability worker offers a further perception of integration.

Extract 6

> *KM*: In the first box...it describes the integration of migrants as being a dynamic two-way process of accommodation. When you saw that, what did you think?
>
> *MS*: One of the (4), I suppose criticisms (2) of let's say, the Muslim kids who came to Mansfield was that they...they would be befriend one another and they would spend time together and there often wasn't integration, and I can quite understand why that would be, because, it's, it's like (sticking to) somebody who speaks the same language as you. If somebody's life is similar to yours and familiar to you, it's so much more comfortable to be with that person. So often you will hear the criticism that "well, these Muslims don't want." There's one group to take as an example, don't want to integrate because they're quite comfortable in their own company and so on and I feel that (2) they're (2) pushed that way as much as they are pulling that way, you know, that there's comfort in it. But, there's often a need to take that comfort because they're feeling unwelcome or ostracised or whatever. (Edinburgh, Nonmigrant 3, "MS")

MS, having moved to Edinburgh from the north of Scotland, is in position 1 on the migration-mobility continuum. She combines rhetorical and empathetic dialogical *I*-positions, to understand separation, not as a less desirable acculturation strategy, or transgressive, but rather as a reasonable response to both social circumstances and a desire to mix with other children who are culturally familiar. MS makes use of an imagined generalized voice of the public. She does not take up the archetypal public position but uses this voice as a resource to make a nonarchetypal argument, demonstrating relative sophistication in unpacking the dominant narrative that one imagines the public has on migration and integration. Nevertheless, MS, when constructing the migrant she has in mind, conflates migration with ethno-cultural category and uses Muslim children as the subject of the debates on integration.

Migrant Descent Position: Language Acquisition in Debate

In the second position, participants tend to draw on their migrant backgrounds to articulate a position around integration. Swedish nonmigrant

TT has a German mother and Swedish father. In discussing integration she commented:

> **Extract 7**
>
> TT: These migrants that have parents that can't speak the language (...). I have always lived with my mum and mum spoke German but mum had two language things that I think are really good, one she even stopped having an accent before I was even two or three or whatever it was, I know that she speaks even cleaner now than she did when I was really young, and even then you could barely hear it, you heard it on the tongue sometimes with U or O but otherwise you couldn't hear that she had another language during almost my whole 25 years,... she learnt to excuse my language she bloody wanted to learn because she was living in Sweden and she was going to stay here... if you are going to be part of the society then you have to learn the language. (Swedish, Nonmigrant 6, "TT")

TT describes herself as "not a normative Swede," saying "I think the German is always a part but I feel Swedish," she explains the problem further.

> **Extract 8**
>
> TT: If I have understood it correctly we have really bad options for learning the language and that is *only* Sweden's fault because we could do that a lot better, and this is frustrating for me because I have worked a lot in old peoples homes, care work a lot and met a lot of migrants that I have a hard time understanding what they mean and it's really frustrating but at the same time there isn't anyone else that would want to take those jobs [NM: No] so you end up in a work team where it's me and one other in a group of ten and all the rest have another ethnic background. (Swedish, Nonmigrant 6, "TT")

Here TT locates her account of integration within the workplace. Getting a job as noted earlier is, of course, one of the key common indicators of integration within Europe. However, TT reveals how the work place becomes the very site where integration is contested. In this one-way assimilationist account, integration is more than simply having a job; it involves the ability to speak to colleagues in the national language without any trace of another accent. TT participated in both the interview and the focus group; here she discusses how young people speak a transcultural language known as *blatte Svenska* (blatte[4] Swedish).

Extract 9

> TT: The problem is also that you then get second generation migrants that can't speak the language they can only speak blatte Svenska (blatte Swedish) which is a language that is developing all the time (6)
> BC: Talking of blatte Svenska that's those in my age that go to school and they don't care about learning the language that's what I think [TT: Exactly]
> BC: They don't care about learning Swedish, they just want to use blatte Svenska
> TT: "I don't want to learn your language I want to speak my language" [BC: yes exactly]
> KB: I actually think that if I don't bother learning the language then I am just going to be a burden but if I learn then I can apply for a job and then you are going to learn a lot more as well. (Stockholm, Focus Group 3—February 2008. Response to newspaper article, Dagens Nyheter [2008])

This illustrates a public perception that uses one's own migrant descent to build an argument for national language acquisition among those also of migrant descent. Learning the language is totemic in integration debates and occurs right across the continuum; its importance is mentioned in all the interviews and focus groups. Perhaps this is not entirely a question of its practical importance within a new country. It suggests a common view of a resistant separation by maintaining one's own language or creating new transcultural languages. This relates less to position along the continuum and is better understood as existing within an underlying social representation at work in the public sphere—a social representation of cohesion.

KB, a migrant who also participated in the focus group, turns the discussion toward the potential mutuality in language acquisition ending "then you are going to learn a lot more as well," suggesting that cultural diversity may have potential benefits. Again a problem migrant is being constructed, which relates to particular cultural ethno-religious categorization. Particular groups of migrants and their descendants sometimes referred to, in some European contexts, as second generation *migrants* or third generation *migrants* are discursively held separately, subordinated, and seen as the focus of integration efforts.

Returnee Position—Resisting the Integration Ideal

In many ways, it is the returnee position, position 4, on the migration-mobility continuum, which led to the development of the continuum.

Participants such as NA (from extract 1), demonstrated their ambiguity toward integration and draw on an outsider perspective. BM, who has also lived abroad several times and then returned to Sweden, comments, when asked the question "are there times when you feel outside of the city?":

Extract 10

> *BM*: I could find situation now where I'm single, I don't have children, I'm not married, I don't belong to the norms. The city (Stockholm) it is pretty and you think of people of being quite national and narrow-minded.
> *KM*: What sort of things can you give me some ideas of what you mean?
> *BM*: You're supposed to live suppose to be married at a certain age you suppose to have studied education and live in certain areas have certain cars (6) you're not suppose to be a foreigner you're not suppose to be (2) gay you're not suppose to be anything that is different.
> *KM*: But you are a white Swedish woman so you.
> *BM*: No I'm fortunate I could always get all these things and be accepted, it's not that I don't feel accepted that's not why. (Stockholm, Nonmigrant 2, "BM")

BM diffuses the debate on the integration of migrants by illustrating further potential categories of exclusion, such as being unmarried, unemployed, or gay. She draws from her own childhood mobility, to explain her position.

Extract 11

> *KM*: But a-part of you doesn't like that?
> *BM*: No I don't like it (1) I don't like the law.
> *KM*: Why is that?
> *BM*: (...) personally I think it's because I had quite a lot in childhood and I know how people be (2) on the outside and are excluded [KM: yeah] so I think I always feel for people not =
> *KM*: = Being included in personal areas.
> *BM*: Although I've never (1) I've never been (1) I have always been included with white upper class sorts of people. I feel I don't (1) I don't like it, I don't feel at home at all.
> *KM*: And if you could magically redesign (1) Stockholm what would you do?
> *BM*: I'd bring in different nationalities different sorts of people all ages. (Stockholm, Nonmigrant 2, "BM")

BM, just like KB, begins to draw on a social representation of mutually beneficial cultural diversity to challenge the emphasis on conformity inherent in integration discourse which positions conformity as central to social cohesion.

These four positions at the nonmobile end of the continuum demonstrate the heterogeneity of nonmigrant public perceptions of integration. Understandings of integration vary between an initial hosting position, assimilation, and separation as a reasonable acculturation strategy. Going further, participants in this case study, with some experience of temporary migration disavow the concept and its ideals in favor of cosmopolitanism or multiculturalism.

Mobile Positions: Constructing the "Problem" Migrant

In examining more mobile positions, perhaps the most striking distinction is between those that relate integration to themselves and those that construct a problem migrant. OU, in position 8 as a settled serial migrant, illustrates the relational challenges of integration (see extract 2), he challenges integration, in the Swedish context, as a pressure to assimilate pointing to the importance of maintaining one's own cultural identities. In contrast, BE, an American academic also in position 8, supports the idea of the migrant demonstrating an adaptive acculturation strategy.

Extract 12

> *BE*: And when I read that (referring to the EU's two-way principle), I wrote a little note here thinking—actually, I never really thought of it as a two-way so much. Or if it is a two-way process, there is much more responsibility on my part, to get along with local rules and customs and cultures, than for the Scottish people to adjust to make my life easier. (Edinburgh, Migrant 6, "BE")

TY and OU, in position 10 and 9 respectively, reveal one of the more intriguing and revealing findings in the analysis. Here they discuss why integration has become a political issue.

Extract 13

> *TY*: I mean first of all by trying to integrate someone you're automatically pointing them out as being different which, you know, might just make integrating them more difficult because you always have, you know, in a lot of communities, in Germany for example, because

> Turkish workers came en mass, you know, so it's very difficult to integrate them whereas where say, you know, Chinese workers came in dribbles. It was a lot easier to integrate them into the community. (Edinburgh, Migrant 2, "TY")

TY in position 10 is of mixed European origins: she has moved several times since childhood and anticipates moving again. OS, a Russian migrant in position 9, has moved several times and in her interview she explains that she is holding on to her Russian citizenship to allow for the possibility of returning to Russia to look after her elderly parents.

Extract 15

> OS: There were some many problems with integration and people don't integrate probably as good as countries would like and of course it's very difficult to integrate people from one for example different religious views it's-it's really difficult I mean looking to the Muslim community. Ahh well their traditions are very strong and of course I mean... often even children who are born in Sweden they are kind of more involved in the Muslim community than you know integrate into Swedish life. (Stockholm, Migrant 2, "OS"[5])

The more mobile end of the continuum demonstrates a heterogeneous and distributed set of perceptions of integration. When interviewed about integration, participants in position 8 relate the issue of integration to themselves, whereas nonsettled mobile positions assume that the discussion is *not* about them. However, there are risks in presuming their nonsettled positions are the principal reason for using such a distancing strategy.

Discussion: New Understandings of Public Perceptions of Integration

The analysis presented within this case study extends accounts of the dialogical self (Bakhtin 1981; Hermans 2001) to the area of public perceptions demonstrating the value of understanding public perceptions of integration as distributed along a migration-mobility continuum. It is hopefully clear by now that it is possible to develop a nuanced understanding of public perceptions as segmented and distributed by combining an analytical device such as the continuum with an understanding of the role of discourse formation or social representations circulating within the public sphere. Positions and arguments set out within this analysis challenge the current terms of reference of both policy focus and acculturation accounts, which approach integration in terms of the imperatives on the migrant to engage in one-way integration into a social undifferentiated dominant group.

Evidently public in Edinburgh and Stockholm readily understand integration in the form of the assimilationist acculturation strategies discussed by Berry (2006). But equally as shown here there are a number of new perceptions, for example, the idea of a hosting position that are worthy of further analysis. Migrants who are fully aware of the pressures to integrate, engage in a dialogue with assimiliationist arguments, and point to the importance of holding on to one's identities as central to developing conceptualizations of integration.

A further site for fruitful research is those processes by which returnee nonmigrants, in position 4 on the continuum, draw from their experiences of being in an outsider position to diffuse and resist the integration ideal. More generally this case study demonstrates, therefore, the value of including nonmigrants in research that aims to understand integration processes and integration policies. Such nonmigrants when discussing integration suggest that separation within a diverse society is not necessarily problematic or transgressive but perhaps a reasonable acculturation strategy.

The analysis and its framing demonstrates how members of the public and policy actors use a *social representation of cohesion* that has become hegemonic to the point that for many it is an unquestioned common sense. Within this social representation, integration becomes constructed as a requirement to reduce cultural distance. Use of the dominant national language is taken as a form of shared citizenship and a totemic outward expression of cohesion. The difficulty with this is those who resist this shared social representation, and emphasize a potentially equally cohesive *social representation of diversity* risk being positioned as transgressive (Bowskill et al. 2007). Actions such as the creative development of a transcultural language, in the Swedish context, or children socializing with their own ethnic group at school in the Scottish context run the risk of being viewed as an obstacle to integration, a sign of dissidence.

It is the existence of a social representation of cohesion that presents separation as a site of risk and conflict, rather than a form of convivial diversity, which perhaps has led to multiculturalism becoming understood as a struggle or a threat within European contexts. Thus the moral privileging of integration as assimilation noted by Bowskill et al. (2007) in England and McPherson (2010) in Australia is shown to occur within the two city contexts of Edinburgh and Stockholm.

A paradoxical feature of integration is that it necessarily constructs a problem migrant where ethno-religious difference, for example, a perceived difference between Muslims and other groups, is conflated with mobility and made salient. Some migrants in the study did not imagine that integration policies related to them. This assumption is not unreasonable when one begins to analyze such talk against the terms of reference of current integration polices outlined in the first part of this chapter. It is not so much that the migrants who took part in this study were not originally non-EU nationals, or facing integration challenges or insecurities in relation to their citizenship status—some of them were. It is that such migrants did not identify as the "problem" migrants they believed integration policies across Europe were attempting to tackle. This exploratory case study begins to delineate the variety of perceptions and arguments that exists on integration within these two city contexts. It points to the fact that a fuller appreciation of integration and public perceptions of integration requires further research to examine how ethno-cultural category intersects with socioeconomic position and mobility.

Conclusion

In this chapter a dialogical analysis has been presented that shows that participants, when discussing features of integration, spoke not as migrants or nonmigrants but constructed several *I*-positions along a *10-point migration-mobility continuum*. The chapter demonstrates differences in the construction and enactment of integration related to position on the continuum from settled nonmigrants to serial migrants. While nonmigrants are revealed to be heterogeneous in their perceptions of integration, use of the dominant national language is viewed as pivotal across the continuum, suggesting a rise in assimilationist understandings of integration. Integration, as conformity, is today constructed, reified, and idealized as a panacea for social cohesion where inherent, paradoxically to the concept, is the construction of a problem migrant. The analysis presented here suggests that a promising challenge for new understandings of integration centers on an examination of the common-sense understandings of the relationship between diversity and social cohesion.

Notes

1. The case study extracts are presented as they are recorded, including the irregularities of speech, to indicate the halting nature of speech and the thought processes involved. The case study transcriptions uses some Jefferson

conventions including ** to denote laughing, (3) to indicate time taken before speaking, = when two people speak at the same time and (...) to denote that some of the transcript has been removed.
2. All participants were made anonymous and contextualized as follows; by city whether they were migrant or nonmigrant; interview number and two anonymous initials.
3. Nicola Magnusson, a researcher on the D-MIC project, conducted the Swedish interviews and focus groups where participants had indicated a preference to speak Swedish.
4. The origins of the term "blatte" are contested, but it is likely to be connected to the Gaelic term "blether" and has come to be associated with the transcultural street talk of certain ethnic minority groups within Sweden. Often used as a pejorative term, it has been appropriated by some groups, for example, the Blatte Deluxe journalism award and the Blatte United football team in Stockholm.
5. Responses to question F24: Why in your view has integration become a political issue? (Enligt din åsikt, varför har integration av invandrare blivit en politisk sak?)

PART III

Law and Order

CHAPTER 7

Asylum Policy Responsiveness in Scandinavia

Frøy Gudbrandsen

Introduction

There are many arguments within the immigration policy literature focusing on the lack of a connection between public opinion and immigration policy: Immigration policymaking is portrayed as elite driven (Freeman 1995; Statham and Geddes 2006), the immigration attitudes of political elites are thought to diverge from that of the general public (Beck and Camarota 2002), and, finally, immigration policies are said to be increasingly shaped at an international level (Joppke and Guiraudon 2001). Yet, this study argues that asylum policies are far from detached from public preferences. On the contrary, Scandinavian governments have changed asylum policies in accordance with shifts in public opinion.

Although almost indistinguishable in some aspects of public policy, Sweden, Norway, and Denmark certainly differ when it comes to immigration. In the early 1980s, asylum policies in all three countries could be described as liberal and open. Since then, policies have been altered in ways that have set them on divergent paths. Indeed, public opinion may contribute to our understanding of these differences. The lack of comparable survey data across time and between countries has limited the scope of public opinion studies on immigration: available data are commonly either cross-national or single-country time series. However, by using data on attitudes toward refugee policies from Sweden, Denmark, and Norway, this study explores the dynamic relationship between public opinion and refugee policies. The data show substantial changes in attitudes in the three Scandinavian countries during the past 30 years, and this study argues that asylum policy developments are closely related to these changes.

Since the 1980s, asylum policies in Scandinavia have gone through numerous changes. The 1983 Danish foreigners' law was considered "the most liberal law in the world". While Sweden currently has liberal immigration policies, Denmark has repeatedly tightened asylum and family immigration policies. In a European perspective, Sweden has the most liberal asylum policies, Denmark has some of the most restrictive, and Norway is situated somewhere in between these two cases. To illustrate the differences, in 2010, Sweden (with a population of 9 million) accepted around 12,000 refugees, Norway (with a population of 5 million) around 5,000, and Denmark (with a population of 5.5 million) just over a 1,000. This picture is also supported by the policy changes studied in this chapter (see overview in appendix 7.1): asylum policy restrictions have been more frequent in Denmark than in the two other countries, whereas it is Sweden that has liberalized its policy most frequently.

This study builds on theories of government responsiveness, suggesting that the electorate's influence is not limited to election day, but extends throughout the electoral period, as politicians respond to changes in public opinion (Page and Shapiro 1983). Many, if not all, of the subsequent studies examining this purported link have come to the same conclusion (Burstein 2003). Still, these findings are not insensitive to the time period, policy field, strength of interest organizations, and—in particular—the saliency of the issue. Yet, when it comes to the impact of public opinion on immigration, there are few studies to draw on. Burstein argues that the effect of public opinion on policy has been overstated, since scholars tend to focus on the issues ranked as most important in surveys (2006). This suggests the need for testing the theory on less salient issues. This study examines two countries where immigration is less predominant (Norway and Sweden), while in Denmark, immigration has persistently been an important issue (Green-Pedersen and Krogstrup 2008). This study also differs from many government responsiveness studies by focusing directly on output—legislative and regulative changes—rather than on policy outcomes. Moreover, case studies from the United States still dominate the government responsiveness field (Canes-Wrone and Shotts 2004; Erikson 2002; Shapiro 2011, 1004). Although comparative studies do exist (Hobolt and Klemmensen 2008; Thomas 2011), this study adds to the literature by expanding the scope of cases that have been subject to analysis.

This chapter is organized as follows: First, I present the theories of responsive government. Second, I give a brief account of the development of asylum policies in Scandinavia. Third, I attend to the measuring of asylum policies, as well as the other variables to be included in the subsequent statistical analysis. The relationship between public opinion and changes to asylum policies in Scandinavia is analyzed through an ordinal logistic regression. Possible determinants of asylum policy, such as asylum applications, media attention, and radical right-wing party support, are controlled for. The analysis suggests that the probability of asylum policy restrictions is higher when public opposition toward refugee immigration increases.

Public Opinion and Policy

This chapter can be situated within the group of studies that "examines changes over time in public preferences and the corresponding changes (or lack of changes) in public policies" (Gilens 2005, 779). Beginning with Page and Shapiro, a number of studies have found that public opinion and policy changes are congruent (1983). Representation occurs indirectly through elections, or directly as governments respond to public preferences (Wleizen 2004: 2). Stimson et al. argue that politicians are well informed about movements in public opinion (1995: 544). They get this information through various sources, including opinion polls, the media, constituencies, and direct contact with the public (Besley and Burgess 2001; Druckman and Jacobs 2011). To increase their chances of reelection, politicians revise their public policies based on their knowledge of what would please their constituency (Stimson, Mackuen, and Erikson 1995: 545). Representation is, therefore, a two-stage process. First, public opinion affects policies via electoral turnover. Second, public opinion is represented when politicians act in accordance with shifts in public opinion.

Government responsiveness studies commonly look at the link between median voter opinion and policy outcomes. Increasingly, however, scholars distinguish between subsections of the electorate and find that some groups of voters are more influential than others. Governments are more responsive to upper-income groups (Bartels 2009; Gilens 2005, 2009), elites, and business leaders (Jacobs and Page 2005). Religious groups also tend to be more influential than the general public opinion (Druckman and Jacobs 2011). Finally, preference representation also varies with partisanship: Republican preferences are better represented than those of Democrats and Independents (Soroka and Wlezien 2008).

This chapter looks primarily at the relationship between the median voter and immigration policy developments. Adapting to the median voter preference means that governments satisfy the majority of the electorate. However, building on research showing that governments adapt more to certain subgroups of the electorate, the chapter looks into the potential impact of one subgroup of the electorate, namely those who cast their vote for the government. But why should governments be more responsive to their own voters than to the median voter, who represent a larger share of the electorate? One reason is that although governments would like to attract new voters, they need to ensure reelection by holding on to their core voters (Budge, Ezrow, and McDonald 2010: 804). If governments pay attention to public attitudes, they should be particularly concerned with those segments that constitute prospective voters. Second, Warwick suggests that government preferences tend to be "bilaterist" rather than centered on the median mandate (2012: 19); parties tend to offer distinct alternatives to the electorate. Third, in Scandinavia there is a close link between the ministerial level and the party organization. Policy preferences of party members can be changing, and these shifts in preferences are likely to be channeled to the government, either formally or informally. Fourth, individual politicians' attitudes are likely to be closer to those of their supporters than those of the general public. Governments also get information about public sentiment through direct, personal contact with citizens (Stimson 1995). Even if politicians strive to meet people from all segments of society, they are more likely to come into contact with their own supporters—thus making them vulnerable to an information bias.

Still, parties differ. Ezrow et al. find that mainstream parties adjust their policy positions to the median voter, while niche parties respond to preference shifts among their supporters (2011). In Scandinavia, during the period under scrutiny, both mainstream and niche parties were in coalitions together. Considering that the mainstream parties were dominant in most coalitions, we would expect governments to be primarily responsive to the median voter, not to the median government supporter. Of course, these preferences may be quite similar. In fact, Best et al. claim that, at least on the left-right scale, "there is an observable one-to-one correspondence between median and government policy position" (2012: 20).

Scholars in the field of responsive government disagree about causality between public opinion and policy change. According to Stimson et al., governments are responsive if they act as a consequence of the changes in public sentiment (1995: 543). Politicians make these choices because they are aware of shifts in attitudes. Wlezien accepts that both the public and the government may react to something else: "All we can say for sure is that the coefficient (B) captures policy responsiveness in a statistical sense, that is, whether and the extent to which public preferences directly influence policy change, other things being equal" (2004: 3). Similarly, Gilens emphasizes that what has been established is an association between public opinion and public policy, not a causal effect. Still, he argues in favor of the latter (2005: 791–792).

Policy Developments in Scandinavia

Although the three Scandinavian countries have different immigration histories, it can be argued that they had a common point of departure in the 1980s. Until the number of asylum seekers began to increase in the 1980s, refugee immigration had been limited, and asylum legislation was liberal. Faced with an increase in asylum applications, all three countries reacted by instituting restrictive policies. The Danish government reacted quickly and made substantial policy changes in 1985 and 1986. In Norway, policies were made stricter in 1987, although to a lesser extent than in Denmark. In Sweden, the restrictions came with the new Aliens Act in 1988 and with the controversial "Lucia decision" in 1989. From then on, policy developments have diverged. While the new Swedish government in 1991 lifted the 1989 restrictions, Danish governments have continued to tighten asylum legislation throughout the 1990s and 2000s, with only a couple of minor liberalizing exceptions. Asylum policy in Norway went through a liberalizing phase from the mid-1990s until the 2001 election. Some aspects of liberalization were substantial, while many must be considered minor and symbolic. For instance, although asylum criteria were liberalized in 1997, it did not change the total number of persons granted residence permits, just the types of permits that were granted.

All three countries adopted legislation to meet the large inflows of refugees from the Balkan Wars. Sweden granted permanent residence permits to refugees from Bosnia, while Denmark and Norway—in line with the rest of Europe—offered only temporary refugee status. After receiving 80,000 refugees in 1993, Sweden later changed legislation so that temporary status could be granted in cases of mass flight.

Norwegian and Swedish policies have been restricted through European Union (EU) legislation (such as the Dublin Convention), whereas Denmark often has been ahead of EU policy regarding restrictions. In addition, the Danish opt-out clauses in the Maastricht Treaty mean that Denmark is not bound by EU minimum standards in asylum policy. Despite increased international attention to immigration, most policy changes related to asylum-based residence permits in Scandinavia have been initiated by national governments. Before moving on to a statistical analysis of the link between these developments and public preferences, the measurement of asylum policy for the statistical analysis will be discussed.

Measuring Asylum Policy

It is not always obvious where to draw the line between relevant and irrelevant policy changes. Although integration measures (such as language courses and job training) are clearly distinct from regulations of residence permits, major changes to integration policy may alter the attractiveness of a country as an asylum destination, which in turn influences the number of refugees admitted. The same is the case for family reunification. Policymakers who seek to reduce refugee immigration not only change asylum regulations, but also family immigration and integration policies that are relevant to asylum seekers' choice of destination. Nevertheless, the policy changes that are included in the statistical analysis deal directly with regulating refugee admissions. As public opinion in one country presumably has little impact on EU-level decisions, I focus on national legislation and exclude the signing of EU agreements. Studies of the influence of public opinion on EU integration find no such link (Hellström 2008; Toshkov 2011). It is up to national governments to decide whether to join new treaties, and public opinion could, therefore, potentially influence the decision to participate. Neither Norway, which is not an EU member, nor Denmark, due to the Maastricht opt-outs, are bound by the EU judicial charter. Thus, in these two states immigration policymaking is less externally dependent than in other European countries.

Policy change is here measured on an ordinal scale, indicating whether immigration policy in a given year was substantially liberalized (−1), restricted (1), or not substantially changed (0). The significance of the change was taken into consideration when both liberal and restrictive changes were made during the same year. In the case of Sweden in 1997, the many amendments in both directions that year did not lead to a substantial shift in either direction. All policy changes are coded in the year of decision, not the year of implementation (see list of policy changes in the appendix). An alternative to this ordinal scale could be to follow Hatton (2009: 201) that uses an asylum policy index, starting at 0 in the base year of 1997 and increasing by one for every major policy change. As he points out, this measure is crude, but it does give an impression of whether policy at a later point in time is more or less restrictive than in 1997. For the purposes of this chapter, this is not necessary. While it is a challenging task to identify the exact importance of various policy measures, it is also possible to say with some certainty whether a legislative or regulative change was intended to restrict or liberalize refugee immigration. Likewise, it is also possible to separate major policy changes from trivial adjustments. Rather than creating a fine-grained scale that gives a false impression of precision, a coarse-grained ordinal scale of three values is used here.

While this study examines asylum policy outputs as regulative and legislative changes, Jennings looks at asylum policy outcome as the number of asylum applications (2009). He argues that the reason he could not detect any thermostatic relationship between public opinion and asylum decisions is due to the nature of asylum decisions that supposedly are immune to political control. However, this is clearly not the case in Scandinavia, where governments have altered asylum criteria on a number of occasions. As long as they are not breaching international agreements, governments are free to change national regulations for asylum decisions. Yet, there are differences within Scandinavia in this respect. After legislative changes in 2010, Danish authorities have been prohibited from granting anyone asylum, unless it would be against international agreements not to do so. In Sweden, on the other hand, legislators have stated that Swedish asylum policy shall always be more liberal than the international minimum standard. The two countries are examples of governments that exploit the potential for national autonomy despite increasing international cooperation on asylum policy.

Analyzing Policy Change

Studies of government responsiveness commonly use a version of the survey question: "What is the most important problem facing your country today?" Here, a question directly linked to policy change is used. In all three Scandinavian countries, national surveys have repeatedly asked respondents about their relative preferences for current refugee policy. The advantage of this survey question is that respondents are actually providing their opinion of whether, and in which direction, governments should change policy in this specific field. Over time within the three countries, the questions are almost identical. Between the countries, questions are not identical, although they are very similar. Levels are, therefore, not comparable between countries, but trends are. The length of the policy process before a political decision on immigration policy is made, varies. It is, therefore not clear which is the correct time interval to use in a statistical analysis of public opinion and asylum policy changes. Commonly, the processes leading up to new laws on foreigners have taken years, but there are also examples of speedy processes that have had a substantial impact on the number of admissions. There are also cases where policy proposals have been substantially altered during consultative rounds just prior to policy passage. Compared to other policy areas, the field of asylum operates more quickly, and as laws on foreigners grant governments the authority to adjust policy regulations without conferring the parliaments, governments can make fast decisions. Yearly intervals are thus not necessarily ideal, but these are the shortest time intervals available.

Two public opinion variables will be tested for their effects on changes made to asylum policies: (1) median voter opinion and (2) opinion of government supporters. In line with Hobolt and Klemmensen, who consider median voter opinion to be "the extent to which government priorities reflect the policy priorities of a majority of the electorate" (2008: 312), median voter opinion is operationalized as the proportion of respondents in each country and each year that would like to restrict refugee immigration.

The core-voter position is operationalized as the proportion of respondents who support government parties preferring to restrict refugee immigration. Respondents in Norway and Denmark were asked which party they would vote for if there would be an election tomorrow. In Norway, the vote choice question was removed from the survey including the refugee attitude question in 2005, limiting the number of Norwegian observations. In Sweden, a question identifying which party respondents thought was the "best party" is included. These variables were then aggregated to generate the variable that measures the opinion of a subsection of the respondents. In years where there is a government change, there will be a large shift in the values of the core-voter variable compared to the median voter variable. This variable, therefore, also indirectly measures the effects of government changes and the different ideologies of parties.

Public opinion is, of course, only one of many possible influences on asylum policy. The number of asylum applications certainly affects how policy is altered. Asylum immigration is characterized by sudden, large, and sometimes unexpected fluctuations, and policy is frequently adjusted accordingly. Government composition and change may also be an important explanation for shifts in policy, as suggested by the partisan theory (Hibbs 1992). Parties can be expected to implement policies in accordance with their ideological preferences. Previous studies have found that center-right governments are more restrictive on immigration than social democratic governments (Gudbrandsen 2010). However, center-right parties have also contributed to liberalizing policy in Scandinavia, and social democratic parties commonly have a complicated relationship to immigration policy (Bale et al. 2010; Hinnfors, Spehar, and Bucken-Knapp 2012). Therefore, the impact that government composition has had on asylum policy is not so clear-cut. Nevertheless, a dummy variable indicating whether the government is right wing or social democratic is included in the analysis.

Radical right-wing parties may also have contributed to more restrictive asylum policies. In Denmark, such parties have been represented in the parliament since 1975—by the Fremskridtspartiet (Progress Party) until 2001 and by Dansk Folkeparti (Danish People's Party) from 1998 onward. Both parties strongly oppose immigration. In Norway, Fremskrittspartiet has been represented in the parliament since the 1970s, and their anti-immigration rhetoric has been pronounced since the mid-1980s. Sweden, arguably, has had two radical right-wing parties. The Sverigedemokraterna (Sweden Democrats), a nationalistic party with a Nazi legacy, first gained parliamentary representation in 2010. This is beyond the study's time frame, which is 1985–2009. Ny Demokrati (New Democracy) was represented only for one electoral term. The party was certainly not immigration-friendly (1991 party manifesto), but its stances were very mild compared to that of the Sweden Democrats, and also that of their sister parties in Norway and Denmark. The vote shares of the radical right-wing parties will be included as explanatory variables. An alternative could be to use survey data that measures support for these parties. This would also give us information about their support in between elections. However, their support has been severely underestimated in surveys, and as the degree of underestimation varies over time, it is better to measure their exact electoral strength.

Togeby argues that Danish attitudes toward refugee immigration have changed in the wake of media attention to refugee immigration (2004: 57). As media coverage concerning asylum seekers and refugees increases awareness of the issue, in addition to putting pressure on policymakers to prioritize the issue, it may impact policy, not just attitudes.

This is also in line with Baumgartner et al., who argue that information is a key "moving part" behind policy shifts (2011: 952). Here, the possible effect of media attention on asylum policy will be measured as the number of newspaper articles mentioning the term "asylum seeker" or "refugee" every year. As the number of newspapers is held constant, the amount of coverage is comparable within (but not between) countries, because the number of electronically searchable newspapers differs. In Sweden and Norway, keyword searches are done through Atekst and Mediearkivet (Retriever). The following newspapers are included: Norway, *VG* and *Aftenposten*; Sweden, *Dagens Nyheter* and *Expressen*. In Denmark, searches are done in Dansk Artikelindeks, which is a different search system with fewer registered articles. The Danish newspapers selected are *JyllandsPosten* and *Politiken*. The media archive InfoMedia is a more complete database, but it only dates back to 1990, which limits the number of time units. Here, searches were done in BT, EkstraBladet, Politiken, Weekendavisen, and Berlingske.

Empirical studies of asylum policies have also found that unemployment in the receiving country has an impact on not only labor immigration but also the reception of asylum seekers (Neumayer 2005). Higher unemployment may create a pressure to limit immigration, and unemployment, as a percent of labor force from Organization for Economic Co-operation and Developmentt (OECD) statistics, will be controlled for. Time trend variables for each country will also be included to control for time-variant omitted variables, to reduce potential autocorrelation, and to obtain an overall estimate of the policy trends. The variables all start at 1 in 1985.

Descriptive statistics indicate that the Danes have been somewhat more negative to refugee immigration than the Swedes and Norwegians (table 7.1). However, since the wording in the questions and time periods are slightly different, cross-national comparisons should be made with caution. A precondition for the median voter and the government supporters to have different impacts on policy is that these respective groups actually hold different attitudes. Enns and Wlezien find that party identification is an important cleavage in the United States, and to some extent, the same appears to be the case for immigration in Scandinavia as well (2011). In Sweden and Denmark, general public attitudes toward refugee immigration have been more restrictive than those of the government supporters. On average, the difference is small: In Denmark the government voters opinion was 3.3 percentage points more restrictive than the median voter opinion, while in Sweden the average difference was only 1.7.

Preliminary correlation analyses indicate that asylum policy changes are related to changes in public opinion. The correlation between the median voter opinion and policy changes is 0.27, whereas the correlation between government supporter opinion and policy changes is 0.43. This provides a hint that the association between policy changes and government voter opinion is stronger than that of the median voter. The result also holds in the ordered logistic regression analysis. Model I (table 7.2) tests whether public opinion has at all an impact

Table 7.1 Descriptive Statistics of Refugee Attitudes of Government Supporters

	Observ.	Mean	Std.Dev.	Min	Max	Norway	Sweden	Denmark
Liberalizations	6	49.76	16.76	26.83	69.53	2	5	0
No substantial change	18	51.44	7.67	37.93	69.80	1	7	10
Restrictions	10	58.09	11.42	42.28	81.17	2	2	5

Sources: Atekst, Dansk Data Arkiv: Gallup omnibus surveys 1985–1991 and ISF omnibus surveys (1993–1998); Borre et al (1993–2005); Nilsson et al (1990–2008); OECD, and Statistics Norway (2006–2008).

Table 7.2 Ordered Logit on Asylum Policy Changes

Asylum policy	Model I		Model II		Model III	
	Coeff.	St.error	Coeff.	St.error	Coeff.	St.error
Government voter	0.46	0.16	0.51	0.17		
Median voter	0.15	0.11			0.22	0.09
Unemployment	−0.23	0.42	0.04	0.33	−0.38	0.41
Asylum seekers	−0.00	−0.00	−0.00	−0.00	−0.00	−0.00
Media attention	0.01	0.01	0.00	0.01	0.00	0.01
Right government	−6.21	2.43	−6.46	2.40	−1.10	1.05
Radical right vote share	0.29	0.38	0.29	0.35	−0.06	0.29
Trend Norway	0.46	0.63	0.56	0.57	0.45	0.51
Trend Sweden	0.56	0.25	0.51	0.24	0.26	0.19
Trend Denmark	0.30	0.23	0.41	0.21	−0.08	0.17
Norway dummy	−1.75	12.21	−1.14	11.53	−9.96	9.69
Sweden dummy	−4.06	4.13	−2.32	3.58	−6.14	3.33
N	34		34		34	
Pseudo R2	0.51		0.47		0.28	
AIC	62.00		62.46		75.85	
BIC	83.35		82.30		95.67	

Sources: Atekst, Dansk Data Arkiv: Gallup omnibus surveys 1985–1991 and ISF omnibus surveys (1993–1998); Borre et al (1993–2005); Nilsson et al (1990–2008); OECD, and Statistics Norway (2006–2008). For sources of policy changes, see Appendix 7.1

on asylum policy change, and both the median voter opinion and government supporters' opinion are included, together with all control variables. Considering the high correlation between the median voter and the government voter opinion (0.68), their effects should be tested collectively. The Wald test shows that their impact on asylum policy changes is jointly significant, with 0.02. The more restrictive public opinion becomes, the more likely governments change policy.

Government composition also has a significant impact on restrictive asylum policy changes: Restrictions have been most frequent during periods with social democratic governments. This result highlights what had been mentioned previously, that the strict Danish immigration policy is not only a product of the 2001 government shift. The social democratic governments during the 1990s have been just as active in restricting policy. However, it should be stressed that there is some degree of variation between the policy changes coded as "restrictive," and that the coding, therefore, is not nuanced enough for us to conclude which type of government has had the most restrictive overall impact on asylum-related immigration. Preliminary analyses showed a weak correlation (0.05) between radical right party vote shares and policy changes, but the effect is not statistically significant in a multivariate model. The coding of New Democracy as a radical right-wing party does not impact on this result. Thus, the regression results do not support the argument that radical right-wing parties outside the government have an impact on asylum policy. Few variables are significant, which is not surprising considering that the total number of units in the analysis is limited to 34: 5 observations from Norway, 14 from Sweden, and 15 from Denmark.

The regression includes a time trend variable for each country, and only the Swedish variable is significant. This means that whereas restrictions have become significantly more frequent over time in Sweden, this has not been the case in the two other countries. For Denmark, insignificant trend variable emphasizes that restricting asylum policy is not a new invention for Danish governments. The number of asylum claims is significant only at a more liberal level, and although this can arguably be defended, bearing in mind the small number of units in the analysis, the variable has an unexpected effect: A higher number of asylum seekers appears to reduce the probability of stricter policies. This is the effect after controlling for time trends, which partly capture the rise in asylum applications since the mid-1980s.

Which of the two public opinion variables best explain asylum policy changes? To judge by this analysis, governments are more responsive to their own electorate. When separate regressions were estimated (Model II and Model III), both of the variables have expected signs and are statistically significant. The goodness-of-fit measures AIC and the BIC are lower for the government voter model, indicating that the preferences of the governments' voters is a better explanation of asylum policy change than that of the median voter. The fully standardized coefficients from model I give the same indication.

Tests of leads and lags suggest that attitudes and policy decisions in the same year are related. As is highlighted in the thermostatic model (Wlezien 1995), not only do governments respond to public opinion, but also the public adjusts their preferences as a result of government actions. It is not possible to trace such a relationship with the data used here. Restrictive policy changes have a positive, significant effect on attitudes in the same year, but a one-year lag of either variable is insignificant. To test for a possible feedback effect (Campbell 2012), a regression of the effects of lagged asylum policy changes on public opinion was done, but without the result of any significant coefficients. In other words, there seems to be a relationship between policy change and public attitudes *in the same year*. Because the data have a panel structure, panel heterogeneity autocorrelated residuals have been considered.

These regression results suggest that there is a correspondence between what Scandinavian governments do on asylum and what their own voters would like them to do. The regression is presented graphically in figure 7.1. The likelihood of a liberalization of asylum policy is at its highest when public opinion holds more liberal attitudes. At middle levels of skepticism toward refugee immigration, policy is unlikely to be substantively changed, whereas it is highly probable that asylum policy is tightened when attitudes become more negative.

Conclusion

The statistical analysis shows that asylum policies are related to public opinion on refugee immigration. Governments may have altered policy on the basis of their knowledge of shifting attitudes among their voters, but it could also be the case that they responded to something else (omitted from the statistical analysis) that was also the cause of changed attitudes among their voters. The data do not allow us to reach firm conclusions on causality, and further studies are certainly needed to understand better the timing and content of immigration policy change. Still, Scandinavian asylum policies have been responsive to public opinion,

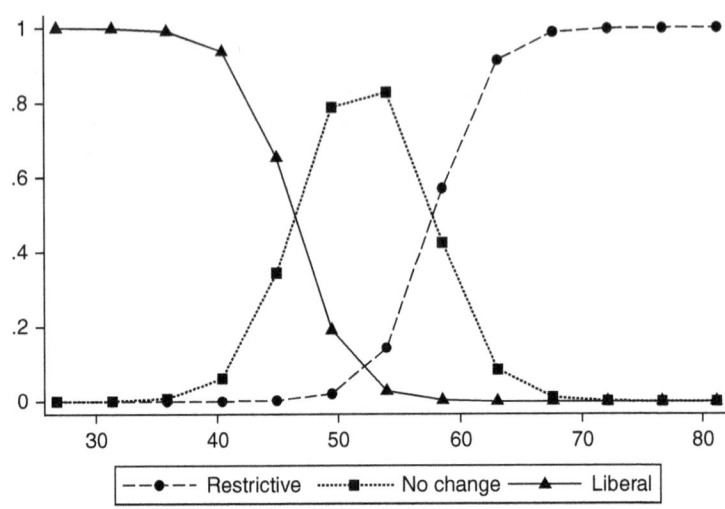

Figure 7.1 Probability of Policy Changes by Share of Government Supporters Who Oppose Refugee Immigration.
Sources: Atekst, Dansk Data Arkiv: Gallup Omnibus Surveys 1985–1991 and ISF Omnibus Surveys (1993–1998); Borre et al. (1993–2005); Nilsson et al. (1990–2008); OECD and Statistics Norway (2006–2008)

in the sense that they have changed in accordance with what the public preferred at different points in time.

Powell (2004: 91) described democratic responsiveness as "what occurs when the democratic process induces the government to form and implement policies that the citizens want." Scandinavian governments have implemented asylum policies in line with changes in citizens' preferences. The link between asylum policies and government voter preferences is tighter than the link between policies and the median voter, which indicates that governments pay closer attention to their core voters and strive to satisfy them first. However, considering the high correlation between the two, the main finding of the analysis is that public opinion is related to policy changes—not that some voter groups may be more influential than other. Robert Dahl (1971: 1–2) considered "the continuing responsiveness of the government to the preferences of the citizens" as one of the key characteristics of a democracy, but was not sure any political system could ever live up to this ideal. This study finds that Scandinavian immigration policies are responsive to citizens' preferences.

Appendix 7.1 Asylum Policy Changes in Scandinavia

Coding of year	Policy changes
Norway	
1987 Restrictive	Limiting the discretionary granting of humanitarian permits, and applying the principle of third country.
1991 Liberal	New law on protection against return. Applicants have the right to individual processing of case.
1992 Restrictive	Fingerprints of all asylum seekers recorded
1995 Liberal	Processing of cases of asylum seekers from Bosnia-Herzegovina put off.
1997 Liberal	Geneva convention should be interpreted more liberally.
1998 Liberal	News groups eligible for asylum. The benefit of the doubt for asylum seekers.
1999 Liberal	Asylum seekers are granted a work permit while application is processed.
2002 Restrictive	The right to residence permit if processing of case takes more than 15 months removed.
2003 Restrictive	Subsistence requirements after asylum applications introduced.
2004 Liberal	Families of children who have been in Norway more than three years granted residence permit.
2005 Restrictive	Asylum seekers are no longer granted permanent residence status on health grounds.
2006 Restrictive	Possibility to deny asylum if applicant can return to other part of home country.
2008 Restrictive	13 restrictions related to asylum immigration
Sweden	
1988 Restrictive	New Law of Foreigners. Amongst other, increased responsibility for transport companies
1989 Restrictive	Lucia decision. The right to asylum limited to only those mentioned in the Geneva convention.
1991 Liberal	Lucia decision lifted.
1992 Liberal	Visa requirements for Bosnia-Herzegovina lifted.
1993 Liberal	Permanent residence permit to refugees from Bosnia-Herzegovina. Visa requirements reintroduced.
1994 Neutral	Amnesty to families. Temporary status in mass flight situations. Temporary status to criminal asylum seekers.
1996 Neutral	New groups eligible for asylum. De facto refugees and conscientious objectors lost right to asylum.
2000 Liberal	Women and children who have been subject to serious abuse may be granted permanent residence status.
2004 Neutral	(Fines on transporters who do not check travel documents – Schengen adjustment.)

continued

Appendix 7.1 Continued

Coding of year	Policy changes
2005 Restrictive	New law of foreigners.
2006 Liberal	Declined asylum seekers who stayed for a long time in Sweden got new assessment of cases.
2007 Restrictive	Refugees from Iraq must be personally at risk to be considered a refugee.
2008 Liberal	Asylum seekers who found work within 6 months can be granted a labour immigration residence permit.

Denmark

Coding of year	Policy changes
1985 Restrictive	"Åpenbar grundlos" procedure.
1986 Restrictive	Principle of third country ("The Danish clause") introduced.
1989 restrictive	Transporter responsibility: Must reject passengers without valid travel documents.
1992 liberal	Suspended processing of applications from Palestine and Yugoslavia. Granted residence permit.
1995 restrictive	Applications from safe countries restricted. Fast track procedure for unfounded applications. Fingerprint system.
1996 restrictive	Asylum seekers lost the right to appeal cases. DNA tests on unsuccessful asylum seekers who resist expulsion.
2002 restrictive	More restrictive protection status. Filing of applications from abroad removed. Cases of refugees who visit home country are re-examined.
2010 restrictive	Access to residence permit on humanitarian grounds restricted. Possibility for permanent residence permit and citizenship restricted.

Note: The codes refer to the whole year, not necessarily all policy changes listed in the table if more than one change that year.

Sources:
Sweden: Swedish government communications to the parliamnent (skrivelser) 1990–2010, OECD SOPEMI annual reports, Spång (2008)
Norway: Government circulations on legislative and regulative changes, Historical overview over immigration policy changes from the Norwegian Immigration Authorities, and OECD SOPEMI annual reports
Denmark: Gammeltoft-Hansen and Whyte (2011), Nour and Zarrehparvar (2011), and OECD SOPEMI annual reports

CHAPTER 8

The Multilevel Governance of Migrant Integration: A Multilevel Governance Perspective on Dutch Migrant Integration Policies

Peter Scholten

Introduction

While migrant integration policies seem to be one of the last strongholds of national sovereignty, migrant integration is in many respects a local process. The concept of "integration" relates both to broad issues like national identity, values, and norms as well as to very local issues like finding a job, meeting people, and going to school. This positions migrant integration policies in an essentially multilevel setting (Alexander 2007; Zincone and Caponio 2006). Besides the multidimensionality of migrant integration as a policy concept, this multilevel setting provides a challenge to the governance of migrant integration.

Yet, migrant integration policies are often described in policy and academic discourse in terms of "national models of integration." Such models involve nationally and historically rooted ways of framing immigrant integration (Brubaker 1992). This means that how integration is defined and acted upon would differ primarily according to specific national histories, differences in national identity, and different views of the role of the state. These national models assume a strong degree of consistency and coherence of integration policies in specific countries (Bowen 2007; Bertossi and Duyvendak 2009; Bommes and Thränhardt

2010; Favell 2005). For instance, French policies would be based on a Republicanist model of assimilation into the French state (Weil 1991), British policies on a race-relations model with a modest conception of state intervention (Favell 2005; Bleich 2003), and Dutch policies on a resilient multicultural model that would continue to inform policy practices (Koopmans 2003; Sniderman and Hagendoorn 2007).

However, local governments and European institutions are often confronted with integration problems in different ways than on the national level (Caponio and Borkert 2010). Local governments often concentrate on concrete social concerns such as interethnic contact and "keeping things together" (De Zwart 2007; Poppelaars and Scholten 2008) and European institutions more on legal topics such as antidiscrimination (Guiraudon 1997). This means that how integration is defined and acted upon may prove much more variable than suggested by national models of integration.

Little is known about how migrant integration policies at various levels interact and produce either policy convergence (such as in national models of integration) or policy divergence (conflicting policies at various levels). Therefore, this chapter focuses on the multilevel governance of migrant integration in the Netherlands, in particular on the national and local level. It asks the question of how immigrant integration has been framed in national and local policies in the Netherlands, how changes and trends in policy framing on these levels can be explained, and what patterns of convergence or divergence can be found in the relation between policy frames on these levels.

The Dutch case provides a test case for the validity of national models of integration in multilevel governance settings. The Netherlands is not just a unitary state where most policy areas are centrally coordinated, according to the literature (Sniderman and Hagendoorn 2007; Koopmans 2003); it can also be taken as an exemplary country for the so-called multicultural model of integration. This chapter will analyze the development of national and local migrant integration policies over the past decades (since the 1980s) and focus in particular on the relation between policies at these levels. For the local level, the chapter focuses on the two largest cities in the Netherlands, Rotterdam and Amsterdam. These cities do not just have the highest percentage of non-Western immigrants among its inhabitants (37 percent and 35 percent respectively, as of 2010), but also differ in terms of types of migrants (mainly Turks and Antilleans in Rotterdam, Moroccans and Surinamese in Amsterdam), in terms of economy (Rotterdam as an industrial city against Amsterdam's services-oriented economy) as well as in terms of local politics (Rotterdam for some time being controlled by a populist party). Selecting these two very different cities with large migrant populations allows us to examine to what extent national policies indeed resonate in local policies under different circumstances, as suggested by the idea of national models of integration.

A Multilevel Governance Perspective on Migrant Integration Policies

"National Models" versus "the Local Dimension" of Migrant Integration Policies

The idea of "national models of integration," inspired by historical-institutionalist thinking, has acquired great resonance in European migration research. A key trait of such national models is that they are expected to be relatively stable over fairly long periods of time, based on the assumption that the conditions that led to a specific model are unlikely to change rapidly and that models themselves tend to develop a certain path-dependency or resistance to change (Brubaker 1992; Hollifield 1997; Koopmans 2005). A key reference is Brubaker's (1992) *Citizenship and Nationhood in France and Germany*. In this book, Brubaker juxtaposes the German and French models of citizenship that provided the foundations for the integration policies in these countries; a differentialist approach in Germany and an assimilationist approach in France. As a true historical institutionalist, Brubaker shows how the historical conditions in both countries led to the construction of these national models: a strongly developed cultural and apolitical sense of national belonging in Germany versus the state-centric tradition of nation building in France.

Bommes and Thränhardt (2010) show that paradigms of migration are inherently bound national states. They argue that these paradigms are national "not just because of their context dependency and insufficient clarifications on the conditions of generalisability, they are national because the modes of presenting and questions are political constituted by the nation states for which migration becomes a problem or a challenge" (10). Similarly, Favell (2005: 47) shows that national models of integration are often the product of the "exclusively internal national political dynamics" or "self-sufficiency" of debates on immigrant integration in politics as well as in migration research. Thus, the development of these national paradigms must be considered a consequence of nation-state centeredness of policy (and academic) discourses, rather than as accurate representations of the uniquely national character of immigrant integration policies. In fact, as Bommes and Thränhardt argue, the national paradigms would have distorted not just international comparative research, often leading to what Favell (2005: 48) describes as "self-justificatory discourse."

In contrast to the focus on national models of integration, there is a growing interest for the local dimension of immigrant integration policymaking (Borkert and Caponio 2010; Penninx and Zincone 2011; Alexander 2007). Cities, often the location where most immigrants live and where integration processes and associated problems take place, have become increasingly active over the past decades in developing their own policies aimed at immigrant integration (Alexander 2007). These local policies are generally more accommodative toward ethnic differences and group-specific measures than national policies. In fact, this thesis implies that policies on the local level could be much more convergent than suggested by the national models of integration. Local opportunity structures would be more open for migrant groups than national opportunity structures, for instance, because policymaking would take place primarily "behind-closed-doors" (Guiraudon 1999) in relative insulation from broader (national) public and political debates, and with a much greater proximity between local governments and local migrant organizations. Studies like Poppelaars and Scholten (2008) and Vermeulen and Stotijn (2010) have indeed revealed instances of "pragmatic accommodation" in local policy practices in cities as Rotterdam, Amsterdam, and Berlin. Though none of these studies adhere to a multiculturalist policy belief (at least not anymore), there were much more pragmatic considerations in concrete policy practices that, for instance, lead these local governments to cooperate with migrant organizations. Both studies show that on the street-level bureaucracy, where policies are put into practice, pragmatic elements of problem-coping and policy routines play a central role in the perseverance of group-specific policies. Uitermark (2007) describes these policies of formally negating ethnic differences but cooperating on a more pragmatic mode with migrant organizations as postmulticulturalist policies.

This thesis is contested by other studies (in particular Mahnig 2004) that show that local migrant policies have been steered much more by "top-down initiatives of political elites aimed at preserving their own political control" than by the bottom-up dynamics suggested by afore-mentioned studies. Migrants would generally have been too weak to mobilize and significantly influence local politics, and local politicians would generally have tended to avoid immigrant issues rather than accommodate them (18–19). Mahnig shows that this top-down logic in local immigrant integration policymaking in fact tends to exclude rather than include migrants. Agenda-setting appears as a key factor in local policymaking according to Mahnig's study: local governments adopt immigrant integration measures only "when their presence began to be widely perceived as threats to the urban society as a whole" (33), thereby staging the agenda-access of this issue on the local political agenda.

Though it remains unclear whether there is convergence or divergence between immigrant integration policies on the local level, these studies lend overwhelming support to the thesis that local policies do have their own policymaking dynamics and involve much more than just the implementation of national policies. However, too little is known about the relation and interaction between national and local immigrant integration policies; interestingly, the growth of studies on local policies alongside the more traditional studies on national policies has not yet resulted in more research on the relation between both levels, or what I define as the multilevel governance of immigrant integration.

A Multilevel Perspective on Policy Framing

This chapter challenges the idea of national models of integration from a multilevel perspective, adopting an empiricist view on whether policies as formulated on the national and local level indeed exhibit strong coherence (as assumed by national models) or exhibit a clear divergence between both levels. This perspective relates first to the broader literature about multilevel governance, and second to the literature of policy framing. The multilevel governance literature has provided much empirical evidence that governance is increasingly dispersed among various policy levels (Rhodes 2007; Kooiman 2003; Bache and Flinders 2004: Hooghe and Marks 2001). Different policy levels tend to pose different opportunity structures that constrain and enable policy actors in very specific ways and that provide different opportunities for various policy frames (Princen and Kerremans 2008). It argues that the structures of multilevel governance differ strongly between policy sectors; there is no universal standard model of multilevel governance (Rosenau 2004).

Three types of factors can be derived from the literature to account for the specific opportunity structures on the different levels; problem, political, and policy factors. First, problems can manifest themselves in different ways on different levels, because of problem trends that are specific to a certain level or because of specific incidents or events

(Hoppe 2010). For instance, whereas national integration policies have tended to be connected with concerns about national identity, local policies are often framed in response to much more concrete and local circumstances such as preventing interethnic tensions and facilitating interethnic contact. Second, every level has its own political setting, including the political balance of power, degree of mediatization, or institutionalized selection principles in topic prioritization (Hilgartner and Bosk 1988). As Alexander (2007) has shown, many local governments have developed their own policy philosophies, in response to specifically local political developments. As we will see in Rotterdam, the rise of a local political party will leave a lasting imprint on local integration policies. Finally, in terms of policy factors, every level has its own policy legacies and presents different opportunities for issue linkages, such as with urban policies on the local level or identity politics on the national level (John 2006). For instance, as we will see for Amsterdam, the established local tradition of policies of tolerance toward different religions will leave a lasting imprint on its policies toward immigrants as well.

This conceptualization of multilevel governance will be connected to a second literature that focuses on policy framing. From a neoinstitutionalist perspective, attention has been drawn to the process of immigrant integration *policymaking* and to the role of narrative construction or "framing" in these policymaking processes (Bleich 2003; Scholten 2011; Boswell Geddes and Scholten 2011). Rather than stressing how national models structure policymaking and public discourse, this framing approach focuses on how social meaning is attributed to immigrant integration by actors within specific institutional settings. A frame thus becomes an inherently selective and normative way of defining, interpreting, and explaining a specific issue (Schön and Rein 1994). A frame helps make sense out of the complex social reality that is often associated with issues such as immigrant integration: they are tools for "naming" and "framing" the problem and determining adequate paths for policy action.

Frames of migrant integration do, first of all, define and conceptualize specific terms; for instance, integration can be phrased as a process of assimilation or rather emancipation. In addition, frames suggest probable causes of the problem, often in terms of causal stories that attribute blame and responsibility; for instance, failing migrant integration can be interpreted as a consequence of deficiencies on the part of migrants as well as a product of institutional discrimination. Frames also define and categorize relevant target groups in specific ways; in the case of migrant integration, this can be specific ethnic minorities as groups, but also more individual categories such as newcomers. Finally, frames suggest proper ways of action, such as fighting discrimination, promoting employability, and preventing spatial concentration.

A hypothesis guiding this analysis is that level-specific configuration of problem, and political and policy factors will matter to the substantive framing of migrant integration on each of the studied levels. If this configuration of factors reveals differences between levels, we expect the multilevel governance of migrant integration to be complicated by frame differences and even frame conflicts between different levels. If the assumption that there are distinct national models of integration holds, we expect to find similar configurations leading to frame congruence between the different levels, thus producing and sustaining a national model of integration.

The Multilevel Governance of Immigrant Integration in the Netherlands

The Dutch case provides a test case for the validity of national models of integration, or, in particular, the so-called Dutch multicultural model. As a unitary state that has become internationally renowned for its multicultural policy approach (see Sniderman and Hagendoorn 2007; Koopmans 2006), one would expect policy coherence between the national and local level.

Rethinking the Dutch Model of Integration

Dutch immigrant integration policies have become internationally (and increasingly also nationally) known for its alleged "multicultural model of integration." A key trait of the Dutch multicultural model would be its tendency to institutionalize cultural pluralism in the belief that cultural emancipation of immigrant minorities is the key to their integration into Dutch society (see also Duyvendak and Scholten 2011). This would reflect a broad acceptance of the transformation of Dutch society into a multicultural society. In the latter respect, a connection is often made with the peculiar Dutch history of pillarization, referring to the period from the 1920s to 1960s when most of Dutch society was structured according to specific religious (protestant, Catholic) or political-ideological (Socialist, liberal) pillars.

The Netherlands first developed an "Ethnic Minorities Policy" in the early 1980s. This policy was targeted at specific cultural or ethnic minorities in Dutch society, such as the foreign workers, the Surinamese, the Moluccans, and the Antilleans. Migrants were framed as "minorities" in Dutch society instead of temporary guests, and government decided to focus on those minorities whose position was characterized by an accumulation of cultural and social-economic difficulties and for whom the Dutch government felt a special historical responsibility (Rath 2001). The Minorities Policy expressed the idea that an amelioration of the social-cultural position of migrants would also improve their social-economic position. The policy objective was to combat discrimination and social-economic deprivation and to support social-cultural emancipation. These policies were not developed to celebrate all kinds of cultural differences—it did not include well-off migrants but just those who were socioeconomically very weak, and even within this category only those ethnic groups for whom Dutch government felt a special historical responsibility. Within this perspective, the government thought the preservation of cultural identities to be useful for instrumental reasons.

Immigrant integration remerged on the national political agenda in various periods since the 1980s. In 1989, the authoritative Dutch Scientific Council for Government Policy denounced this policy model, as it focused too much on "culture and morality" and tended to make minorities too much dependent on state facilities because of its group-specific measures (WRR 1989). According to the WRR, the institutionalization of cultural pluralism should no longer be considered an independent policy objective. Rather, government should focus on stimulating individual migrants to stand on their own feet. Several years after this report, a broad national debate emerged that picked up on important points of the 1989 WRR report. In addition, this national minorities debate added a much more critical tone to the Dutch accommodative approach toward cultural differences in general, and Islam in particular. Subsequently, in the early 1990s, government policy changed in several important regards. The Minorities Policy was reframed into an Integration Policy that stressed the social-economic participation of immigrants as citizens or "allochthonous" rather than emancipation of minorities. Promoting "good" or "active" citizenship became the primary policy goal, stimulating individual migrants to live up to their civic rights as well as their duties and to become economically independent participants in society.

Later, just after the turn of the millennia, immigrant integration again reemerged on the agenda, resulting in what would be seen as an assimilationist turn in Dutch integration policies. A (second) broad national debate was triggered in 2000 by claims that Dutch policy had become a "multicultural tragedy" (Scheffer 2000). Also, the populist politician Fortuyn made the alleged failure of the Dutch integration approach into one of his central political issues. This set in motion a gradual assimilationist turn, which was codified in an "Integration Policy New Style.' Whereas the Integration Policy had stressed 'active citizenship," the Integration Policy "New Style" stressed rather the "common citizenship," which meant that "the unity of society must be found in what members have in common (...) that is that people speak Dutch, and that one abides to basic Dutch norms" (TK 2003–2004, 29203, nr. 1: 8.). Persisting sociocultural differences were now considered a hindrance to immigrant integration. Also, the integration policy was more and more linked to a broader public and political concern about the preservation of national identity and social cohesion in Dutch society. It was in this period that the framing of the "multicultural model" took place as a "counterdiscourse" against which new policy developments were to be juxtaposed. This assimilationist turn may have contributed to a discursive reconstruction of the history of integration policies that put much greater stress on its alleged multiculturalist traits.

This brief policy analysis shows that there has not been one dominant model or framing in the Netherlands. In spite of the singular image of the Netherlands as representing the multicultural model, Dutch policy has been inspired, beyond the multicultural model, by at least two different frames. One of these competing frames is the more liberal-egalitarian (social-economic) frame, which became particularly influential in the 1990s. And the other is the more assimilationist frame that emerged during the 1990s and became more prominent after the turn of the millennium. In fact, there never really has been a "national multicultural model," as defining slogans as "integration with preservation of cultural identity" were rejected already in the 1980s; only later this slogan would be projected on this period in public and political discourse. Neither pillarization nor multiculturalism were really embraced as normative ideals; statements of multiculturalism rather referred in a more descriptive sense to the increase of diversity in society. As far as references to pillarization or multiculturalism were used, these seem to have been much more pragmatic than normative. Therefore, the multiculturalism rather seems to have developed into a counterdiscourse, or a discourse used for juxtaposition against the assimilationist turn taking place since the early 2000s.

Immigrant Integration Policies in Amsterdam

The city of Amsterdam is one out of several well-researched European cities in terms of local immigrant integration policies. In many cases (e.g., Lucassen and Penninx 1995), Amsterdam's policy of tolerance, pluralism, and recognition of ethnic groups is perceived as an exemplary case for the so-called Dutch multicultural model of integration. Indeed, for a long time it seems that Amsterdam's immigrant integration policy largely followed in suit with national policy developments. In the late 1970s and during the 1980s, Amsterdam developed a more pluralist "Minorities Policy," in many ways resembling the national Ethnic Minorities Policy from that period. This policy formed a response to the national developments in this period, in addition to the mounting social problems that the city was faced with in the 1970s, for instance, in the sphere of housing. In a 1978 policy memorandum on foreign workers in Amsterdam, the government observed that most foreign workers would indeed settle permanently. A 1982 memorandum subsequently established the foundation of Amsterdam's policies. Clearly revealing a multiculturalist policy framing, this memorandum defined the objective as "based on the idea that minorities should integrate while also maintaining their cultural identity" (Kraal 2001: 20). This policy involved many group-specific measures, such as the establishment of ethnic minority advisory councils and other measures in the social-economic domain (Vermeulen 2006), like promoting ethnic entrepreneurship, affirmative action policies by the city government, and very tolerant policies toward the establishment of (mainly Muslim) religious facilities (Alexander 2007).

By the end of the 1980s, it became evident that the local minorities policy was not, or at least not sufficiently, successful (City of Amsterdam 1989). More or less simultaneous with the debate triggered by the 1989 report from the Scientific Council for Government Policy (WRR), this put immigrant integration back on the local agenda, though not immediately leading to significant changes in local policies. The first National Minorities Debate that took place in 1992 did, however, find its way onto the local political agenda of Amsterdam during the local elections of 1994. This would, though perhaps more gradually than on the national level, mark a turning point away from Amsterdam's pluralist policies of the 1980s. The new climate brought the anti-immigrant Center Party into the City Council with four seats. The replacement of the mayor Ed van Thijn, a proclaimed multiculturalist, further facilitated a policy frame shift in the years to follow (Alexander 2007: 186).

This resulted, though no earlier than 1999, in a newly formulated Diversity Policy, involving a reframing from what Kraal (2001) defined as "group-specific policies" toward "problem-oriented policies." Many group-specific measures were abandoned, at least in formal policy, for a more generic and individual or citizen-oriented approach. Wolff (1999) describes the three main aims of the new Diversity Policy as guaranteeing equal opportunities, combating discrimination, and promoting individual participation. Some group-specific social-economic measures were abandoned, the role of migrant organizations (at least formally) diminished significantly, and generic policies in both areas and in areas as spatial policies stepped up in order to promote participation and interethnic contact, a change that can be interpreted as a shift from bonding within communities to the bridging of ethnic differences. As part of such a more generic approach, the role of migrant organizations was decreased significantly, in favor for a more individualized and diverse "migration council" that did not represent any group in particular. In addition, Amsterdam developed, in correlation with national developments and developments in a number of other cities, civic integration programs on the local level. Even going beyond the requirements of the civic integration of Newcomers Law that entered force in 1998, Amsterdam developed civic integration programs for newcomers, "oldcomers" (long-term resident migrants who still suffer language or other associated integration problems), and adults. Amsterdam's often proactive and tolerant policies toward cultural and religious matters were largely abandoned, claiming that these matters belonged to the private realm rather than the public realm (Maussen 2006: 69).

Immigrant integration reappeared prominently on the local political agenda after the turn of the millennium. The murder of filmmaker Theo van Gogh by a Dutch-Moroccan Muslim radical was a particularly powerful focus event in this respect. Following this event, Amsterdam published a new memorandum "We, the people of Amsterdam" (City of Amsterdam 2005). This memorandum made a more explicit issue connection between immigrant integration and antiradicalization policies. This new policy initiative seems to reinforce the trend toward what Maussen (2006, 2009) describes as a dialogical approach to immigrant integration, involving an approach less oriented at groups or even cultural and religious matters in general, but more at participation and interethnic contact. Rather than choosing an assimilative approach, as was the case on the national level in this period, this local dialogical approach stressed the diversity possibilities for identification with the city of Amsterdam as a means of creating social cohesion on the city level. In public debate, Amsterdam's mayor Cohen's slogan "keeping things together" became exemplary for this pragmatic approach. Indeed, studies reveal that migrants tend to identify much more with the city they live in than with Dutch national identity at large (Van der Welle and Mamadouh 2009).

However, in terms of policy practices, various studies indicate that in spite of the frame shifts in official policies, many instances of pragmatic accommodation of ethnic differences were continued well into the 1990s and even later. De Zwart (2005) reveals that Amsterdam's city government as well as many district governments continued to cooperate with migrant organizations or accommodate ethno-cultural differences for various pragmatic reasons. For street-level bureaucrats, cooperating with these organizations was often a primary means for staying in touch with policy target groups, gaining information on these groups, and assuring cooperation from these groups. Similarly, Vermeulen and Stotijn (2010) found that local policies toward unemployment among immigrant youth also took the ethno-cultural factor into account along with street-level bureaucrat processes.

Immigrant Integration Policies in Rotterdam

In the city of Rotterdam, the development of local immigrant integration policies followed a different path. The issue of immigrant integration emerged on the political agenda relatively early, following ethnic riots in 1972 about housing problems in the Rotterdam neighborhood Afrikaanderbuurt. Furthermore, Rotterdam's industrial character of the local economy meant that the city was strongly affected by the economic recession in the 1970s, following the oil crises. This recession hit the immigrant population particularly hard, with problems of social segregation, deprivation, and criminality concentrated in specific sections around the city's center. This meant that the city of Rotterdam was faced relatively early with the consequences of discrepancy between the norm of not being an immigration country and the fact of increasing and prolonged settlement of migrants in specific neighborhoods.

Consequently, Rotterdam adopted a policy aimed at integration by the end of the 1970s, starting form a 1978 memorandum that already concluded that most immigrants would indeed be there to stay. In contrast to national policies, Rotterdam's policies were much more oriented at social deprivation than at cultural emancipation (Veenman 2001: 10). In contrast with Amsterdam's pluralist policies, Rotterdam's policies combined elements of an integrationist with a more dialogical approach (Maussen 2003: 113). A 1985 policy memorandum states that "minorities should to a great extent adapt [to Dutch society] (...) integration inevitably means learning Dutch language, knowledge of and participating in Dutch social relations and the acquisition of some Dutch norms and values (...) however, foreigners do not need to become like average Dutchmen" (City of Rotterdam 1985). The policy's main focus was on integration in the spheres of labor market, education, and housing, and overall on stimulating interethnic contact (Veenman 2001: 10).

Rotterdam was not only a frontrunner in developing immigrant integration policies (even establishing a specific Minorities Policy in 1981, just before the establishment of the national Ethnic Minorities Policy in 1983); it continued to be a policy entrepreneur in terms of influencing national policies. In the 1988, it issued a Memorandum on Minorities Policy in the 1990s (City of Rotterdam 1988), in which it advocated specific policies that mainly targeted social-economic areas. This was, evidently, in line with the policies Rotterdam had developed in the 1980s already. With this memorandum, it attempted to influence a report from the Scientific Council for Government Policy that would be issued a bit later (1989). It did so very successfully (Veenman 2001: 11), especially so given the tremendous influence this 1989 WRR report would have on national policy developments (see earlier in this chapter: p. 158). In this context, Rotterdam also continued to plea for more policy decentralization, as it considered national policies aimed at social renewal a failure (18). During the 1990s, Rotterdam would largely continue this policy approach aimed at integration through social-economic participation, though in the early 1990s it would gradually decrease many of its subsidies to specific programs, adopting an approach that rather aimed to simulate initiatives from individual migrants and their organizations themselves (13).

Like Amsterdam, Rotterdam experienced a gradual shift throughout the 1990s to a Diversity Policy that was oriented at promoting (and even celebrating) the diversity of the city. This was, for instance, manifested in Rotterdam's liberal policies in this period toward the establishment of new mosques, which were seen as tokens of the diverse character of the city (Maussen 2003). The tone of this Diversity Policy was much more positive than the earlier integration policies aimed primarily at social deprivation. A difference with Amsterdam's diversity policies was that Rotterdam continued to cooperate with migrant organizations even under the banner of the Diversity Policy. In particular, these migrant organizations were taken as instruments for the integration of these groups, rather than as instruments for the accommodation of cultural differences. In addition, the City of Rotterdam was a frontrunner in the early 1990s in the development of civic integration programs for newcomers. Already, in 1991, Rotterdam began a municipal Project Integration for Newcomers (Van den Bent 2010: 152). Much earlier, Rotterdam made participation in these courses mandatory for migrants who received social benefits (153). With these programs, the cities' policies shifted attention from settled minority groups to the ongoing influx of newcomers to the city.

The years 2002 and 2003 marked a major turning point in Rotterdam's local politics (Tops 2007: Van den Bent 2010). Immigrant integration figured prominently in local media and was a key stake in the local elections of 2002. In these years, Pim Fortuyn made his first moves on the Dutch political stage, as leader of the center-right populist party "Liveable Rotterdam" that eventually managed to win the 2002 local elections. In these elections, immigrant integration was framed in relation to issues such as criminality, Islam, radicalization, and the decline of social cohesion. In response, an assimilationist policy was developed that concentrated in particular on neighborhoods where migrants are relatively overrepresented (Uitermark and Duyvendak 2008). In this context, the municipality pushed national government to adopt the so-called Rotterdam law (formally called "Special Measures for Urban Issues," which was advocated by Rotterdam and implemented in Rotterdam only, hence the Rotterdam law) that was implemented in January 2005 and provided the municipalities with means for preventing the settlement of people from low-income categories or with social security benefits in designated urban areas (Uitermark and Duyvendak 2008). Clearly, not just social-economic participation, but also interethnic contact and acculturation were seen as important factors for immigrant integration. Also, Rotterdam adopted new measures to promote interethnic contacts in particular. For instance, it developed a project ("Welcome to Rotterdam") where "old" and "new" citizens of Rotterdam would meet on an individual basis to do something together and get acquainted with each other (Muijres and Aarts 2011).

Following what has been described as the "white backlash" with the rise of Liveable Netherlands in 2002, subsequent elections brought the Labour Party back to power, aided significantly by rising immigrant support for this party. This strongly suggests political polarization along ethnic lines between Liveable Rotterdam and the Labour Party (van den Bent 2010: 254), which continue to be almost equally strong in terms of electoral support. Whereas the ethnic vote does not seem to have played a role of much significance before (Odmalm 2005), since 2002 this ethnic vote thus has become central to Rotterdam's local electoral politics. This seems to be supported by data that shows that even in national elections, the percentage of migrants who went to the ballot box increased significantly in Rotterdam. Migrants voted overwhelmingly for leftist parties (such as the Labour Party) in response to the rise of center-right parties, whereas it decreased in Amsterdam where center-right parties never gained the level of power that they did reach in Rotterdam.

The Multilevel Dynamics of Migrant Integration Policies in the Netherlands

The preceding analysis of national and local migrant integration policies reveals a progressive divergence between both levels. It must be said that in the earliest periods, especially in the late 1970s and 1980s, there was some convergence. The policies of Amsterdam and, though less so, Rotterdam to a large extent followed suit with national policy developments; local and national policies defined immigrant settlement as a permanent phenomenon and developed policies aimed at immigrant integration in which migrant organizations obtained an important role. The seemingly coherent multilevel governance of integration in this period seems to be the consequence of a more or less simultaneous realization that immigrant settlement was permanent, than a consequence of policy coordination.

However, since the 1990s, the case studies of Amsterdam and even more so Rotterdam show signs of progressive divergence in relation to national policies. Both cities have clearly become increasingly responsive to the specifically local developments, including local problem developments as well as political developments and focus events. Already in the late 1980s, Rotterdam appears to have been an important policy entrepreneur in the frame shift toward a more social-economically oriented integration policy in the 1990s; this policy advocacy was a consequence of the severe problem pressure the City of Rotterdam experienced in social-economic areas as labor, housing, and education, which it felt was insufficiently addressed by the national Ethnic Minorities Policy (Veenman 2001). Furthermore, responding to the gradual alleviation of many of the most immediate social problems in the economic upsurge of the late 1990s, both cities adopted Diversity Policies that (at least for brief period) celebrated cultural diversity of both cities (Maussen 2003), this in contrast with national developments in the Integration Policy of that period.

In terms of multilevel governance, the first decade of the twenty-first century marks a period of not only national-local divergence, but also a period where policies at both levels seem to have become increasingly contradictory and the differences between Amsterdam's and Rotterdam's policies more marked. In response to the rise to power of the Populist Liveable Rotterdam Party in 2002, Rotterdam adopted an assimilationist policy approach even before the assimilationist turn on the national level (providing a stage to Pim Fortuyn who would later play a key role in national developments). Rotterdam clearly continued to be a policy entrepreneur rather than a policy follower. Furthermore, much more than on the national level where policies increasingly left assimilation to individual migrants themselves, Rotterdam continued to play a very active role in projects aimed at problems of migrants (especially Moroccans and Antilleans) and at promoting interethnic contact (such as the Welcome to Rotterdam project). In addition, it went much further than national policies in terms of promoting social mixing in specific neighborhoods, with the renowned "Rotterdam law" (Uitermark and Duyvendak 2008). In contrast, Amsterdam continued much of its Diversity Policy, in spite of the national assimilationist turn. However, especially following the Van Gogh murder in 2004, Amsterdam followed a much more pragmatic policy of "keeping things together." Especially by promoting diversity and interethnic contact, rather than accommodating group demarcations in society, Amsterdam aimed to "bond" migrants and natives together in a common Amsterdam community. Much more than being oriented at specific groups, Amsterdam's policies have become increasingly oriented at specific problems (Kraal 2001).

Besides the discrepancy between the national and local level, the frame perspective adopted in this chapter helped identify policy dynamics or frame shifts over time as well. Rather than there being one dominant model deeply embedded in Dutch institutions and resistant to change, there has been a series of frame shifts in Dutch policies. There have been at least several discourses or frames that have competed over the policy agenda over the past decades (Roggeband and Vliegenthart 2007). Each frame is characterized by its own selectivity in terms of focusing on specific facets of immigrant integration. This has confused the debate about policy successes and failures in the Dutch; whereas "universalists" point to evidence of the labor market and education sectors as proof of policy success, both multiculturalists and assimilationist point at evidence from the social-cultural sphere to claim policy failure (though, of course, both valuing evidence very differently). In fact, the ongoing controversies over the success or failure of the Dutch approach are less indications of the doubtful effect of Dutch policies than they are indications of ongoing deep-seated frame controversies (Scholten 2011).

The frame shifts that have occurred in the Dutch case over the past decades must be understood against the background of changing situational factors that helped put a particular frame on the agenda in specific periods. The rise of the Ethnic Minorities Policy in the 1980s cannot be understood without reference to broader social and political belief in that period that this problem should be resolved rationally (technocratically) and should be systematically depoliticized, and that with the given levels of immigration, Dutch society could effectively be turned into a multicultural society. These factors explain what Vink described as the "pillarization reflex" in the early 1980s (Vink 2007). Similarly, the rise of the Integration Policy in the early 1990s cannot be understood without reference to the broader politics of state retrenchment and welfare state reform in the Netherlands in the late 1980s, as well as the progressive individualization of Dutch society in that period. Finally, the assimilationist turn at the beginning of the twenty-first century cannot but be considered as a direct consequence of broader turn to the political right in Dutch politicians, with immigrant integration as a pivotal concern not just for populist but also for most center-right parties (and increasingly also the Labour Party).

Conclusions: The Multilevel Governance of Immigrant Integration in the Netherlands

From a multilevel governance perspective on how migrant integration policies have been framed at the national and the local level (Rotterdam and Amsterdam) in the Netherlands, this chapter has revealed that national and policies have developed in very different ways. This calls for a rethinking of the idea of national models of integration. Actual integration policies are much less consistent over time and their mutual relation is much less coherent as suggested by "national models of integration." Rather than an effective state-centered mode of policy coordination, the Dutch case has revealed many instances where local governments formulated migrant integration policies in response to very specific local factors, such as local focus events (the Van Gogh killing), local political circumstances (the rise of Liveable Rotterdam), and local policy factors (such as the broader approach to socioeconomic problems in Rotterdam and the broader pluralist tradition in Amsterdam). This seems to support claims of Caponio and Borkert (2010) and Alexander (2007) that there is a specific local dimension of policymaking, much more responsive to local problem pressure and local political conditions and events than merely being responsive to the national level.

The local dimension of migrant integration policymaking reveals itself not just in the differences in how migrant integration is framed at the national and the local level, but also in the interaction between both levels. Rather than a top-down mode of policy coordination, the analysis presented in this chapter revealed many instances of interaction between both levels. In fact, both the cities of Rotterdam and Amsterdam have on occasion acted as policy entrepreneurs that have tried to influence national developments in order to broaden the scope for local policy action. Take, for instance, the entrepreneurship of Rotterdam in the formulation of civic integration policies for newcomers and for the adoption of a national law that would allow local governments to adopt special measures for promoting spatial dispersion (the so-called Rotterdam Law).

Besides differences between national and local policies, the analysis in this chapter revealed differences between both city cases as well. Whereas Rotterdam already from the early 1980s followed a more integrationist and socioeconomic approach, Amsterdam's policies put much more emphasis on diversity and sociocultural emancipation. As such, this chapter does not support the thesis that local policies, because of their proximity to migrants, are always more accommodative to ethnic differences. In fact, to reflect more the thesis by Mahnig (2004), local policies can even be much more "integrationist" with sometimes even "exclusionary" consequences than national policies. This applies in particular to the city of Rotterdam where local political circumstances even triggered an assimilationist turn before the national level. Even in the City of Amsterdam, known for its policy of "keeping things together," the extent to which ethnic differences are accommodated is not so much a conscious policy choice but rather a pragmatic policy practice oriented at resolving specific problems.

Furthermore, reconceptualizing "models" as frames helps accounting for the dynamic ways in which frames are produced, reproduced, or challenged. At least for the Dutch case, subjective and strategic factors of policy framing seem to have been much more influential on policymaking than the objective problem conditions (as in Freeman) or historical legacies (as in Brubaker). For international comparative studies, this will support efforts to surmount the replication of differences between national models of integration and account for the dynamic ways in which policies develop and possibly also discover patterns of convergence in policymaking as well as empirically found the observations on policy divergences.

CHAPTER 9

Ideology and Entry Policy: Why Center-Right Parties in Sweden Support Open-Door Migration Policies

Andrea Spehar, Gregg Bucken-Knapp, and Jonas Hinnfors

The Puzzle of Center-Right Parties Favoring Open Immigration Entry Policies

On September 20, 2010, Swedes woke up to a new political landscape. The openly xenophobic Sweden Democrats (SD [Sverigedemokraterna]) had, with 5.7 percent of the votes at the general election, comfortably gained *Riksdag* (parliament) representation for the first time. However, although newly elected, signs had existed for nearly a decade of its impending political breakthrough, as SD had steadily increased its representation in the country's regional and local political administrations. Moreover, while the party's success may have been a sea change in Swedish politics, it was not the first time a far right populist party had broken through nationally. The New Democracy (NYD [Ny Demokrati]) party gained nearly 7 percent of the seats during the 1991 Riksdag election, before losing practically all of its votes in 1994.

Conventional wisdom, as presented in previous research, would expect existing parties, and center-right parties in particular to react to the new party system context and voter threat by adopting anti-immigration policies (Bale 2003, 2004). Strict immigration policies as a feature of right-of-center parties have been described as the

European norm (Neumayer 2005), as well as for the Nordic countries (Green-Pedersen and Odmalm 2008; Gudbrandsen 2010). Thus, the pressure toward stricter policies among Swedish non-Socialist parties should have been apparent during the 1991–1994 period and increasingly, from the early 2000s onward.

However, throughout this period, Swedish non-Socialist parties have refrained from adapting to anti-immigration sentiments and moving toward stricter entry policies. Moreover, they have done the exact opposite, formulating more open policies, and when in government, implementing these measures. Sweden appears to be a deviant case (Dahlström and Esaiasson 2011). In different entry policy instances, and at different times, various center-right parties have been present and leading the charge to make it easier for people to enter and settle in Sweden. It is not an exaggeration to say that where there is a debate over entry policy in Sweden, at least one center-right party advocating a less restrictive stance has been present.

This puzzling development of non-Socialist parties formulating open entry policies appears to be a distinctive feature of the overall 1991–2011 period. However, it applies particularly well to the 1991–1994 period as to the post-2002 period. Not only was the xenophobic threat heightened then, but center-right parties were either serious contenders for government or in governing coalitions, and, therefore, should have been disposed toward restrictive entry policies.[1]

Moreover, several of these comparatively open entry policies were formulated amid fierce opposition from the Social Democratic Party (SAP). In 1993, the center-right government granted 50,000 Bosnian refugees permanent residence permit—the SAP instead proposed temporary permits and efforts to keep the refugees closer to their homeland, a policy the party had introduced in 1989. Likewise, against strong SAP opposition, in 2008 the center-right government lifted most bars, in place since the late 1960s, against labor migration for third-country nationals (TCNs) (Hinnfors et al. 2011). While these less restrictive measures were heavily criticized by xenophobic parties, center-right parties did not respond by supporting more restrictive migration policies.

In sum, we are presented with several puzzles concerning the surprising immigration entry policy openness found among Swedish non-Socialist parties. Why do non-Socialist parties formulate open policies where previous research would expect them to be restrictive? In this chapter, we consider various potential explanations for these comparatively open stances adopted by Swedish non-Socialist parties. Table 9.1 provides a preliminary overview of Swedish parties' 1989–2011 immigration entry policy stances.

Table 9.1 Swedish Parties, 1989–2011: Immigration Entry Policy Stances*

Swedish Governments	Key Policy Decision and Restrictiveness/Openness (R = Restrictive, O = Open)	Supporting Party(ies)
1989–1991 SAP	**R**: Strict application of the Geneva convention + temporary residence permits only (1989)	SAP + M
1991–1994 CENTER-RIGHT (M, L, C, K)	**O**: Permanent residence permits reintroduced; notion of "refugee" widened (1993);	CENTER-RIGHT (L, C, K, M)
	O: Decision to grant permanent residence to Bosnian refugees;	CENTER-RIGHT (L, C, K, M)
	R: Temporary residence permits reintroduced (permanent possible).	CENTER-RIGHT (L, C, K, M) + SAP
1994–2006 SAP	**R**: Labor migration restrictions regarding new EU member states** (2004);	SAP
	O: No labor migration restrictions regarding new EU member states** (2004);	CENTER-RIGHT + GREENS (M, L, C, K, G)
	R: Deportation possible even in cases where child suffers from "apathy stress syndrome" (2006);	SAP + M
	O: Enactment of a temporary Asylum Act. The Act made it easier to obtain a residence permit for, primarily, families with children who have been in Sweden for a long time.	CENTER-RIGHT + GREENS (L, C, K, G) + Left Party
2006–2011 CENTER-RIGHT (M, L, C, K)	**O**: Labor market immigration from non-EU countries reintroduced (2007);	CENTER-RIGHT + GREENS (M, L, C, K, G)
	O: Measures to facilitate greater circular migration debated and proposed;	CENTER-RIGHT + GREENS (M, L, C, K, G)
	O: Asylum seekers whose application for residency has been rejected but who remain in the country without permission have received an increased right to education, health care, and the right to run businesses.	CENTER-RIGHT + GREENS (M, L, C, K, G)

Note: SAP: Social Democratic Party; M: Moderate Party; L: Liberal Party; C: Center Party; K: Christian Democrats; G: Green Party.

*R = Restrictive = Parties refer to their policies as "strict" and/or declare that the number of entrants should be limited and/or declare that current legislation should be implemented "efficiently" and/or declare that entry legislation should become tighter/stricter and/or declare that asylum should be given on the condition of return and/or declare that various abuses of the asylum system should be penalized; O = Open = Parties refer to their policies as "open" or "liberal" or "humane" and/or declare that the number of entrants should be increased and/or declare that current legislation should be interpreted liberally and/or declare that immigration rights should be extended to new groups (Gudbrandsen 2010: 254f).

** Note that the minority SAP government's restrictive proposal for transitional arrangements for citizens from the new EU member states was defeated in parliament by the joint votes from non-Socialist and Green parties in favor of an open policy.

In this chapter, our aim is twofold. First, we describe the entry policy preferences of Swedish political parties toward labor migrants, refugees, and asylum seekers, with a special focus on non-Socialist parties. Second, following our documentation of the open stance adopted by non-Socialist parties, we discuss some explanatory challenges regarding why parties formulate open entry policies, calling attention to ideology as an underutilized variable and strong contender in the cases at hand. We stress that our focus is only on formal entry policies, and does not address integration policy measures for those migrants who have been legally admitted.

Theoretical Challenges

We argue that conventional explanations alone are insufficient for understanding the entry policy preferences of non-Socialist parties. Mainstream parties all, to a greater or lesser extent, operate in a strategic climate where interparty competition, public opinion, and the desire to implement effective policy matter for shaping preferences. But, as we will show, none of these factors—alone or in conjunction with one another—are sufficient determinants of the stances adopted by non-Socialist parties. A more nuanced understanding of how non-Socialist parties make sense of the strategic environment associated with entry policies also requires consideration of the potential role played by party ideology.

Obviously, party ideologies are not static, and may vary over time, forcing parties to reevaluate long-held value and policy commitments. We derive our data for the party ideology variable from a number of primary sources, including party programs, parliamentary and party congress protocols, op-ed pieces, press interviews, and other relevant reports. Our definition of party ideology is greatly influenced by Berman's discussion (1998) of programmatic beliefs as the key ideational source of the specific policy preferences developed by parties.

Our aim is not to present a white-washed picture of the migration policy preferences of non-Socialist parties. Indeed, as we will show, these parties have not consistently supported liberal migration policies, particularly in the instance of asylum policy. Our data does allow us to make two claims though. First, the portrayal of non-Socialist parties' migration policies as being predominantly restrictive is dramatically exaggerated. Over the past several decades it is traditional center-right parties, and the Greens, that have been at the forefront of the push for more open doors when it comes to immigration to Sweden, and not the center-left (in particular the SAP). Second, not all non-Socialist parties have consistently formulated open policies. On many issues, the Moderate Party formed an alliance with the SAP. However, in 1991–1994, as well as from the early 2000s onward, the appearance of the xenophobic parliamentary threat triggered a chain of events resulting in drastically more open Moderate Party policies, in line with the three other coalition partners and the Greens.

The stance of the Moderate Party only adds to our puzzlement. Overall, the non-Socialist group of parties has behaved in a way that contradicts the image of "right" being restrictive and "left" being "open." What is more, each individual non-Socialist party, including the Moderates, has acted completely against what would be expected when the threat from xenophobic parties was at its peak. In this chapter we discuss these puzzles, which boil down to the key question: why have Swedish non-Socialist parties formulated open immigration policies?

A popular theme in the migration policy literature is an emphasis on vote maximizing as a key explanatory variable (Money 1999). Right-wing and populist parties are by far the most common objectives of these studies (Bale 2008; Green-Pedersen and Krogstrup 2008; Green-Pedersen and Odmalm 2008; Kitschelt 1997; Rydgren 2005; Rydgren and Widfeldt 2004; Smith 2008). Naturally, vote maximizing is important as parties need to win elections. However, something has been missing in earlier research. Our analysis shows that non-Socialist support for generous entry policies is largely consistent over the past several decades, regardless of efforts by far right populist parties, or the left-of-center parties, to see more restrictive entry policies enacted. Nor have non-Socialist parties' policies varied according to public opinion development. Swedish center-right parties have been at the fore of all major liberalizations in Swedish migration policy in the past two decades, including wide-scale permanent residence permits for refugees, and a dramatic liberalization of labor migration policies. Thus, we feel it is warranted to put a question mark around vote maximization, and minimization of party system threats, as explanatory variables on their own.

Alongside these more traditional accounts, we call attention to the potential explanatory role of ideology. In mapping migration policy formulation within the European Parliament, Hix and Noury (2007: 198) conclude that regardless of the MEP's left-right position as such "MEPs from member states with general more liberal political cultures are more pro-migration." This suggests that the extent of "liberalism" might be a key aspect behind the degree of openness. In the same vein, several previous studies dwell fleetingly on ideology, but, consistently within a vote maximizing context. For instance, Freeman and Kessler (2008: 669) note: "Left parties [being] torn between fealty to the indigenous working-class component of their base and responding to their intellectual and professional supporters' concern to protect the interests of migrant workers," reflecting an ideological concern over welfare state goals and economic policies. Similarly, Perlmutter (1996: 377) claims that "mass parties are more likely to downplay the issue, because they face cross-cutting cleavages that affect their core constituencies." Odmalm (2011: 1071; cf. Schain 2008) suggests "a set of potentially conflicting ideological streams—market liberalism vs. value conservatism (for the center-right) and international solidarity vs. welfare state/labour market protectionism (for the center-left)—create framing dilemmas," thus highlighting the fact that contradictory ideological pulls within the same party might dissuade the party leaders from politicizing immigration. Moreover, as suggested by Hinnfors et al. (2012) ideology appears to have played an important role behind the SAP's formulation of entry policies.

Obviously, neither strategic considerations alone, such as voters' opinions, nor pure ideological goals fully determine any party's policies. However, within a certain ideological context, certain policies appear more palatable, and others less appealing. Parties do not just emulate their opponents or follow the majority voter position (Bale et al. 2010) in a crude Downsian fashion. They normally operate within a certain ideological framework, which substantially will reduce the policy options open to a party leadership.

Rather than highlighting one variable at the expense of others, we stress the interplay between ideology and strategy (Lewin 1988). While it may not be possible to specify the exact percentage between the variables, we have applied the following data logic approach to assess public opinion, interparty competition, and ideology as causal factors: When a party's policy preference is in keeping with public opinion trends, or when party-system pressure exists in the form of influential anti-immigration parties, such a correlation will be seen as strengthening the likelihood that these strategic factors played a role in shaping policy preferences. However, when a given party opts for a policy at odds with public opinion, or does not reflect interparty competition pressures, we consider the role of ideology. We will examine whether, and how, relevant aspects of party ideology were called upon by key party figures and in documents when motivating specific policies. When ideology and preference formulation square, we will interpret it as an indicator of ideological influence.

Labor Migration Policy Debates: Third-Country Nationals (TCNs), EU Enlargement, and Circular Migration

As the Swedish economy rapidly expanded at the start of the new millennium, and as demographic forecasts pointed toward the specter of a rapidly graying workforce, the Confederation of Swedish Employers (SN [Svenskt Näringsliv]) began a sustained campaign to relax Sweden's strict TCN labor migration policies (Fahimi 2001). Since the early 1970s, similar to most other European states, labor migration to Sweden had been sharply limited, with short-term temporary work permits being the norm, and with virtually no opportunities for conversion to permanent residency. In an initial report, authored by an upcoming Liberal Party politician, a key proposal was that employers—and not labor market authorities—should have decision-making authority as to whether a given potential migrant should be granted a permit (Fahimi 2001: 16). SN economists followed up with a more detailed 2002 report, as that autumn's parliamentary election campaign increasingly took shape, reasserting the need for employers to have discretion over work permit applications as well as freedom of movement for the migrant throughout the sectors of the economy and a relatively quick path to permanent residency (Ekenger and Wallen 2002). The ruling SAP opposed these proposals, with Prime Minister Göran Persson (2002) dismissing such calls as "the dumbest thing we could do" and MPs characterizing the proposals as a "neo-liberal wedge" designed to break up the Swedish welfare model (Riksdagen: *svar på fråga* 2002–2003: 696).

Both the Greens, who had declared that "a more open Sweden leads to a richer society" (Miljöpartiet 2002) and the Liberals, who stressed that "Sweden needs more immigrants, not fewer" (Folkpartiet 2002), were enthusiastic supporters of the calls for substantially less restrictive labor migration policies. The four center-right parties collectively mocked the ruling SAP for "happily criticizing us for our desire to let more people come to our land and contribute to both their own and everyone's well-being" (Lundgren et al. 2002). Similar criticisms of the SAP insistence that labor migration was not desirable while domestic unemployment rates remained high was also expressed by individual center-right parties, such as the Moderate Party's admonishment that "it's up to us to decide whether immigration (will be seen as) as a resource for, or a drain on, our society" (Moderaterna 2002). The central argument advanced by all five parties in favor of more open labor migration policies was the demand for labor—both short term as evidenced in the number of jobs that were going unfilled in certain sectors, as well as long term, in the face of dire labor shortages that would have an impact across the Swedish economy.

Despite the SAP victory in the 2002 election, the issue returned in early 2003 when the Greens published a proposal for a socially responsible labor migration. SAP policy was portrayed as embodying the principles that "global development involves open borders for goods and capital, but closed borders for people" and "those who live here first have to get jobs before we let others in" (Miljöpartiet 2003). In its place, the Greens proposed regulations largely similar to those of SN and the Liberals. This paved the way for a Blue-Green-sponsored parliamentary committee investigation into the relaxation of TCN labor migration policy, a move firmly opposed by the SAP. When the committee released its final report in autumn 2006, one month after the SAP suffered a historic defeat at the hands of the four-party center-right alliance, the majority SAP (Left Party) proposals offered little in the way of concrete relaxation of the existing rules other than the possibility for limited permit renewals and eventual sector-wide access for migrants to job opportunities (Bucken-Knapp 2009). Yet, with the support of the Greens, the center-right government implemented its desired reform in 2008, stripping unions of their veto power over applications, and creating a path to permanent residency for labor migrants that provided them with ever broader access to the sectors of the Swedish economy (Regeringens proposition 2007–2008: 147). In justifying its far-reaching reforms, Minister of Migration Tobias Billström stressed how a more liberal entry policy could be important for preserving a desirable dependency ratio, as well as having knock-on employment effects (Sveriges Radio 2007).

Simultaneous to the battle over the reform of Sweden's TCN entry policy, parties were embroiled in a debate as to whether transitional rules for citizens from the ten states acceding to the EU in May 2004 ought to be adopted.

Initially, the SAP opposed rules that would block the free movement of labor to Sweden from Europe's newest citizens (Svenska Dagbladet 2002). Yet, this changed in the spring of 2003, when a parliamentary committee report highlighted the prospect that generous Swedish social services could serve as a powerful pull factor for Eastern European migrants (SOU 2002: 116). Following the broadcast of an investigative television program focusing on the impact of EU enlargement for Swedish welfare state services, Prime Minister Göran Persson speculated that transitional rules might be necessary to prevent cases of "benefits tourism" (Aftonbladet 2003). By spring 2004, the SAP had shifted firmly in favor of transitional rules, proposing that work permits and job offers be required for the first year that citizens from new EU member states were resident in Sweden, and reserving the possibility that tests of labor market conditions could be introduced if deemed necessary— thus potentially putting new EU citizens and TCNs on similar footing when seeking employment in Sweden (Skr. 2003–2004: 119).

While the four non-Socialist parties were opposed to the SAP's proposal, they did not adopt a joint stance rejecting transitional rules. Centre Party leader Maud Olofsson sharply criticized Göran Persson, noting that "in the zeal to maintain power, and to avoid taking responsibility (Persson) is feeding an unhealthy welfare nationalism" (TT Nyhetsbanken 2004a). Leading Christian Democratic candidates for the 2004 EU parliamentary elections also underscored the party's opposition to transitional rules, arguing that "free movement (of people) is a fundamental right" and that any conditions imposed on entry would further foster the sense within the new EU member states that they were not being admitted as equal members (TT Nyhetsbanken 2004b). In contrast, both the Liberals and the Moderates emerged with separate counterproposals to that of the SAP. The Liberals advocated that migrants would need to be in possession of sufficient funds for their first year in Sweden (a stance consistent with concerns about TCN access to welfare state services), but opposed strict work permit rules. This was, however, a deeply divisive issue within the party and key members, such as current minister for integration Erik Ullenhag and current EU minister Birgitta Ohlsson, openly opposed the parliamentary party's decision. Non-Socialist allies also expressed disappointment, with one leading Christian Democrat noting that it felt "particularly difficult that a party that stands for social liberalism would succumb to the government's populism" (TT Nyhetsbanken 2004c). Senior Moderate Party politicians attacked the ruling SAP's call for transitional rules, noting that while previously "a wall kept people trapped in Eastern Europe, the Social Democrats want to erect a wall around Sweden that will shut them out." Yet, the Moderates too advocated some brand of transitional rules. Stressing that the party valued "free movement and the right of people to build an independent life based on their own work," the Moderates proposed residence (not work) permits be granted to migrants with offers of employment, and suggesting that phased-in social benefits be considered (Reinfeldt, Carlsson, and Westerberg 2004). For their part, the Greens had focused their efforts on joint propositions with the Left Party, emphasizing better regulation of migrants seeking independent contractor status. Despite a last-minute effort by the SAP to secure a compromise deal with the Liberals, in which support would be thrown behind legislation allowing for implementation of work permits "at a later date" if necessary, no deal was reached (Sveriges Television 2004). Although the SAP, Liberals, and Moderates initially contemplated various forms of transitional rules, in the end only the SAP kept the initial restrictive line. At the final Riksdag vote all parties except SAP opposed transitional rules.

While the Blue-Green reform of TCN labor migration policy in 2008 paved the way for non-EU citizens to work and settle permanently in Sweden, the governing center-right alliance was also keenly interested in exploring the degree to which circular migration of foreign labor to Sweden could be better facilitated, establishing a parliamentary committee of investigation to that end in 2009 (Dir 2009: 53). Here too, the Greens played a key role, with a leading Green MP, Mikaela Valtersson, named chair of the committee. Given our contention that Sweden's non-Socialist parties have been at the forefront of efforts to implement more open entry policies, it may seem counterintuitive that the current government's support for circular migration—an ongoing pattern in which migrants regularly spend time in both the sending and receiving countries—should be counted in that column. Yet, is should be stressed that support from non-Socialist parties for circular migration does not represent a retreat from the policy allowing TCNs to settle permanently in Sweden. Indeed, the governing alliance and the Greens regularly highlight their desire to extend their liberal migration policies, where possible. Rather, circular migration was deemed warranted for its potential contribution to develop policy goals (Skr. 2007–2008: 89). While the government acknowledged clear economic benefits for Sweden (Svenska Dagbladet 2010), such as through increased tax receipts, a particular emphasis was placed on how circular migration could boost both the economy of the sending country and its level of social capital (Dir 2009: 53, 2). The committee's final report, published in 2011, proposed several measures embracing the principle that migrants ought to have the opportunity to move back and forth between their homelands and Sweden. Underpinning all proposals was a broad logic that increased migration contributed to counteracting demographic trends within Sweden, improving economic development opportunities within sending countries, and "to the extent where it is possible, people should get to choose where and how they will live their lives" (SOU 2011: 28, 73). Key among these was the proposal that Swedish permanent residents would be able to leave Sweden for a period of five years without having their permit revoked, as opposed to the current one-year rule, provided written notification was submitted to the Swedish Migration

Board (SOU 2011: 28, 102). The authors also proposed that migrants in possession of Swedish unemployment insurance could, under certain conditions, continue to receive payments for a period of three months while looking for employment abroad (28–188), and those students who have completed their education can receive a six-month residency permit to pursue employment (28, 150).

Refugee Migration Policy Debates

After the 1991 election, the new center-right government was formed by four parties: the Center, the Liberals, the Moderates, and the Christian Democrats. One of the new government's first actions was to withdraw the previous SAP government's bill, "An active immigration and refugee policy," proposed in early 1991. This bill proposed that refugees seeking asylum in Sweden should be granted temporary residence permits rather than permanent ones. Refugees should be encouraged to return to their home countries as soon as possible, as this was argued to constitute a more humanitarian and "holistic" policy than encouraging refugees to become Swedish citizens with possible future burdens on the welfare state system (Appelqvist and Tollefsen-Altamirano 1998). The Liberals, with 9.1 percent of the vote, paid extra attention to the new government's asylum policies. The Liberals held the Department for Cultural Affairs (and the immigration portfolio) and were able to mold government refugee policies in an increasingly open direction. According to Birgit Friggebo, Liberal minister of immigration, members of her party regarded the refugee policy of the previous SAP government as increasingly restrictive (Riksdagens snabbprotokoll 1993–1994: 76).

The principal object of the Liberals' criticism was the SAP government's December 1989 "Lucia decision." The "St. Lucia" (a Swedish December 13 festival related to Christmas) decision was tantamount to a drastic tightening of asylum rules; only a strict application of the Geneva convention was to be utilized. Maj-Lis Lööw, then SAP minister for immigration affairs, held that limitations to refugee numbers were essential in order to safeguard a dignified reception in the new country (Lundh and Ohlsson 1994: 91). However, the new center-right government took immediate action to reverse this policy by replacing the interpretation of the SAP with the previously generous practices of the Aliens Act.

The next step toward more open immigration policies was taken in 1993. On the initiative of the Liberals, the center-right government granted 50,000 Bosnian refugees permanent residence permits. To grant permanent residence to Bosnian refugees was by no means straightforward or simple. Three policy alternatives were debated prior to the Bosnian decision (Appelqvist 2000; Appelqvist and Tollefsen-Altamirano 1998). The first option was to bide one's time, that is, take no action. The second option was to grant the Bosnians temporary residence permits with a subsequent conversion into permanent residence permits should the Bosnian situation deteriorate. The third option was to grant permanent residence permits from the outset. The SAP and Moderate Party advocated temporary permits. The SAP argued that the Bosnian National Organisation wanted its citizens back for postwar reconstruction and that those who received permanent residence permits would lose touch with their motherland. As the Swedish standard of living would be higher than in the country of origin, it was argued that refugees would lack incentives to return and thus, Sweden would not contribute to reconstruction. Instead, Sweden should make repatriation easy and thereby avoid creating new groups of social security dependants. Repeatedly, the SAP were eager to avoid extra presumed burdens on the welfare state. Initially, this position was shared by the Moderates. However, the Liberals opposed temporary permits and instead advocated permanent residency. Contributing to the Liberal stance was the fact that many refugees had been in the country for quite some time. Security and the refugees' right to regain control over their lives were important arguments in favor of permanent residency (Riksdagens snabbprotokoll 1993–1994: 76; Appelqvist and Tollefsen-Altamirano 1998: 104).

After internal center-right government negotiations, permanent residency became government policy, a dramatic break with earlier shifts toward ever-stricter policies. The decision to grant permanent residence can be interpreted as an expression of liberal ideology. The motives guiding the Liberals' decision focused upon the individual and his or her needs in terms of coping with the situation. During the Bosnian crisis, the Liberals stressed that very few suggested an improvement in conditions in Bosnia-Herzegovina and that it would be unreasonable and inhuman to individual refugees to wait for the situation to settle. The party's arguments emphasized core liberal ideas about individual freedoms. It is also important to understand the center-right government's decision in a wider perspective, related to the Liberals' understanding of refugee policymaking in general. During periods of opposition, the Liberals were known to criticize the refugee policy of both the SAP and the Moderates. On various occasions, the Liberals articulated the view that the generous humanitarian goal of Swedish refugee policy was diminishing. Seen from this perspective, the granting of permanent residency to Bosnians represented an articulation of the particular interests of the Liberals, who with three other parties comprised a coalition government. Once in power, the Liberals were in a position to reverse a policy it regarded as deeply restrictive.

The 1993 decision on permanent residence permits can be regarded as a brief parenthesis of openness. When the SAP returned to office in 1994, they reverted to policies of the late 1980s. The 1995 parliamentary investigation "Refugee Policies in a Global Perspective" held that "it's a human right to be able to return to your country. Encouraging voluntary returns should constitute an important part of refugee policies" (SOU 1995: 75 205). A 1996 government bill added emphasis to the policy by facilitating voluntary returns for all, including those with permanent residency (Government bill 1996–1997: 25). Furthermore, a heated debate erupted over purported simulation of semi- or total paralysis and apathy among young children in families soon to be deported after being denied residence permits. The SAP minister in charge, Barbro Holmberg, strongly defended a report from the Cabinet's special coordinator, which claimed the children were "up and running" at nights, and that the children were either intoxicated or induced by their parents to act in order to persuade immigration authorities to grant residence permits to the family. The allegations caused a furor among parts of the center-right opposition and five of the Riksdag's parties. The Liberals, the Christian Democrats, the Centre Party, the Left Party, and the Greens demanded that the children and their families be given amnesty, including permanent residency. The demand was turned down by combined votes of the SAP and Moderates.

After 1995, the numbers of newly arrived asylum seekers fell rapidly (Migrationsverkets statistik). In 2006 and 2007, however, Sweden once again became an important destination country for asylum seekers. In 2007, the Swedish Board of Migration registered a total of 36,207 applications for asylum, more than any other EU state. The high figures experienced by Sweden can primarily be explained by a significant increase in the flow of refugees from Iraq since 2006, a result of the enactment of a temporary Asylum Act. The Act made it easier to obtain a residence permit, especially for families with children who had been in Sweden for lengthy periods. In spite of initial concerns by SAP and Moderates, the Act was pushed through after a public opinion outcry among grassroots movements, religious communities, and other political parties.

In spring 2011 the four government parties (Moderates, Christian Democrats, Centre, and Liberals) forged a comprehensive framework agreement with the Greens. Among other things, the agreement aims to give illegal immigrants the right to health care and education and would give them the right to run businesses. The move follows long negotiations between the three smaller governing parties, who have long argued for such rights, and the Moderates, which opposed the idea. Migration minister Tobias Billström (M) has previously argued that giving such entitlements would legitimize people with no right to be in Sweden (SR Ekot 30/10 2008).

The Role of Ideology

It is comparatively easy to demonstrate how the Swedish case does not square perfectly with the logic of prevailing accounts. Unlike literature emphasizing how shifts in the party system will provide certain inducements for center-right actors to back restrictive entry polices—chiefly as a result of the increased electoral fortunes of populist parties—this has not been the case in Sweden, as shown in table 9.2. In the four electoral cycles when anti-immigration have constituted a realist party threat to the established parties—1991–1994, 2002–2006, 2006–2010, and 2010—Swedish non-Socialist parties have made support for various open entry policy measures a visible component of their politics, both in terms of labor migration and refugee/asylum seekers. Over the course of the last three periods, the populist SD steadily grew in strength, capturing significant numbers of seats in local government and achieving its long-held goal of Riksdag representation in 2010. Yet, Swedish non-Socialist parties have remained the key actors pushing for implementation of policies making it comparatively easier for foreigners to come and settle in Sweden. Even prior to the formal advent of SD, non-Socialist parties made their mark on Swedish migration policy by implementing a distinctly more open entry policy for refugees and asylum seekers in the early 1990s—the period in which the populist New Democracy had its brief but strong parliamentary success. Moreover, although the populist ND and SD parties were heavily criticized by all mainstream parties it has not been the case that strict immigration entry policies have been anathema as such. As strict labor migration policies were continuously standard SAP policy and, at times, stricter refugee/asylum policies too, it would have been perfectly easy for the non-Socialist parties to join them in order to stave off any right-wing threats—but they did not do so. Moreover, in spite of the SAP's overall party system interest in creating a Red-Green bloc against the center-right government post-2006, the SAP has not been able to share policies with the Greens on the issue of immigration entry policies. Our suggestion is that the underlying ideologies differed between the SAP and the non-Socialist parties, thus preparing the triumph for different policies.

By the same token, public opinion is only of limited utility for making sense of the stance by Swedish non-Socialist parties in support of open entry policies. For example, surveys in 2002 and 2003 showed that substantial majorities favored allowing TCNs with employment offers to come to Sweden (Bucken-Knapp 2009). Likewise, studies show that public opinion regarding refugee numbers have dropped from the 1990s to the 2000s (although still relatively high). At first glance, such evidence would appear to cast doubt on our claim that public opinion is not crucial for shaping a given party's entry policy preferences. After all, if public opinion is strongly supportive of labor migration, and political parties visibly support it, wouldn't one argue this has the makings of a causal linkage? And if voters become more understanding and accepting about relatively high refugee numbers, and parties actually formulate and implement more open policies, wouldn't that indicate an explanatory relationship? However, we doubt that public opinion is such a strict determinant of entry policy preferences for one important reason: at the same time as the Swedish public was strongly in support of more relaxed entry policies, the ruling SAP was vehemently opposed to it. Indeed, in 2002, support for a less restrictive migration policy was high even among SAP voters (63 percent) and a majority of LO members (59 percent). Further, in 2003, the respective percentage of SAP supporters and LO members supporting labor migration had increased (Bucken-Knapp 2009). In the same vein, we notice that while voter support for refugees increased (Demker 2010), the SAP refrained from joining the various center-right policy agreements regarding less strict legislation concerning refugees. If parties formulate entry policies with one eye on voters, be it the electorate as a whole, or their most loyal support base, then we would have expected that all mainstream Swedish parties would have moved sharply in the direction of open entry policies and not just the non-Socialists. Moreover, there was no denying that populist parties had in fact attracted substantial numbers of voters who supported restrictive entry policies. Indeed, the SAP's unwillingness to move in a more open direction could be interpreted as a Downsian form of policy adaptation to public opinion moods. Again, a comparison between the parties reveal flaws in the argument, as non-Socialist parties took a completely opposite policy path from that of the SAP. Given that there is nothing in the public opinion hypothesis that suggests it is limited to only one party of families, we find this hypothesis lacking.

Table 9.2 Immigration Policy Decisions in Relation to Several Strategic Contexts

Swedish Governments	Anti-Immigration Party Election Result	Degree of Anti-Immigration Party Threat	Degree of Public Opinion Xenophobic Threat	Key Policy Decision and Restrictiveness/Openness (R = Restrictive, O = Open)	Supporting Party(ies)
1989–1991 SAP	0	None	No Data	R: Strict application of the Geneva convention + temporary residence permits only (1989)	SAP + M
1991–1994 CENTER-RIGHT (M, L, C, K)	91–94 (ND): 6.7%	HIGH	HIGH	O: Permanent residence permits reintroduced; notion of "refugee" widened (1993);	CENTER-RIGHT (L, C, K, M)
				O: Decision to grant permanent residence to Bosnian refugees;	CENTER-RIGHT (L, C, K, M)
				R: Temporary residence permits reintroduced (permanent possible).	CENTER-RIGHT (L, C, K, M) + SAP
1994–2006 SAP	94 (ND): 1.2% 98 (SD): 0.4% 02 (SD): 1.4%	LOW	94–98: HIGH 99–01: MEDIUM 02–03: MEDIUM/ HIGH 04: HIGH 05–06: MEDIUM	R: Labor migration restrictions regarding new EU member states (2004); NB rejected by Riksdag);	SAP + Left Party
					CENTER-RIGHT + GREENS (M, L, C, K, G)
				O: No labor migration restrictions regarding new EU member states (2004); NB carried by Riksdag);	SAP + M

2006–2011 CENTER-RIGHT (M, L, C, K)	06 (SD): 2.9% 10 (SD): 5.7%	HIGH		CENTER-RIGHT + GREENS (M, L, C, K, G) (L, C, K, G) + Left Party
			R: Deportation possible even in cases where child suffers from "apathy stress syndrome" (2006).	
			O: Enactment of temporary Asylum Act. The Act made it easier to obtain a residence permit for, primarily, families with children who have been in Sweden for a long time	
		07–11: MEDIUM	O: Labor market immigration from non-EU countries reintroduced (2007);	CENTER-RIGHT + GREENS (M, L, C, K, G)
			O: Measures to facilitate greater circular migration debated and proposed;	CENTER-RIGHT + GREENS (M, L, C, K, G)
			O: Asylum seekers whose application for residency has been rejected but who remain in the country without permission have received an increased right to education, health care, and right to run businesses.	CENTER-RIGHT + GREENS (M, L, C, K, G)

Yet, if non-Socialist parties are not driven to support open entry policies on the basis of interparty competition or the pulls of public opinion, is it possible that opening Sweden's borders to increased levels of migration can simply be regarded as the rational act of policymakers solely interested in solving pressing economic problems or ensuring compliance with international norms for humanitarian treatment of displaced and persecuted peoples? Here too, at first glance, one might think the Swedish case lends support to the thesis of policymakers as problem-solvers. As Bleich (2002) notes, this literature portrays actors as "responding to problems by implementing new and better policy solutions arrived at through processes of learning." Cross-national differences in policy responses are thought to stem from differences in local conditions and the lessons learned from previous attempts at solving the given policy problem. However, this more technocratic account is ill-suited for application to the Swedish case. Given that both non-Socialist parties and the SAP are facing the same policy challenge—be it in the form of demographic shortages or foreign citizens seeking protection—a problem-solving perspective cannot be utilized for making sense of sharply divergent responses by competing actors.

Thus, if both conventional accounts of migration policy preference formation, and more technocratic accounts of policymakers as problem-solvers have clear limitation, what possible explanation is left? Overall, there is a sufficient trail of evidence pointing toward the role of ideology in shaping the entry policy preferences of Swedish non-Socialist parties. Quite consistently, open policies have been supported by referring to liberal principles about basic human liberties. Regarding labor migration, a recurrent theme has been about market-led immigration rather than state planning as the norm. Likewise, arguments about more open policies have been sharply critical of social democratic, corporatist solutions involving tripartite arrangements where the state, the unions, and the employers strike bargains and reach political compromises.

The non-Socialist parties have not always acted as a unified bloc regarding entry policies. Occasionally, the Moderates have perceived refugee migration flows to Sweden as problematic. However, given the Swedish party structure, the Moderates have had many reasons to close ranks with the other non-Socialist parties to present a government alternative. These strategic fundamentals would lend some credence to the "party system" explanatory factor and we do indeed acknowledge its importance. However, at the same time, we emphasize that it has been the Moderates' overarching ideological goal to challenge the SAP's vision of how Swedish society ought to be organized and administered.

Moreover, even prior to the establishment of the four-party non-Socialist alliance in 2004, the Moderate Party has advocated—on its own and in conjunction with the other non-Socialist parties—a labor migration reform chiefly relying on market dynamics.

Throughout, the Liberals and the Christian Democrats have advocated strong moral and ethical values inherent in the responsibility to protect refugees with the Christian Democrats referring to Christian moral values and the Liberals to individual rights. For example, during the Bosnian refugee crisis the 'individualism line" held that it would be unreasonable, inhuman, and destructive to the individual refugee to wait for the situation to settle or to take individual responsibility for any "national" or "state" Bosnian considerations.

Swedish debates over immigration policy have, in fact, substantially mirrored the respective visions held by the Socialist bloc (SAP and the Left Party) and the non-Socialist bloc (the Moderate, Centre, Liberal, and Christian Democrat, and perhaps Greens) toward both the welfare state and the regulation of the labor market. Even though welfare state institutions rarely change overnight, it appears that the political paradigms of different welfare states represent useful analytical tools when it comes to understanding different attitudes toward migration. The Swedish Socialist parties traditionally advocate a strong welfare state with benefits, rights, and duties for all its citizens. This system is thus highly redistributive in accordance with its norm of ensuring equality. On the contrary, the Swedish Liberals construct their policies on the political and ideological assumption that does not center on the dismantling of the Swedish welfare state. Rather, while the Liberals and other non-Socialist parties broadly support that the broad entitlements of the welfare state should remain intact, these should be accessed only after the individual has exhausted most reasonable attempts at securing employment.

Concluding Remarks

The contribution of this chapter is a modest, albeit important, one to debates over political parties and entry policy preference formation. At the most empirical level, it has clearly documented that non-Socialist parties in Sweden have been at the forefront of open-door policies, both with regard to labor migration and those concerning refugees and asylum seekers. This stands in sharp contrast to both research literature—and a popular perception—that parties of the center-right and allies are generally the sources of restrictive immigration policies. Whether this pattern is borne out in other settings remains to be seen. In terms of prevailing theoretical accounts of parties and entry policy preferences, the Swedish case highlights the need to consider more a nuanced set of dynamics. There is no doubt that parties have a chief aim of securing votes in order to govern or exercise influence. To that end, both an awareness of interparty competitive dynamics and the tides of public opinion are crucial. But parties do not move about in this strategic environment blindly when formulating entry policy. As we have argued, they do so with the aid of ideology. The task for researchers now is to better specify how ideology exerts an influence on the formation of migration policy preferences—both for non-Socialist and Socialist parties, and both in Sweden and beyond. To a great extent, this will involve a reanalysis of many settings where the politics of migration policy have previously been examined. This is undoubtedly a complex and time-consuming process-tracing exercise, but it is a valuable one.

Note

1. The Moderates, the Liberals, the Center Party, and the Christian Democrats.

The Discourses and Politics of Migration: Policy, Methodology, and Theory

Umut Korkut, Jonas Hinnfors, and Helen Drake

Where do migration discourses and politics come from? This volume highlights the value of a focus on discourse and politics in the field of migration studies that looks beyond migration issues. We observe that migration discourse and politics are related to a range of other issue areas and are dealt with at multiple levels of governance. Roma immigration and their securitization; gendered and informal immigration; perceptions of integration by migrants themselves; the role of economic interests and economic nationalism in shaping migration preferences; ideology and entry policies, as well as the linguistic and institutional evolution of asylum systems: these are all examples in which migration discourse and politics are charged with concerns about other issue areas as well.

The contributors to this volume explore the underlying but implicit discursive frames that affect the politics of immigration and that have institutional, legal, and policy implications. The book investigates the expression of discourse within formal institutional mechanisms, and through informal ideational framing mechanisms such as party propaganda and campaigning activities. These mechanisms all, crucially, charge policy and ideational environments with stable, structure-like patterns. Furthermore, questions about the direction, content, and intensity of the impact of formal institutions on immigration policies inform this volume.

In order to understand how discursive and political mechanisms interrelate, this volume pursues the formulation of three narratives. First, we ask questions about the discursive construction of foreigners.

Second, we raise issues concerning host countries and host societies. Third, we explore diverse problematics regarding law and order. We argue that the challenge of problem definition cuts through these narratives, and that this challenge also frames the interrelationship between discursive and political institutional research: once a definition becomes dominant, such as in the case of the differentiation between "Good and Bad Immigrants" suggested by the True Finn Party in Finland as shown in chapter 5, it excludes policies that are not consistent with that way of describing the issue. As such, discursive and political mechanisms shape how immigration is dealt with in public and policy spheres.

Throughout this volume, accordingly, we utilize the discursive research method as an approach that emphasizes the study of politics as a process that is not purely mechanical. Political mechanisms relate to formal institutional as well as informal ideational settings, and we recognize that abstract ideas may trump formal institutions in terms of their effect on/in relation to migration policies and administrative traditions. Thus, for example, our study of discourse, politics, and policies in relation to the topic of migration presents us with evidence that framing and problem definition have played a considerable role in the construction of the foreigner (as shown by McGarry and Drake in chapter 4); in defining the roles played by host states and societies vis-à-vis the foreigner; and, finally, regarding matters of law and order, and that the challenge of definition is, inevitably, a contested process among political actors. Moreover, our authors demonstrate that it is not necessarily only the elite that appropriates the means of problem definition; indeed, the process of problem definition allows for a diversity of views among many voter groups within the population.

Furthermore, having underlined that voter demand is a powerful and legitimate factor behind policy developments, we demonstrate with empirical evidence gathered from various democratic nation-states, that political parties are key actors in setting/determining migration policy. They enjoy substantial room for maneuver regarding the kind of policies they offer to their voters, despite a range of constraints such as economic forces or structural institutional settings. By framing their policies differently, political parties are able to reach out to different voter groups either at different times or simultaneously. Moreover, politics is not only played out at the national level. As Scholten highlights in chapter 8, local and regional level politics contribute to policy diversity even while national models seem to persist. It is also evident that political parties formulate national policy against the backdrop of international obligations, such as EU membership.

The volume provides an interpretation of empirical evidence regarding migration in a plethora of European countries—the Netherlands, France, United Kingdom, Turkey, Switzerland, Norway, Sweden, Finland, and Poland—using the tools of policy and discursive analysis—and by engaging with a diversity of thematic contexts, such as gender, and the economic relations that can relate to immigration systems. These relations do not necessarily have to be formal. For instance, the lack of coherence between national, formal programs and rules in Turkey and actual local outcomes is striking. As Eslen-Ziya and Korkut demonstrate in chapter 2, gender-related developments among Turkish middle-class families with regard to work, children, and family commitments have contributed to enforcing a semiacceptance by otherwise anti-immigration authorities of unauthorized immigrants. Yet, such acceptance comes with conditions that migrants remain within a narrowly defined labor market and work as maids, child minders, and caretakers. The Turkish case thereby offers an interesting comparison with that of Sweden 50 years ago where a similar setting led to a completely different outcome, when the strong labor movement suggested closing the borders and advocated an increase in female gainful employment. The argument was that in periods of economic slump, women would "flexibly" be able to go back to housework and, after some hesitation, the Social Democrats opted for abolishing the then open system of large labor migration and launched an ambitious day-care system (Hinnfors 1999) that reduced the previous middle-class demand for nannies and maids. By contrast, Eslen-Ziya and Korkut show in the Turkish case that similar interests affected migrants differently because Turkish middle-class families do not have any day-care sector at their disposal. At the same time, lax immigration policies provide a constant flow of vulnerable immigrants for nanny and maid positions in middle-class families. This sociopolitical context enfeebles immigrants and force them into gendered and fragile roles in the informal labor market within which they can only survive in the host states. Therefore, the needs of the host states and host societies, in a way, force immigrants into a semiclandestine status.

Taking the study of such needs further, Afonso studies immigration policy as a policy area with distributive consequences. As long as immigration serves the needs of the host nation, even conflicting policy interests can find representation on the same political platform. As he shows in chapter 1, the political elite in the Swiss People's Party (SVP) has developed a strikingly pragmatic immigration discourse. Much in the same vein as important parts of the agenda-setting and framing-orientated literature would suggest (Rose and Baumgartner

2012), the SVP has managed to conceal differences between itself and important sections of its electorate in order to reconcile the elite's perceived needs of the labor market and economy with the needs of important sectors of the SVP electorate. Thus, we see a balancing act between different socioeconomic interests, on the one hand, and by the craft of political elite image construction, on the other. Such a balancing act between contending ideological elements is by no means totally set in stone, as Afonso has shown for the SVP. There, the dilemma of balancing ideological purity with voter maximization considerations has led the party to develop somewhat contradictory policies with different voter group targets, but has managed to do so underneath a loosely coherent image umbrella. The revelation of this mixture of images and policy contents, and an understanding of how these images and contents were made to fit into different parts of the SVP's overarching concerns about ideology and voters, was possible through a careful use of the discursive method.

The discursive approach also presented itself as a vital tool in terms of studying how the environment of immigration politics looks to "deviant" groups. As such, Roma, regardless of their status as European citizens, can fall prey to security concerns, implying that they do not belong. Hence, what follows as the policy course is not to enable their rights and freedoms, but to deal with their vulnerability as if it threatens the security of the host society and challenges the established norms in this society. McGarry and Drake show, in the case of France, how the Roma are constructed in political discourse, and how hostile policies are, accordingly, enacted to exclude them. Thereby, they present an exemplary use of law-and-order rhetoric by a host state to discriminate against an ethnically defined and problematically constructed immigrant population. Moreover, their study can be used to add an important building block to the so-called securitization debate. While much of the previous research in this field has focused on issue areas such as the economy, the political system, or, perhaps rather self-evidently, the military system, becoming securitized within an international politics logic, other strands of the literature have looked at how environmental and migration issues might become securitized within a part domestic, part international politics framework (Borbeau 2011; Waever 1995). Mcgarry and Drake demonstrate how in the case of the French handling of Roma immigration, domestic notions about law and order were fed into more traditionally international notions about securing the borders, notions that are themselves made increasingly complex by the role of the European Union (EU) level in domestic and international decision making. Indeed, we see how French policies were partly in breach of EU laws and regulations, and how, accordingly, the whole notion of "host country," "host society," and "immigrant" become increasingly muddled when the immigrants—the Roma—are legally legitimate citizens of the EU.

Our volume also demonstrates how a discursive approach can lay bare the functioning of economic policy justifications of immigration as a strategic choice. An economic rationale can depoliticize and deradicalize immigration policy. As Kuisma has shown in his study of the True Finns (chapter 5), political actors, rather than directly dealing with the far more sensitive ethno-cultural aspects of immigration, can construct "the foreigner" as good or bad in terms of the foreigner's purported burden on the economic system. Hence, a heavily charged question such as whether the reconciliation of an ethnically diverse society with a generous welfare regime is possible or not, was instead framed partly as a practical question of who would correspond to a good or a bad immigrant in economic terms. As such, the policy framing activities of political actors function in the service of their political objectives (obviously, they may sometimes backfire); namely, in the case of the True Finns, voter maximization without jeopardizing ideological objectives, much in the same vein as the Swiss People's Party has managed to do, as discussed earlier. Thus, on the one hand, although ideological foundations may be relatively anti-immigrant or even strongly xenophobic, less coherent patterns may emerge regarding more day-to-day, focused policymaking than might be expected. On the other hand, Kuisma shows that a range of considerations regarding center-periphery and establishment-nonestablishment issues (e.g., about the Finnish-EU relations, and about the "little man in the street" versus anonymous structures) can blend into anti-immigration stances even when not necessarily originating from a truly anti-immigration or racist ideology as such. The nature of this seemingly complex blend and of how "economic nationalism" has functioned as an overarching logic binding the various policy strands together is revealed by the discursive method. Significantly, this volume also shows that immigration politics is not exclusively a field whereby elites can "construct" images freely regardless of any voter opinion. Gudbrandsen's chapter demonstrates that Scandinavian asylum policies have in general been developed in tandem with overall public opinion formation, in the sense that they have changed in accordance with what the public preferred at different points in time.

However, as to the direction of causality, the picture is still less clear. Do elites follow voter opinion or do the elites in fact lead? Here, the jury is still out as Spehar, Bucken-Knapp, Hinnfors, in chapter 9, on Swedish non-Socialist parties suggest. In spite of the looming threat from the openly anti-immigration Sweden Democrats, the non-Socialist parties did in fact move toward a decidedly more open immigration policy. The same paradoxical policy development had already taken place in 1991–1994 when the then non-Socialist government opted for drastically more open refugee policies in spite of the presence of the new (and, it would prove, short-lived) anti-immigration New Democracy Party (Hinnfors, Spehar, and Bucken-Knapp 2012). While voter opinion and party system development are strong explanatory factors in these cases, it seems that we cannot disregard party ideology as an equally strong variable accounting for why it is that parties interpret the same developments differently. Moreover, the open-border policies were not necessarily based purely on a migration agenda per se. Instead, behind their policies, strong ideological convictions about the need to reform the overall labor market and welfare state systems contributed to easing legislation on immigrants, which—the parties have calculated—might put pressure on the established systems by virtue of putting pressure downward on wages.

Beyond parties, our volume shows that it is not only the voting public, or political parties, at the national level that are important players in the game of migration and asylum policies. In addition, there are multilevel aspects of such policies, such as those that take place between state and superstate levels (as shown by Mcgarry and Drake). Sarah Craig's chapter shows the ongoing battle over jurisdiction between EU member states and the European courts on the matter of migration policy. She reveals how the discretion of the member states is gradually being eroded, with supranational courts increasingly having a stronger say. Key to how the battle is evolving appears to be the extent to which legal directives offer a margin of discretion to member states. For example, any omission or gap in the protection of asylum seekers' procedural rights increases the policy freedom of member states. Yet, as Craig shows, both the European Court of Human Rights and the European Court of Justice have increasingly managed to impose protection duties on EU member states. Thus, while various national models of immigration exist within the EU, an "EU national model" is slowly developing, with policy repercussions at the national level.

Similarly, multilevel approaches to studying migration issues are equally fruitful at the domestic level. As convincingly illustrated by Scholten in chapter 8, via a careful application of discourse analysis on the immigration policy and politics context in Amsterdam and

Rotterdam, Dutch integration policies vary considerably between different cities, and do so consistently. Thus, the local context appears to be at least as powerful as national policy structures. As Scholten's chapter shows, integration relates to such heavily charged issues as national identity, values, and norms, as well as local politics, bread-and-butter issues, and employment, social well-being, and education. Thus, the framing of immigration, integration, and identity are crucial in that they qualify the development of national paradigms and models. In this sense, how social meaning is attributed to immigrant integration by the actors within specific institutional settings relates to the scope of this volume. Moreover, Scholten's study also illustrates that beyond the discrepancies in framing integration between the national and local level, shifts in policy dynamics over time can also be detected. In the same vein, in chapter 6, Mahendran reveals a gap between national, formal, models of integration and local, public perceptions of integration. In addition, these differences may vary according to people's position on a continuum from settled nonmigrants to serial migrants.

This book has been informed by the value of studying migration policies by means of a range of discursive methodologies. Though the chapters have had different empirical objects—political-administrative actors and institutions (parties, bureaucracies, courts, the general public) at the national and local levels—they have all applied, in common, qualitative discursive methods. Thus, the authors have been able to reveal, on the one hand, complex webs of ideas behind seemingly plain and simple notions of migration policy. On the other hand, they have been able to show how seemingly irreconcilable ideas have been brought together under a policy umbrella that forms a coherent logic.

Careful discursive analyses, as they have been applied in the chapters in this book, have demonstrated a range of different ways in which political actors can form migration policies. Theoretically, we have shown how much of this discourse—and especially in terms of actual, implemented policy—is the outcome of a battle of ideas, or a struggle over ideology. However, "ideology" has proved to be rather more pliable and less coherent than has often been presumed. While an element of coherence according to some kind of connecting logic appears to be essential, a surprisingly eclectic range of subideology notions, views, and standpoints have been shown to be possible to squeeze under the overarching ideology umbrella. Moreover, the outcome of the battle of ideas or the struggle over ideology is by no means set in stone. As can be inferred from the arguments in this book, the very same "objective factors," such as the number or character of immigrants, national administrative-bureaucratic models, or the presence of so-and-so many voters showing support or opposition regarding certain aspects of life can result in totally different policy formulations. One important reason behind this surprising freedom to maneuver is, we would suggest, the rather forgiving attitude shown by ideologies toward superficially contradictory ideas.

We would like to conclude by emphasizing that in spite of the growth of huge bureaucracies with notions about technocratic policy regimes, the importance of ideas and ideologies is most definitely not to be ruled out.

Bibliography

Abdelal, Rawi. "Nationalism and International Political Economy in Eurasia." In *Economic Nationalism in a Globalizing World*, ed. Eric Helleiner and Andreas Pickel, 21–43. Ithaca, NY: Cornell University Press, 2005.

Acton, Thomas and Ilona Klímová. "The International Romani Union: An East European Answer to a West European Question?" In *Between Past and Future. The Roma of Central and Eastern Europe*, ed. Will Guy, 157–219. Hatfield: University of Hertfordshire Press, 2001.

Afonso, Alexandre. "Europeanisation, Policy Concertation and New Political Cleavages: The Case of Switzerland." *European Journal of Industrial Relations* 16 (2010): 57–72.

———. "Policy Change and the Politics of Expertise: Economic Ideas and Immigration Control Reforms in Switzerland." *Swiss Political Science Review* 13 (2007): 1–38.

———. "When the Export of Social Problems Is No Longer Possible: Immigration Policies and Unemployment in Switzerland." *Social Policy & Administration* 39 (2005): 653–668.

Aftonbladet. "Göran Persson orolig för 'social turism.'" (November 21, 2003).

"Ajankohtainen kakkonen—Halla-Ahon Kampanja: Hurmoksesta Hämmennykseen." YLE TV2, 2009.

Akalın, Ayşe. "Hired as a Caregiver, Demanded as a Housewife: Becoming a Migrant Domestic Worker in Turkey." *European Journal of Women's Studies* 14 (2007): 209–225.

Akpınar, Taner. "Türkiye'ye yönelik kaçak işgücü göçü." *AnkaraÜniversitesi SBF Dergisi* 65 (2010): 1–22.

Albertazzi, Daniele and Duncan McDonnell. *Twenty-First Century Populism: The Spectre of Western European Democracy*. Basingstoke: Palgrave Macmillan, 2007.

Alesina, Alberto and Edward L. Glaeser. *Fighting Poverty in the US and Europe: A World of Difference*. Oxford: Oxford University Press, 2004.

Alexander, Michael. *Cities and Labour Immigration: Comparing Policy Responses in Amsterdam, Paris, Rome and Tel Aviv*. London: Ashgate, 2007.

Ålund, Alexsandra and Carl-Ulrick Schierup. *Paradoxes of Multiculturalism: Essays on Swedish Society*. Aldershot: Avebury, 1991.

Amnesty International. *Greece: No Place for an Asylum-Seeker.* London. (February 27, 2008).

———. *Recommendations to the Council of Europe High-Level Meeting on Roma and Travellers.* Strasbourg. (October 20, 2010).

Andersen, Jørgen Goul. "Denmark: The Progress Party—Populist Neo-liberalism and Welfare State Chauvinism." In *The Extreme Right in Europe and the USA*, ed. Paul Hainsworth, 193–205. London: Pinter, 1992.

———. "Restricting Access to Social Protection for Immigrants in the Danish Welfare State." *Benefits* 15 (2007): 257–269.

Andersen, Jørgen Goul and Tor Bjørklund. "Structural Changes and New Cleavages: The Progress Parties in Denmark and Norway." *Acta Sociologica* 33 (1990): 195–217.

———. "Radical Right-Wing Populism in Scandinavia: From Tax Revolt to Neo-liberalism and Xenophobia." In *The Politics of the Extreme Right: From the Margins to the Mainstream*, ed. Paul Hainsworth, 69–87. London: Pinter, 2000.

Anderson, Benedict R. *Imagined Communities: Reflections on the Origin and Spread of Nationalism.* London: Verso, 1991.

Anderson, Bridget. *Doing the Dirty Work: The Global Politics of Domestic Labour.* London: Zed Books, 2000.

Apap, Joanna, Sergio Carrera, and Kemal Kirişçi. "EU Turkey Relations in the Pre-accession Period: Implementing the Schengen Regime and Enhancing Border Control." *CERP Report.* 2005.

Appelqvist, Maria. "Flyktingmottagandet och den svenska välfärdsstaten under 1990-talet." In *Välfärdens förutsättningar*, ed. Johan Frizell, 181–222. Stockholm: Fritzes, SOU 2000, 37.

Appelqvist, Maria och and Aina Tollefsen-Altamirano. "Svensk flyktingpolitisk utveckling under 1990-talet." In *En ny flyktingpolitikk i Norden?: Utviklingen av midlertidig beskyttelse på 1990-talet*, ed. Tollefsen-Altamirano, Brekke Appelqvist, and Vedsted-Hansen, 89–146. Köpenhamn: Nordiska ministerrådet.

Aradau, Claudia, Jef Huysmans, and Vicki Squire. "Acts of European Citizenship: A Political Sociology of Mobility." *Journal of Common Market Studies* 48, no. 4 (2010): 945–965.

Arter, David. "The Breakthrough of Another West European Populist Radical Right Party? The Case of the True Finns." *Government and Opposition* 45, no. 4 (2010): 484–504.

Asylum Aid. *I Feel Like as a Woman I Am Not Welcome.* London. (January 2012).

Bache, Ian and Matthew Flinders. "Themes and Issues in Multi-level Governance." In *Multi-level Governance,* ed. Ian Bache and Matthew Flinders, 1–14. Oxford: Oxford University Press, 2004.

Bader, Veit. "Institutions, Culture and Identity of Trans-national Citizenship: How Much Integration and 'Communal Spirit' Is Needed?" In *Citizenship, Markets and the State*, ed. Colin Crouch and Eder Klaus, 192–212. Oxford: Oxford University Press, 2001.

Baillot Helen, Sharon Cowan, and Vanessa Munro. "Hearing the Right Gaps: Enabling and Responding to Disclosures of Sexual Violence within the UK Asylum Process." *Social and Legal Studies* 21, no. 3 (2012): 269–296.
Bakhtin, Mikhail, M. and Michael Holquist. *The Dialogic Imagination: Four Essays.* Vol. 1. Texas: University of Texas Press, 1981.
Bakhtin, Mikhail, M. Michael Holquist, and Liapunov Vadim. *Toward a Philosophy of the Act.* Texas: University of Texas Press, 1993.
Bale, Tim. "Cinderella and Her Ugly Sister: The Mainstream and Extreme Right in Europe's Bipolarising Party System." *West European Politics* 26 (2003): 67–90.
———. "Turning Round the Telescope. Centre-Right Parties and Immigration and Integration Policy in Europe." *Journal of European Public Policy* 15 (2008): 315–330.
Bale, Tim, Christopher Green-Pedersen, Krouwel André, Kurt R. Luther, and Nick Sitter. "If You Can't Beat Them, Join Them? Explaining Social Democratic Responses to the Challenge from the Populist Radical Right in Western Europe." *Political Studies* 58, no. 3 (2010): 410–426.
Banting, Keith G. "Looking in Three Directions: Migration and the European Welfare State in Comparative Perspective." In *Immigration and Welfare: Challenging the Borders of the Welfare State*, ed. Michael Bommes and Andrew Geddes, 13–33. London: Routledge, 2000.
Barbara Ehrenreich and Arlie Russell Hochschild (eds.). *Global Woman: Nannies, Maids and Sex Workers in the New Economy.* London: Henry Holt, 2002.
Bartels, Larry M. "Economic Inequality and Political Representation." In *The Unsustainable American State*, ed. L. Jacobs and D. King. New York: Oxford University Press, 2009.
Barth, Frederik. *Ethnic Groups and Boundaries: The Social Organization of Cultural Difference.* Boston: Little Brown, 1969.
Bauböck, Rainer. *Transnational Citizenship: Membership and Rights in International Migration.* Aldershot: Edward Elgar, 1994.
Bauman, Zygmunt. *Mortality, Immortality and Other Life Strategies.* Stanford: Standford University Press, 1992.
Baumeister, Andrea T. "Habermas: Discourse and Cultural Diversity." *Political Studies* 51, no. 4 (2003): 740–758.
———. *Liberalism and the "Politics of Difference."* Edinburgh: Edinburgh University Press, 2000.
Baumgartner, Frank R., Bryan D. Jones, and J. Wilkerson. "Comparative Studies of Policy Dynamics." *Comparative Political Studies* 44, no. 8 (2011): 947–972.
Beck, Roy and Steven Camarota. *Elite vs. Public Opinion. An Examination of Divergent Views on Immigration.* Washington, DC: Center for Immigration Studies, 2002.
Béland, Daniel. "Ideas and Social Policy: An Institutionalist Perspective." *Social Policy and Administration* 39, no. 1 (2005): 1–18.
Béland, Daniel and Robert Henry Cox. "Introduction: Ideas and Politics." In *Ideas and Politics in Social Science Research*, ed. Daniel Béland and Robert Henry Cox, 3–22. Oxford: Oxford University Press, 2011.

Berman, Sheri. *The Social Democratic Moment: Ideas and Politics in the Making of Interwar Europe*. Cambridge, MA: Harvard University Press, 1998.

Berry, John W. "Globalisation and Acculturation." *International Journal of Intercultural Relations* 32, no. 4 (2008): 328–336.

———. "Mutual Attitudes among Immigrants and Ethnocultural Groups in Canada." *International Journal of Intercultural Relations* 30, no. 6 (2006): 719–734.

———. "Psychology of Acculturation." In *Nebraska Symposium on Motivation, 1989: Cross-cultural Perspectives. Current Theory and Research in Motivation*, ed. John J. Berman, 201–234. Lincoln, Nebraska: University of Nebraska Press, 1990.

Bertossi, Christophe and Jan Willem Duyvendak. "Modèles d'intégration et intégration des modèles ? Une étude comparative entre la France et les Pays-Bas." *Migrations Société* 21, no. 122 (2009): 39–76.

Besley, Timothy and Robin Burgess. "Political Agency, Government Responsiveness and the Role of the Media." *European Economic Review* 45, nos. 4–6 (2001): 629–640.

Best, Robin E., Ian Budge, and Michael D. Mcdonald. "Representation as a Median Mandate: Taking Cross-national Differences Seriously." *European Journal of Political Research* 51, no. 1 (2012): 1–23.

Betz, Hans-Georg. "The New Politics of Resentment—Radical Right-Wing Populist Parties in Western Europe." *Comparative Politics* 25, no. 4 (1993): 413–427.

———. *Radical Right-Wing Populism in Western Europe*. Basingstoke: Macmillan, 1994.

Betz, Hans-Georg and Stefan Immerfall (eds.). *The New Politics of the Right: Neo-populist Parties and Movements in Established Democracies*. Basingstoke: Macmillan, 1998.

Bhatia, Sunil. "Acculturation, Dialogical Voices and the Construction of the Diasporic Self." *Theory & Psychology* 12, no. 1 (2002): 55–77.

Bleich, Erik. "Integrating Ideas into Policy-Making Analysis. Frames and Race Policies in Britain and France." *Comparative Political Studies* 35 no. 9 (2002): 1054–1076.

———. *Race Politics in Britain and France: Ideas and Policymaking since the 1960s*. New York: Cambridge University Press, 2003.

Blyth, Mark. *Great Transformations: Economic Ideas and Institutional Change in the Twentieth Century*. New York: Cambridge University Press, 2002.

Body-Gendrot, Sophie. "European Policies of Social Control Post-9/11." *Social Research* 77 (Spring 2010): 181–204.

Bogardus, Emory S. "A Social Distance Scale." *Sociology & Social Research* 17 (1993): 265–271.

Bommes, Michael and Dietrich Thränhardt. *National Paradigms of Migration Research*. Munster: Institute for Migration Research and Intercultural Studies.

Bommes, Michael and Ewa Morawska. *International Migration Research: Constructions, Omissions and the Promises of Interdisciplinarity*. London: Ashgate, 2005.

Bornschier, Simon. *Cleavage Politics and the Populist Right: The New Cultural Conflict in Western Europe, Social Logic of Politics.* Philadelphia, PA: Temple University Press, 2010.

Borre, Ole, Jørgen Goul Andersen, Johannes Andersen, and Hans Jørgen Nielsen. *Danish Election Surveys.* Odense: Dansk Data Arkiv, 1993–2005.

Boswell, Christina and Andrew Geddes. *Migration and Mobility in the European Union.* Basingstoke: Palgrave, 2010.

Boswell, Christina, Andrew Geddes, and Peter Scholten. "States, Knowledge and Narratives of Migration: The Construction of Immigration in Migration Policy-Making in Europe." *British Journal of Politics and International Relations* 13, no. 1 (2011): 1–11.

Bourbeau, Philippe. "Resiliencism: Premises and Promises in Securitisation Research." *Resilience: International Policies, Practices and Discourses* 11, no. 1 (2013): 3–17.

Bowen, John. "A View from France on the Internal Complexity of National Models." *Journal of Ethnic and Migration Studies* 33, no. 6 (2007): 1003–1016.

Bowskill, Matt, Evanthia Lyons, and Adrian Coyle. "The Rhetoric of Acculturation: When Integration Means Assimilation." *British Journal of Social Psychology* 46, no. 4 (2007): 793–813.

Brown, Wendy. *States of Injury: Power and Freedom in Late Modernity.* Princeton, NJ: Princeton University Press, 1995.

Brubaker, Rogers. *Citizenship and Nationhood in France and Germany.* Cambridge, MA: Harvard University Press, 1992.

———. "Neither Individualism Nor 'Groupism': A Reply to Craig Calhoun." *Ethnicities* 3, no. 4 (2003): 553–557.

Bucken-Knapp, Gregg. *Defending the Swedish Model: Social Democrats, Trade Unions and Labor Migration Policy Reform.* Lanham, MD: Lexington Books, 2009.

Budge, Ian, Lawrence Ezrow, and Michael D. McDonald. "Ideology, Party Factionalism and Policy Change: An Integrated Dynamic Theory." *British Journal of Political Science* 40, no. 4 (2010): 781–804.

Buğra, Ayşe and Burcu Yakut-Çakar. "Structural Change, Social Policy and Female Employment in Turkey." *Development and Change* 41 (2010): 517–538.

Buitelaar, Marjo. "'I Am the Ultimate Challenge' Accounts of Intersectionality in the Life-Story of a Well-Known Daughter of Moroccan Migrant Workers in the Netherlands." *European Journal of Women's Studies* 13, no. 3 (2006): 259–276.

Burstein, Paul. "The Impact of Public Opinion on Public Policy: A Review and an Agenda." *Political Research Quarterly* 56, no. 1 (2003): 29–40.

———. "Why Estimates of the Impact of Public Opinion on Public Policy Are Too High: Empirical and Theoretical Implications." *Social Forces* 84, no. 4 (2006): 2273–2289.

Buzogány, Áron. "Swimming against the Tide. Contested Norms and Anti-discrimination Advocacy in Central and Eastern Europe." In *The Europeanisation of Gender Equality Policies,* ed. Maxime Forest and Emanuela Lombardo, 145–167. New York: Palgrave, 2011.

C-411/10 NS and C-493/10 ME [2012] 2 Common Market Law Reports 9.
Calhoun, Craig. "'Belonging' in the Cosmopolitan Imaginary." *Ethnicities* 3, no. 4 (2003): 531–553.
Campbell, Andrea Louise. "Policy Makes Mass Politics." *Annual Review of Political Science* 15, no. 1 (2012): 333–351.
Campbell, John. "Language Analysis in the United Kingdom's Refugee Status Determination System: Seeing through Policy Claims about 'Expert Knowledge.'" *Ethnic and Racial Studies* (2012). DOI 10.1080/01419870.2011.634506.
Canes-Wrone, Brandice and Kenneth W. Shotts. "The Conditional Nature of Presidential Responsiveness to Public Opinion." *American Journal of Political Science* 48, no. 4 (2004): 690–706.
Caponio, Tiziana and Maren Borkert. *The Local Dimension of Migration Policymaking*. Amsterdam: AUP, 2010.
Carrera, Sergio and Anaïs Faure Atger. *L'Affaire des Roms: A Challenge to the EU's Area of Freedom, Security and Justice*. Brussels: Centre for European Policy Studies, September 2010.
Castles, Stephen and Godula Kosack. "The Function of Labour Immigration in Western European Capitalism." *New Left Review* 1, no. 73 (May–June 1972): 3–21.
Çelik, Nihal. "Immigrant Domestic Women Workers in Ankara and Istanbul." MA Dissertation. Ankara: The Graduate School of Social Science, Middle East Technical University, 2005.
Cerny, Philip G. *The Changing Architecture of Politics: Structure, Agency, and the Future of the State*. London: Sage, 1990.
Cindoğlu, Dilek and Saime Özçürümez. "Region, Gender and Migration: The Case of Turkey." *Gender Migration and Intercultural Interaction in South-East Europe—WP6 National Report*. 2008.
City of Rotterdam. "Memorandum on the Integration of Minorities." City of Rotterdam: Policy memorandum, 1995.
———. "Wij zijn allemaal Amsterdammers." City of Amsterdam: Policy memorandum, 2005.
Cole, Alistair. "The Fast Presidency? Nicolas Sarkozy and the Political Institutions of the Fifth Republic." *Contemporary French and Francophone Studies* 16, no. 3 (2012): 311–321.
Collett, Elizabeth. A. *One Size Fits All?: Tailored Integration Policies for Migrants in the European Union*. Brussels: European Policy Centre, 2006.
"Commissioner for Human Rights, Mr. T Hammarberg." Report prepared following his visit to Greece from December 8 to 10, 2008. (February 4, 2009).
Conseil Fédéral. "Message Concernant La Loi Fédérale Contre Le Travail Au Noir." *Feuille Fédérale* (2002a): 3371–3437.
———. *Message Concernant La Loi Sur Les Étrangers*. Berne: Administration Fédérale, 2002b.
Corliss, Stephen. "Asylum in Turkey: Today and Future Prospects." In *Migration and Labour in Europe: Views from Turkey and Sweden*, ed. Emrehan Zeybekoglu

and Bo Johansson. Marmara University Research Centre for International Relations, Swedish National Institute for Working Life, Istanbul, 2003.

Costello, Cathryn. "The Asylum Procedures Directive and the Proliferation of Safe Country Practices: Deterrence, Deflection and the Dismantling of International Protection." *European Journal of Migration and Law* 7 (2005): 35–69.

Council of Europe. *European Convention on Human Rights*. 1950.

———. "Recent Rise in National Security Discourse in Europe: The Case of Roma. Parliamentary Committee." Doc. 12386. October 5. Strasbourg: Council of Europe, 2010.

Council of the European Union. *Regulation (EC) No 2725/2000 of 11 December 2000 concerning the Establishment of "Eurodac" for the Comparison of Fingerprints for the Effective Application of the Dublin Convention*. OJ L 316/1. 2000.

———. *Regulation (EC) No 407/2002 of 28 February 2002 Laying Down Certain Rules to Implement Regulation (EC) No 2725/2000 concerning the Establishment of "Eurodac" for the Comparison of Fingerprints for the Effective Application of the Dublin Convention*. OJ L 62/1. 2002.

———. *Directive 2003/9/EC of 27 January 2003 Laying Down Minimum Standards for the Reception of Asylum Seekers*. OJ L 31. February 6, 2003a: 18–25 (Recast compromise package agreed on July 11, 2012).

———. *Regulation (EC) No 343/2003 of 18 February 2003 Establishing the Criteria and Mechanisms for Determining the Member State Responsible for Examining an Asylum Application Lodged in One of the Member States by a Third-Country National*. OJ l 50/1. *(The Dublin Regulation)*. 2003b.

———. "Immigrant Integration Policy in the European Union." Brussels, 14615/04 (Presse 321) (November 19, 2004).

———. *Directive 2005/85/EC of 1 December 2005 on Minimum Standards and Procedures for Granting and Withdrawing Refugee Status*. OJ L 326/13. December 13, 2005. (APD).

———. *Amended Proposal for a Eurodac Regulation (339556) 10638/12 COM (12) 254*. 2012.

Craig, Sarah. "The Use of Language Analysis in Asylum Decision-Making in the UK—A Discussion." *Journal of Immigration Asylum and Nationality Law* 26, no. 3 (2012): 255–268.

Craig, Sarah and Maria Fletcher. "Deflecting Refugees: A Critique of the EC Asylum Procedures Directive." In *The Challenge of Asylum to Legal Systems*, ed. Prakash Shah, 53–83. London, Cavendish, 2005.

Crawley, Heaven. *Chance or Choice? Understanding Why Asylum Seekers Come to the UK*. London: Refugee Council, January, 2010.

Crowley, John. "The Politics of Belonging: Some Theoretical Considerations." In *The Politics of Belonging: Migrants and Minorities in Contemporary Europe*, ed. Andrew Geddes and Adrian Favell, 15–41. Aldershot: Ashgate, 1999.

Crul, Maurice and Liesbeth Heering. *The Position of the Turkish and Moroccan Second Generation in Amsterdam and Rotterdam. The TIES Study in the Netherlands*. Amsterdam: Amsterdam University Press, 2008.

Culpepper, Pepper. *Quiet Politics: Business Power and Corporate Control*. Cambridge: Cambridge University Press, 2010.

Dagens Nyheter. *Krav på svenskkunskaper skärps för invandrare*. (February 18, 2008).

Dahl, Robert A. *Polyarchy: Participation and Opposition*. New Haven: Yale University Press, 1971.

Dahlström, Carl and Peter Esaiasson. "The Immigration Issue and Anti-immigrant Party Success in Sweden 1970–2006: A Deviant Case Analysis." *Party Politics* (2011) (DOI 1354068811407600, first published on June 10, 2011).

Dansk Data Arkiv. Gallup Omnibus Surveys: 1985–1991.

———. Socialforskningsinstituttets Omnibus Surveys: 1993–1998.

Daróczi, Gábor. "Inclusion of the Roma: Europe's Joint Responsibility." In *Roma: A European Minority. The Challenge of Diversity*, ed. Monika Flašíková-Beňová, Hannes Swoboda, and Jan Marinus Wiersma, 79–88. Brussels Alliance of Socialists and Democrats in the European Parliament. 2011.

Dauvergne Catherine. "Sovereignty, Migration and the Rule of Law in Global Times." *Modern Law Review* 67, no. 4 (2004): 588–515.

Davies, Celia, Margeret S. Wetherell, and Elizabeth Barnett. *Citizens at the Centre: Deliberative Participation in Healthcare Decisions*. Bristol: Policy Press, 2006.

De Genova, Nicholas. "The Legal Production of Mexican/Migrant Illegality." *Latino Studies* 2 (2004): 160–185.

De Lange, Sarah. "A New Winning Formula? The Programmatic Appeal of the Radical Right." *Party Politics* 13 (2007): 411–435.

De Zwart, Frank. "The Dilemma of Recognition: Administrative Categories and Cultural Diversity." *Theory and Society* 34, no. 2 (2005): 137–169.

Deaux, Kay. *To Be an Immigrant*. New York: Russell Sage Foundation, 2006.

Demker, Marie. "Svenskarna långsiktigt alltmer positiva till invandrare." In *Nordiskt ljus*, ed. Sören Holmberg and Lennart Weibull. Göteborg: SOM, 2010

Dhima, Giorgio. *Politische Ökonomie Des Schweizerischen Ausländerregelung*. Chur/Zurich: Rüegger, 1991.

Diken, Bülent. "From Refugee Camps to Gated Communities: Biopolitics and the End of the City." *Citizenship Studies* 8, no. 1 (March 2004): 83–106.

Downs, Anthony. *An Economic Theory of Democracy*. New York: Harper, 1957.

Druckman, James N. and Lawrence R. Jacobs. "Segmented Representation: The Reagan White House and Disproportionate Responsiveness." In *Who Gets Represented?*, ed. Christopher Wlezien and Peter K. Enns. New York: Russell Sage Foundation, 2011.

Duyvendak, Jan Willem and Peter Scholten. "Beyond National Models of Integration: The Coproduction of Integration Policy Frames in the Netherlands." *Journal of International Migration and Integration* 12, no. 3 (2011): 331–348.

Eatwell, Roger. "Introduction: The New Extreme Right Challenge." In *Western Democracies and the Extreme Right Challenge*, ed. Roger Eatwell and Cas Mudde, 1–16. London: Routledge, 2004.

———. "The Rebirth of the 'Extreme Right' in Western Europe?" *Parliamentary Affairs* 53, no. 3 (2000): 407–425.

Ege, Gamze. "Foreign Domestic Workers in Turkey: A New Form of Trafficking in Turkey?" Master's Thesis. Ankara: Graduate School of Social Science, Middle East Technical University, 2002.

Ekenger, Karin and Fabian Wallén. "Invandring för tillväxt och nya jobb." *Svenskt Näringsliv* (July 2002).

Engle, Lauren B. *The World in Motion: Short Essays on Gender and Migration.* Geneva: IOM, 2004.

Enns, Peter K. and Christopher Wlezien. *Who Gets Represented?* New York: Russell Sage Foundation, 2011.

Epstein, Lee and J. A. Segal. "Measuring Issue Salience." *American Journal of Political Science* 44 (2000): 66–83.

Erder, Sema and Selmin Kaşka. *Irregular Migration and Trafficking in Women: The Case of Turkey.* Geneva: IOM, 2003.

Erikson, Robert S., Michael B. MacKuen, and James A. Stimson. *The Macro Polity.* New York: Cambridge University Press, 2002.

Europe 1. "Le ministre de l'intérieur a invoqué des 'conditions de vie insupportables,'" (August 27, 2010), available at http://www.europe1.fr/Politique/Evry-Valls-justifie-l-expulsion-des-Roms-1215999/ (Accessed October 11, 2012).

European Commission, DG Employment and Social Affairs. "The Situation of Roma in an Enlarged European Union. Fundamental Rights and Discrimination." April 22, 2004.

———. *Communication from the Commission to the European Parliament, the Council, the ECOSOC and Committee of the Regions: Policy Plan on asylum – an integrated approach to protection across the EU,* 17 June 2008, COM (2008) 360 final. 2008.

———. "Statement on the Latest Developments on the Roma Situation." Speech delivered by Viviane Reding. September 14, 2010a.

———. "Statement by Viviane Reding." Vice President of the European Commission, EU Commissioner for Justice, Fundamental Rights and Citizenship Brussels. October 19, 2010b.

———. "The Imperative of Roma Integration: More Than Just a 'Summer Story.'" Speech by Viviane Reding, at the Council of Europe High-Level Meeting on Roma and Travellers, Strasbourg. October 20, 2010c.

———. "Communication from the Commission to the European Parliament, the Council, the European Economic and Social Committee of the Regions: An EU Framework for National Roma Integration Strategies up to 2020." COM (2011) 173/4. Brussels. 2011

European Parliament. *Resolution on the Situation of Roma and on the Freedom of Movement in the European Union.* September 9, 2010. Brussels. P7_TA.

European Parliament and Council. *Amended Proposal for a Directive on Common Procedures for Granting and Withdrawing International Protection Status (Recast APD)* EU: COM (2011) 319 Celex No. 511P CO319. 2011a.

———. *Directive 2011/95/EU of 13 December 2011 on Standards for the Qualification of Third-Country Nationals or Stateless Persons as Beneficiaries of International Protection, for a Uniform Status for Refugees or for Persons Eligible for Subsidiary Protection, and for the Content of the Protection Granted (Recast)* OJ L (December 20, 2011b): 337–339.

———. *Proposal for a Regulation Establishing the Criteria and Mechanisms for Determining the Member State Responsible for Examining an Application for International Protection in One of the Member States by a Third-Country National or Stateless Person (Recast)* COM (2008) Final, December 3, 2008.

European Presidency. "Common European Asylum System: State of Play." *Note 13340/12* (September 4, 2012).

———. *Conclusions*. Tampere (October 15–16, 1999).

European Roma Policy Coalition (ERPC). *Analysis of the National Roma Integration Strategies*. Brussels: EPRC, 2012.

European Roma Rights Centre (ERRC). *Roma Rights in Jeopardy*. Factsheet. Budapest: ERRC, 2012.

European Roma Rights Centre/European Roma Policy Coalition (ERRC/ERPC). *EU Framework Weak on Discrimination against Roma*. Budapest: EPRC, April 5, 2011.

European Union. *Charter of Fundamental Rights of the European Union*. OJ (C83) 389. March 30, 2010.

———. *Treaty on the Functioning of the European Union* (Consolidated Version). OJC 115/47(TFEU). 2008.

Ezrow, Lawrence, Cathrine De Vries, Marco Steenbergen, and Erica Edwards. "Mean Voter Representation and Partisan Constituency Representation: Do Parties Respond to the Mean voter Position or to Their Supporters?" *Party Politics* 17, no. 3 (2001): 275–301.

Facchini, Giovanni and Anna Maria Mayda. "From Individual Attitudes towards Migrants to Migration Policy Outcomes: Theory and Evidence." *Economic Policy* 56 (2008): 653–713.

Fahimi, Bijan. *Öppna den svenska arbetsmarknaden*. Stockholm: Svenskt Näringsliv, 2001.

Faist, Thomas, and Andreas Ette. *The Europeanization of National Policies and Politics of Immigration: Between Autonomy and the European Union*. New York: Palgrave Macmillan, 2007.

Fassin, Didier. "The Biopolitics of Otherness. Undocumented Foreigners and Racial Discrimination in French Public Debate." *Anthropology Today* 17, no. 1 (February 2001): 3–7.

Favell, Adrian. "Integration Nations: The Nation-State and Research on Immigrants in Western Europe." In *International Migration Research: Constructions, Omissions and the Promises of Interdisciplinarity*, ed. Michael Bommes and Ewa Morawska, 41–68. Aldershot: Palgrave, 2005.

Feuz, Patrick. "Die Kehrtwenden der SVP sind legendär." *Tages Anzeiger* (May 25, 2011): 5.

Finseraas, Henning. "Anti-immigration Attitudes, Support for Redistribution and Party Choice in Europe." In *Changing Social Equality: The Nordic Welfare*

Model in the 21st Century, ed. Jon Kvist, Johan Fritzell, Bjørn Hvinden, and Olli Kangas. 23–44. Bristol: Policy Press, 2012.

Fischer, Alex, Sarah Nicolet, and Pascal Sciarini. "Europeanisation of Non-EU Countries: The Case of Swiss Immigration Policy towards the EU." *West European Politics* 25 (2002): 143–170.

Fischer, Manuel, Alex Fischer, and Pascal Sciarini. "Power and Conflict in the Swiss Political Elite: An Aggregation of Existing Network Analyses." *Swiss Political Science Review* 15 (2009): 31–62.

Fleck, Gabor and Rughiniş Cosima. *Come Closer: Inclusion and Exclusion of Roma in Present Day Romanian Society*. Bucharest: National Agency for Roma, 2008.

Folkpartiet. *En ny integrationspolitik* (August 2002).

Fraser, Nancy. "From Redistribution to Recognition." *New Left Review* 1, no. 212 (July–August 1995): 68–93.

Freeman, Gary. "Migration and the Political Economy of the Welfare State." *Annals of the American Academy of Political and Social Science* 485 (1986): 51–63.

———. "Modes of Immigration Politics in Liberal Democratic States." *International Migration Review* 29 (1995): 881–908.

Freeman, Gary P. and Alan K. Kessler. "Political Economy and Migration Policy." *Journal of Ethnic and Migration Studies* 34, no. 3 (2008): 655–678.

Gammeltoft-Hansen, Thomas and Zachary Whyte. "Dansk asylpolitik 1983–2010." In *Asylbørn i Danmark: en barndom i undtakelsestilstand*, ed. Kathrine Vitus and Signe Smith Nielsen. Copenhagen: Hans Reitzel, 2011.

Gamson, Joshua. "Rubber Wars: Struggles over the Condom in the United States." *Journal of the History of Sexuality* 1 (1990): 262–282.

Gheorghe, Nicolae. "Romania Is Shirking Its Roma Responsibilities." *Guardian* (November 3, 2010), available at http://www.guardian.co.uk/commentisfree/2010/nov/03/romania-shirking-roma-responsibilities (Accessed October 13, 2012).

Giddens, Anthony. *The Third Way: The Renewal of Social Democracy*. Cambridge: Polity Press, 1998.

Gilens, Martin. "Inequality and Democratic Responsiveness." *Public Opinion Quarterly* 69, no. 5 (2005): 778–796.

———. "Preference Gaps and Inequality in Representation." *PS: Political Science and Politics* 42, no. 2 (2009): 335–341.

Gillespie, Alex and Flora Cornish. "Intersubjectivity: Towards a Dialogical Analysis." *Journal for the Theory of Social Behaviour* 40, no. 1 (2009): 19–46.

Givens, Terry and Rahsaan Maxwell (eds.). *Immigrant Politics: Race and Representation in Europe*. Boulder, CO: Lynne Rienner, 2012.

Gourevitch, Peter. *Politics in Hard Times: Comparative Responses to International Economic Crises*. Ithaca, NY, and London: Cornell University Press, 1986.

Government of France. *Une place égale dans la société française: Stratégie du gouvernement français pour l'inclusion des Romsdans le cadre de la communication de la Commission du 5 avril 2011 et des conclusions du Conseil du 19mai 2011*. Paris: 2012.

Government bill 1996/1997:25, "Svensk migrationspolitik i globalt perspektiv."

Green-Pedersen, Christoffer and Jens Krogstrup. "Immigration as a Political Issue in Denmark and Sweden." *European Journal of Political Research* 47, no. 5 (2008): 610–634.

Green-Pedersen, Christoffer and Pontus Odmalm. "Going Different Ways? Right-Wing Parties and the Immigrant Issue in Denmark and Sweden." *Journal of European Public Policy* 15, no. 3 (2008): 367–381.

Gudbrandsen, Frøy. "Partisan Influence on Immigration: The Case of Norway." *Scandinavian Political Studies* 33, no. 3 (2010): 248–270.

Guglielmo, Rachel, and Timothy William Waters. "Migrating towards Minority Status: Shifting European Policy towards Roma." *Journal of Common Market Studies* 43, no. 4 (2005): 763–786.

Guiraudon, Virginie. *Policy Change behind Gilded Doors: Explaining the Evolution of Aliens' Rights in France, Germany and the Netherlands, 1974–94.* New Haven: Harvard University Press, 1997.

Hainsworth, Paul (ed.). *The Extreme Right in Europe and the USA.* London: Pinter, 1992.

——— (ed.). *The Extreme Right in Western Europe.* London: Routledge, 2008.

——— (ed.). *The Politics of the Extreme Right: From the Margins to the Mainstream.* London: Pinter, 2000.

Hall, Peter. "Policy Paradigms, Social Learning and the State: The Case of Economic Policy-Making in Britain." *Comparative Politics* 25, no. 3 (1993): 275–296.

Hammar, Tomas. "Closing the Doors to the Swedish Welfare State." In *Mechanisms of Immigration Control: A Comparative Analysis of European Regulation Policies*, ed. Grete Brochmann and Tomas Hammar. Oxford: Berg, 1999.

Hammarberg, Thomas. *The Human Rights of Roma and Travellers in Europe.* Strasbourg: Council of Europe, 2012.

Haney, Lynne. *Gender and the Politics of Welfare in Hungary.* Berkeley, Los Angeles, and London: University of California Press, 2002.

Hannula, Milla. *Maassa Maan Tavalla: Maahanmuuttokritiikin Lyhyt Historia.* Helsinki: Otava, 2011.

Hardin, Russell. "Migration and Community." *Journal of Social Philosophy* 36 (Summer 2005): 273–287.

Harlen, Christine Margerum. "A Reappraisal of Classical Economic Nationalism and Economic Liberalism." *International Studies Quarterly* 43, no. 4 (1999): 733–744.

Harmes, Adam. "The Rise of Neoliberal Nationalism." *Review of International Political Economy* 19, no. 1 (2012): 59–86.

Haste, Helen and Salie Abrahams. "Morality, Culture and the Dialogic Self: Taking Cultural Pluralism Seriously." *Journal of Moral Education* 37, no. 3 (2008): 377–394.

Hattam, Victoria and Carlos Yescas. "From Immigration and Race to Sex and Faith: Reimagining the Politics of Opposition." *Social Research* 77 (Spring 2010): 133–162.

Hatton, Timothy J. "The Rise and Fall of Asylum. What Happened, and Why?" *Economic Journal* 119, no. 535 (2009): F183–F213.

Heinisch, Reinhard. "Success in Opposition-Failure in Government: Explaining the Performance of Right-Wing Populist Parties in Public Office." *West European Politics* 26 (2003): 91–130.

Helbling, Marc. "Naturalisation Politics in Switzerland: Explaining Rejection Rates at the Local Level." In *The Local Dimension of Migration Policymaking*, ed. Tiziana Caponio and Maren Borkert, 33–56. Amsterdam: AUP, 2010.

Helleiner, Eric. "Economic Nationalism as a Challenge to Economic Liberalism? Lessons from the 19th Century." *International Studies Quarterly* 46, no. 3 (2002): 307–329.

Hellström, Johan. "Who Leads, Who Follows? Re-examining the Party-Electorate Linkages on European Integration." *Journal of European Public Policy* 15, no. 8 (2008): 1127–1144.

Helsingin Sanomat. "KKO Tuomitsi Halla-Ahon Myös Kiihottamisesta Kansanryhmää Vastaan." (June 8, 2012).

Hermans, Hubert, J. M. "The Dialogical Self: Toward a Theory of Personal and Cultural Positioning." *Culture & Psychology* 7, no. 3 (2001): 243–281.

Hermans, Hubert, J. M. and Giancarlo Dimaggio. "Self, Identity, and Globalization in Times of Uncertainty: A Dialogical Analysis." *Review of General Psychology* 11 no. 1 (2007): 31–61.

Hermans, Hubert, J. M. and Thorsten Gieser. *Handbook of Dialogical Self Theory*. Cambridge: Cambridge University Press, 2012.

Hibbs, Douglas A. "Partisan Theory after Fifteen Years." *European Journal of Political Economy* 8 (1992): 361–373.

Hilgartner, Stephen and Charles Bosk. "The Rise and Fall of Social Problems: A Public Arenas Model." *American Journal of Sociology* 94, no. 1 (1988): 53–78

Hinnfors, Jonas. "Stability through Change." *Journal of Public Policy* 19, no. 3 (1999): 293–312.

Hinnfors, Jonas, Andrea Spehar, and Gregg Bucken-Knapp. "The Missing Factor: Why Social Democracy Can Lead to Restrictive Immigration Policy." *Journal of European Public Policy* 19, no. 4 (2012): 585–603.

Hix, Simon and Abdul Noury. "Politics, Not Economic Interests: Determinants of Migration Policies in the European Union," *International Migration Review* 41, no. 1 (2007): 182–205.

Hobolt, Sarah Binzer and Robert Klemmensen. "Government Responsiveness and Political Competition in Comparative Perspective." *Comparative Political Studies* 41, no. 3 (2008): 309–337.

Hochschild, Arlie Russell. "Global Care Chains and Emotional Surplus Value." In *On the Edge: Living with Global Capitalism*, ed. W. Hutton and A. Giddens. London: Jonathan Cape, 2000.

Hochschild, Arlie Russell. *The Managed Heart: Commercialization of Human Feeling*. Berkley: University of California Press, 2003.

Hollifield, James. "Immigration and Integration in Western Europe: A Comparative Analysis." In *Immigration into Western Societies—Problems and Policies*, ed. Emec Ucarer and Donald Puchala. London: Pinter.

Hont, István. *Jealousy of Trade: International Competition and the Nation-State in Historical Perspective*. Cambridge, MA: Belknap Press of Harvard University Press, 2005.

Hooghe, Liesbeth and Gary Marks. *Multi-level Governance and European Integration*. Lanham: Rowman and Littlefield, 2001.

Hoppe, Rob. *The Governance of Social Problems: Puzzling, Powering, Participation*. Bristol: Polity Press, 2010, available at http://ec.europa.eu/justice/discrimination/files/roma_france_strategy_fr.pdf (Accessed May 5, 2012).

Howarth, Caroline. "A Social Representation Is Not a Quiet Thing: Exploring the Critical Potential of Social Representations Theory." *British Journal of Social Psychology* 45, no. 1 (2006): 65–86.

Howarth, Caroline, Wolfgang Wagner, Nicola Magnusson, and Gordon Sammut. "'It's Only Other People Who Make Me Feel Black': Acculturation, Identity and Agency in a Multicultural Community." *Political Psychology* 34 (2013).

Huang, S. and B. S. A. Yeoh. "Ties That Bind: State Policy and Migrant Female Domestic Helpers in Singapore." *Geoforum* 27 (1996): 479–493.

İçduygu, Ahmet. "Demographic Mobility over Turkey: Migration Experiences and Government Responses." *Mediterranean Quarterly* 15, no. 4 (2004): 88–99.

———. "Irregular Migration in Turkey." *Migration Research Series* 12. Geneva: International Organization for Migration, 2003.

İçduygu, Ahmet and Fuat Keyman. "Globalization, Security and Migration: The Case of Turkey." *Global Governance* 6 (2000): 383–398.

İçduygu, Ahmet and Köser-Akcapar Şebnem. *The Labor Dimensions of Irregular Migration and Human Trafficking in Turkey*. Geneva: ILO, 2005.

Ignazi, Piero. *Extreme Right Parties in Western Europe*. Oxford: Oxford University Press, 2003.

Ireland, Patrick. *Becoming Europe: Immigration, Integration and the Welfare State* Pittsburgh: University of Pittsburgh Press, 2004.

———. *The Policy Challenge of Ethnic Diversity: Immigrant Politics in France and Switzerland*. Cambridge, MA: Harvard University Press, 1994.

ISMMO. "Yabanci Kacak Isciler ve Turkiye'de Goc Hareketi Raporu," available at http://archive.ismmmo.org.tr/docs/basin/2012/yazilibasin/25062012/yabancI_kacak_isciler_ve_turkiyeye_goc_hareketI_raporu.doc (Accessed September 13, 2013).

Ivarsflaten, Elisabeth. "Threatened by Diversity: Why Restrictive Asylum and Immigration Policies Appeal to Western Europeans." *Journal of Elections, Public Opinion & Parties* 15 (2005a): 21–45.

———. "The Vulnerable Populist Right Parties: No Economic Realignment Fuelling Their Electoral Success." *European Journal of Political Research* 44 (2005b): 465–492.

Jacobs, Lawrence R. and Benjamin I. Page. "Who Influences US Foreign Policy?" *American Political Science Review* 99, no. 1 (2005): 107–123.

Jennings, Will. "The Public Thermostat, Political Responsiveness and Error-Correction: Border Control and Asylum in Britain, 1994–2007." *British Journal of Political Science* 39, no. 4 (2009): 847–870.

John, Peter. "The Policy Agendas Project: A Review." *Journal of European Public Policy* 13, no. 7 (2006): 975–986.
Joppke, Christian. "Beyond National Models: Civic Integration Policies for Immigrants in Western Europe." *West European Politics* 30, no. 1 (2007): 1–22.
Joppke, Christian and Virgine Guiraudon. *Controlling a New Migration World. EUI Studies in the Political Economy of Welfare.* London and New York: Routledge, 2001
Jovchelovitch, Sandra. *Knowledge in Context: Representations, Community and Culture.* New York: Routledge, 2007.
Judt, Tony. "Edge People." *New York Review of Books* (February 23, 2010), available at http://www.nybooks.com/articles/archives/2010/mar/25/edge-people/ (Accessed March 16, 2010)
Kaşka, Selmin. "The New International Migration and Migrant Women in Turkey: The Case of Moldovan Domestic Workers." Mireko̧c Migration Research Program at the Koç University Research Projects, 2005–2006. Istanbul: Koç University, 2006.
Kastoryano, Riva. "Codes of Otherness." *Social Research* 77 (Spring 2010): 79–100.
Keough, Leyla. "Driven Women: Reconceptualizing the Traffic in Women in the Margins of Europe through the Case of Gagauz Mobile Domestics in Istanbul." *Anthropology of East Europe Review* 21, no. 2 (2003): 73–78.
Kestilä, Elina. "Is There Demand for Radical Right Populism in the Finnish Electorate?" *Scandinavian Political Studies* 29, no. 3 (2006): 169–191.
Kingdon, John W. *Agendas, Alternatives and Public Policies.* New York: Longman, 2003.
Kitschelt, Herbert. "Diversification and Reconfiguration of Party Systems in Postindustrial Democracies." *Europäische Politik* 3 (2004): 1–23.
———. *The Radical Right in Western Europe—A Comparative Analysis.* Ann Arbour: University of Michigan Press, 1997.
Kitschelt, Herbert and Anthony J. McGann. *The Radical Right in Western Europe: A Comparative Analysis.* Ann Arbor, MI: University of Michigan Press, 1995.
Koç, Yıldırım. *Türkiye'de Yabancı Kaçak İşçilik.* Ankara: Türk-İş, 1999.
Kollman, Kelly. "European Institutions, Transnational Networks and National Same-Sex Unions Policy: When Soft Law Hits Harder." *Contemporary Politics* 15 (2009): 37–53.
Kooiman, Jan. *Governing as Governance.* London: Sage, 2003.
Koopmans, Ruud. "Good Intentions Sometimes Make Bad Policy: A Comparison of Dutch and German Integration Policies." In *Migration, Multiculturalism, and Civil Society*, ed. Friedrich Ebert Stiftung, 163–168. Berlin: Friedrich Ebert Stiftung, 2005.
———. "Uitvluchten kan niet meer...Repliek op Bocker en Thranhardt." *Migrantenstudies* 1 (2003): 45–56.
Koopmans, Ruud, Statham Paul, Marco Giugni, Florence Passy. *Contested Citizenship. Immigration and Cultural Diversity in Europe.* Minneapolis: University of Minnesota Press, 2005

Korkut, Umut. *Liberalization Challenges in Hungary: Elitism, Progressivism, and Populism*. New York: Palgrave/NYU European Studies Series, 2012.

Korkut, Umut and Hande Eslen-Ziya. "The Impact of Social Conservatism on Population Politics in Poland and Turkey." *Social Politics* 18, no. 3 (2011): 387–418.

Kraal, Karen. "Amsterdam: From Group-Specific to Problem-Oriented Policy." In *Multicultural Policies and Modes of Citizenship in European Cities*, ed. Rogers and Tillie, 15–39. Aldershot: Ashgate, 2001

Kriesi, Hamnspeter and Alexander Trechsel. *The Politics of Switzerland: Continuity and Change in a Consensus Democracy*. Cambridge: Cambridge University Press, 2008.

KRS v United Kingdom (Appln. No. 32733/08) (2009) 48 European Human Rights Reports SE8.

Küçük, Bülent. "The Diversity and the European Public Sphere: The Case of Turkey." *EUROSPHERE Country Report* 4 (2010): 1–63.

Kuisma, Mikko and Magnus Ryner. "Third Way Decomposition and the Rightward Shift in Finnish and Swedish Politics." *Contemporary Politics* 18, no. 3 (2012): 325–342.

Kümbetoğlu, Belkis. "Enformelleşme Süreçlerinde Genç Göçmen Kadınlar ve Dayanışma Ağları." *Folklor/Edebiyat* 11 (2005): 5–25.

Kymlicka, Will and Keith Banting. "Immigration, Multiculturalism, and the Welfare State." *Ethics and International Affairs* 20, no. 3 (2006): 281–304.

Labour Administration and Inspection Programme. *Labour Inspection in Europe: Undeclared Work, Migration, Trafficking*. Geneva: International Labour Office, 2010.

Lamont, Michèle and Marcel Fournier (eds.). *Cultivating Symbolic Boundaries and the Making of Inequality*. Chicago: University of Chicago Press, 1992.

Larsen, Christian Albrekt. "Ethnic Heterogeneity and Public Support for Welfare: Is the American Experience Replicated in Britain, Sweden and Denmark?" *Scandinavian Political Studies* 3, no. 4 (2011): 332–353.

L'Express. "Pétition contre le ministère de l'Immigration" (June 22, 2007), available at http://www.lexpress.fr/actualite/politique/petition-contre-le-ministere-de-l-immigration_465119.html (Accessed October 11, 2012).

Le Temps, "Loi Sur les Etrangers." *Le Temps* (May 7, 2004).

Levi-Faur, David. "Friedrich List and the Political Economy of the Nation-State." *Review of International Political Economy* 4, no. 1 (1997): 154–178.

Lewin, Kurt. "Resolving Social Conflict." In *Selected Papers on Group Dynamics*, ed. Gertrude W. Lewin. New York: Harper & Row, 1948.

Lewin, Leif. *Ideology and Strategy*. Cambridge: Cambridge University Press, 1988

Lipset, Seymour Martin and Stein Rokkan. *Party Systems and Voter Alignments: Cross-national Perspectives*. New York: Free Press, 1967.

Lubbers, Mark, M. Gijsberts, and P. Scheepers. "Extreme Right-Wing Voting in Western Europe." *European Journal of Political Research* 41 (2002): 345–378.

Lucassen, J. and Rinus Penninx Newcomers. *Immigrants and Their Descendants in the Netherlands 1550–1995*. Amsterdam: Het Spinhuis, 2005.

Lundgren, Bo, Alf Svensson, Maud Olofsson and Lars Leijonborg "Borgerliga partiledarna gör utfästelser för nästa mandatperiod: 'Tillväxten' skall upp till 3 procent." *Dagens Nyheter* (August 11, 2002).

Lundhm, Christer and Rolf Ohlsson. *Från arbetskraftsimport till flyktingsinvandring*. Stockholm: SNS Forlag, 1999.

Lutz, Helma. "Life in the Twilight Zone: Migration, Transnationality and Gender in the Private Household." *Journal of Contemporary European Studies* 12 (April 2004): 47–55.

Mahendran, Kesi. "Introducing Four Psychologies of Unemployment and Their Implications for Intervention." In *Unemployment, Precarious Work and Health*, ed. Thomas Kieselbach and Simo Mannila, 53–72. Hiedelberg: VS Verlag, 2011.

———. "The Transition of a Scottish Young Person's Centre—A Dialogical Analysis." In *Rethinking Communicative Interaction*, ed. Colin B. Grant, 235–256. Amsterdam/Philadelphia: John Benjamins, 2003.

Mahnig, Hans. "The Politics of Minority-Majority Relations: How Immigrant Policies Developed in Paris, Berlin and Zurich." In *Citizenship in European Cities: Immigrants, Local Politics and Integration Policies*, ed. Rinus Penninx, 17–38. Ashgate: Farnham, 2004.

Marková, Ivana. *Dialogicality and Social Representations: The Dynamics of Mind*: Cambridge: Cambridge University Press, 2003.

Maussen, Marcel. "Constructing Mosques: The Governance of Islam in France and the Netherlands." PhD Thesis, University of Amsterdam, 2009.

———. *Ruimte voor de Islam? Stedelijk beleid, voorzieningen, organisaties*. Amsterdam: Het Spinhuis, 2006.

Mayer, Nonna. *Ces Français Qui Votent Le Pen*. Paris: Flammarion, 2002.

McGann, Anthony and Herbert Kitschelt. "The Radical Right in the Alps: Evolution of Support for the Swiss Svp and Austrian FPÖ." *Party Politics* 11 (2005): 147–171.

McGarry, Aidan. "The Dilemma of the European Union's Roma Policy." *Critical Social Policy* 32, no. 1 (2012): 126–136.

———. "Political Participation and Interest Articulation of Roma in Romania." *Journal on Ethnopolitics and Minority Issues in Europe* 1 (2008): 1–25.

———. "The Roma Voice in the European Union: Between National Belonging and Transnational Identity." *Social Movement Studies* 10, no. 3 (2011): 283–297.

———. *Who Speaks for Roma? Political Representation of a Transnational Minority Community*. London: Continuum, 2010.

McPherson, Melinda. "'I Integrate, Therefore I Am': Contesting the Normalizing Discourse of Integrationism through Conversations with Refugee Women." *Journal of Refugee Studies* 23, no. 4 (2010): 546–570.

Mead, Lawrence M. *Beyond Entitlement: The Social Obligations of Citizenship*. New York: Free Press, 1986.

Mehta, Jal. "The Varied Roles of Ideas in Politics: From 'Whether' to 'How.'" In *Ideas and Politics in Social Science Research*, ed. Daniel Béland and Robert Henry Cox, 23–46. Oxford: Oxford University Press, 2011.

Menz, Georg. "'Useful' Gastarbeiter, Burdensome Asylum Seekers, and the Second Wave of Welfare Retrenchment: Exploring the Nexus between Migration and the Welfare State." In *Immigration and the Transformation of Europe*, ed. Craig Parsons and Timothy M. Smeeding, 393–418. Cambridge: Cambridge University Press, 2006.

Miljöpartiet de Gröna. *Arbetskraftsinvandring med socialt ansvar – 10 förslag* (March 4, 2003).

———. "Peter Eriksson om arbetskraftsinvandring: Lyssna på företagen!" (May 17, 2002).

Mirekoç Policy Briefing. *Briefing on Migration and Asylum Seeking Movements to Turkey and Relevant Policies* no. 1, 2009.

Moderaterna, *Valmanifest 2002*.

Momsen-Henshall, Janet (ed.). *Gender, Migration and Domestic Service*. London: Routledge, 1999.

Money, Jeannette. *Fences and Neighbors: The Political Geography of Immigration Control*. Ithaca, NY: Cornell University Press, 1999.

Moravcsik, Andrew. "Active Citation: A Precondition for Replicable Qualitative Research." *PS: Political Science and Politics* 43 (2010): 29–35.

Moreno-Lax, Violeta. "Dismantling the Dublin System: MSS v Belgium and Greece." *European Journal of Migration and Law* 14 (2012): 1–31.

Moscovici, Serge. "The Generalized Self and Mass Society." In *Societal Psychology*, ed. Hilde T. Himmelweit and George Gaskell, 66–91. London: Sage, 1990.

Moscovici, Serge and Gerard Duveen. *Social Representations: Explorations in Social Psychology*. Cambridge: Polity Press, 2000.

MSS v Belgium and Greece (Appln. No. 30696/09) (2011) 53 European Human Rights Reports 2.

Mudde, Cas. *Populist Radical Right Parties in Europe*. Cambridge: Cambridge University Press, 2007.

———. "Racist Extremism in Central and Eastern Europe." *East European Politics and Societies* 19, no. 2 (2005): 161–184.

Muijres, Mieke and Noelle Aarts. *Welkom in Rotterdam! : een studie naar interculturele ontmoetingen tussen "oude" en "nieuwe" Rotterdammers*. Wageningen: Wageningen University.

Mykkänen, Pekka. "Presidentti Halonen Vaatii HS-Haastattelussa Arkirohkeutta Rasismia Vastaan. " *Helsingin Sanomat* (November 13, 2011).

Nacu, Alexandra. "The Politics of Roma Migration: Framing Identity Struggles among Romanian and Bulgarian Roma in the Paris Region." *Journal of Ethnic and Migration Studies* 37, no. 1 (2011): 135–150.

Nancheva, Nevena. "What Are Norms Good For? Ethnic Minorities on Bulgaria's Way to Europe." *Journal for Communist Studies and Transition Politics* 23, no. 3 (2007): 371–395.

Neue Zürcher Zeitung. "24 SVP Parlamentarier für die Freizügigkeit." *Neue Zürcher Zeitung* (November 25, 2008): 13.

———. "Arbeitgeber-Direktor gegen Blocher." *Neue Zürcher Zeitung* (October 31, 2004): 14.

———. "Die SVP gegen das Freizügigkeits-Päckli." *Neue Zürcher Zeitung* (December 1, 2008): 13.

Neumayer, Eric. "Asylum Recognition Rates in Western Europe—Their Determinants, Variation, and Lack of Convergence." *Journal of Conflict Resolution* 49, no. 1 (2005): 43–66.

Niessen, Jan, Thomas Huddleston, Laura Citron, Andrew Geddes, and Dirk Jacobs. *Migrant Integration Policy Index.* London: British Council, 2007.

Nilsson, Lennart, Sören Holmberg, and Lennart Weibull. Riks-SOM. Ed. Göteborgs universitet SOM-institutet: SND Svensk National Datatjänst, 1990–2008.

Nominal Vote on Free Movement of Workers, available at http://www.parlament.ch/ab/frameset/d/n/4706/117777/d_n_4706_117777_117893.htm?Display TextOid=117894 (Accessed November 19, 2012).

Nominal Vote on Swiss Law on Undeclared Work, available at http://www.parlament.ch/poly/Abstimmung/47/out/vote_47_2257.pdf (Accessed November 19, 2012).

Nour, Susanne and Mandana Zarreuparvar. "Bilag A: Konventioner, love og lovændringer på asyl- og udlændingeområdet fra 1949 til I dag." In *Asylbørn i Danmark: en barndom i undtakelsestilstand,* ed. Vitus, Kathrine and Signe Smith Nielsen, 261–269. Copenhagen: Hans Reitzel, 2011.

Nuiva vaalimanifesti, available at http://www.vaalimanifesti.fi (Accessed September 28, 2011).

Odmalm, Pontus. *Migration Policies and Political Participation: Inclusion or Intrusion in Western Europe?* Basingstoke: Palgrave Macmillan, 2005.

———. "Political Parties and 'the Immigration Issue.'" *West European Politics* 34, no. 5 (2011): 1070–1091.

Oesch, Daniel. "The Changing Shape of Class Voting." *European Societies* 10 (2008a): 329–355.

———. "Explaining Workers' Support for Right-Wing Populist Parties in Western Europe: Evidence From Austria, Belgium, France, Norway, and Switzerland." *International Political Science Review/Revue internationale de science politique* 29 (2008b): 349–373.

Oesch, Daniel and Line Rennwald. "The Class Basis of Switzerland's Cleavage between the New Left and the Populist Right." *Swiss Political Science Review* 16 (2010): 343–371.

Page, Benjamin I. and Robert Y. Shapiro. "Effects of Public-Opinion on Policy." *American Political Science Review* 77, no. 1 (1983): 175–190.

Parla, Ayse. "Irregular Workers or Ethnic Kin? Post-1990s Labour Migration from Bulgaria to Turkey." *International Migration* 45 (2007): 157–181.

Parliament of Switzerland. "Loi Contre Le Travail Au Noir – Note De Synthèse," 2006, available at http://www.parlament.ch/f/suche/pages/legislaturrueckblick.aspx?rb_id=20020010.

Parliament Suisse Loi Contre Le Travail Au Noir—Note De Synthèse, available at http://www.parlament.ch/f/suche/pages/legislaturrueckblick.aspx?rb_id=200 20010 (Accessed October 20, 2011).

Parliamentary Committee. "Recent Rise in National Security Discourse in Europe: The Case of Roma." Political Affairs Committee, Doc. 12386, Strasbourg. October 5, 2010.

Pedersen, Søren. *Holdninger til flygtninges adgang til Danmark: Rockwook Fondens Forskningsenhed.* Odense: Dansk Data Arkiv, 1999–2002

Peers, Steve. *EU Justice and Home Affairs Law.* Oxford: Oxford University Press, 2006.

Penninx, Rinus and Giovanna Zincone. "The Multi-level Governance of Immigrant Integration and Migration." In *Migration Policy Making in Europe*, ed. Zincone Borkert and Penninx, 269–304. Amsterdam: AUP, 2011.

Perlmutter, Ted. "Bringing Parties Back In: Comments on 'Modes of Immigration Politics in Liberal Democratic Societies.'" *International Migration Review* 3, no. 1 (1996): 375–388.

Perussuomalaiset. "Matias Turkkila Perussuomalainen-Lehden Päätoimittajaksi," available at http://www.perussuomalaiset.fi/ajankohtaista?issue=1301 (Accessed September 20, 2012).

———. *Oikeutta Kansalle.* Perussuomalaisen Puolueen Yleisohjelma: Olen Perussuomalainen, 1995.

———. Perussuomalaisten Eurovaaliohjelma 1999: Perussuomalainen Kriittisenä Euroopassa.

———. Perussuomalaisten Kunnallisvaalijulistus 2000: Peruspalveluiden Ja Perusturvan Puolesta.

———. Perussuomalaisten Lähiajan Tavoiteohjelma, 2001.

———. Perussuomalaisten Eduskuntavaaliohjelma 2003: Uusi Suunta Suomelle—Korjauksia Epäkohtiin, 2003a.

———. Perussuomalaisten Lähiajan Tavoiteohjelma—Lappeenranta 2003b.

———. Perussuomalaisten EU-Vaaliohjelma 2009: Suomalaisena Euroopassa—Kansanvallan Puolesta.

———. Suomalaiselle Sopivin. Perussuomalaiset r.p.:n Eduskuntavaaliohjelma, 2011.

Pickel, Andreas. "Explaining, and Explaining with, Economic Nationalism." *Nations and Nationalism* 9, no. 1 (2003): 105–127.

Piguet, Etienne. *L'Immigration En Suisse. 50 Ans D'Entrouverture.* Lausanne: PPUR, 2004.

Piore, Michael. *Birds of Passage: Migrant Labour and Industrial Societies.* Cambridge: Cambridge University Press, 1979.

Polittrends. "Analysis of Referendum Vote on Free Movement of Workers," available at http://www.polittrends.ch/abstimmungen/abstimmungsanalysen/vox-analysen/052509f.html#1 (Accessed September 28, 2012).

Poppelaars, Caelesta and Peter Scholten. "Two Worlds Apart. The Divergence of National and Local Integration Policies in the Netherlands." *Administration & Society* 40, no. 4 (2008): 335–357.

Powell, G. Bingham. "The Chain of Responsiveness." *Journal of Democracy* 15, no. 4 (2004): 91–105.

Princen, Sebastiaan and Bart Kerremans. "Opportunity Structures in the EU Multi-level System." *West European Politics* 31, no. 6 (2008): 1129–1146.

Putnam, Robert D. *Bowling Alone: The Collapse and Revival of American Community.* New York: Simon and Schuster, 2000.
Quassoli, Fabio. "Migrants in the Italian Underground Economy." *International Journal of Urban and Regional Research* 23, no. 2 (1999): 212–231.
Racial Equality Directive. 2000/43/EC.
Raggatt, Peter, T. F. "Forms of Positioning in the Dialogical Self: A System of Classification and the Strange Case of Dame Edna Everage." *Theory & Psychology* 17, no. 3 (2007): 355–382.
———. "Positioning in the Dialogical Self: Recent Advances in Theory Construction." In *Handbook of Dialogical Self Theory*, ed. Hubert Hermans and Thorsten Gieser. Cambridge: Cambridge University Press, 2012.
Rath, Jan. "Research on Immigrant Ethnic Minorities in the Netherlands." In *The Politics of Social Science Research. Race, Ethnicity and Social Change*, ed. Peter Ratcliffe. New York: Palgrave.
Regeringens direktiv. *Cirkulär migration och utveckling*, Dir. 2009: 53.
Regeringens proposition 2007/2008:147. *Nya regler för arbetskraftsinvandring.* April 29, 2008.
Regeringens skrivelse. *Särskilda regler under en övergångsperiod för arbetstagare från nya medlemsstater enligt anslutningsfördraget.* Skr. 2003/2004:119.
Rein, Martin and Donald Schön. *Frame Reflection: Toward the Resolution of Intractable Policy Controversies.* New York: Basic Books, 1994.
———. "Problem Setting in Policy-Research." In *Using Social Science in Public Policy*, ed. Carol H. Weiss, 235–251. Lexington, MA: D.C. Heath, 1977.
Reinfeldt, Fredrik, Gunilla Carlssson, and Per Westerberg, "Ingen mur runt Sverige!" *Svenska Dagbladet* (March 18, 2004).
———.,*Från skattemissnöje till etnisk nationalism. Högerpopulism och parlamentarisk högerextremism i Sverige.* Lund: Studentlitteratur, 2005.
Reneman, Marcelle. "An EU Right to Interim Protection During Appeal Proceedings in Asylum Cases?" *European Journal of Migration and Law* 12, no. 4 (2010): 407–434.
Results Referendum on Swiss Aliens Law 2006, available at http://www.parlament.ch/f/dokumentation/dossiers/dossiers-archiv/auslaendergesetz/Pages/auslaendergesetz-abstimmung.aspx (Accessed October 10, 2011).
Rhodes, Rod, "Understanding Governance: Ten Years On." *Organization Studies* 28, no. 8 (2007): 1243–1264.
Ribas-Mateos, Natalia. "How Can We Understand Immigration in Southern Europe?" *Journal of Ethnic and Migration Studies* 30, no. 6 (2004): 1045–1063.
Riksdagen. *Svar på fråga 2002/03:696 om kommuners och läns behov av arbetskraft från tredjeland* (March 26, 2003).
Riksdagens snabbprotokoll 1993/94:76.
Roggeband, Conny and Rens Vliegenthart. "Divergent Framing: The Public Debate on Migration in the Dutch Parliament and Media, 1995–2004." *West European Politics* 30, n. 3 (2007): 524–548.
Romani CRISS. "Letter of Protest of Romanian President Băsescu." European Feminist Forum, Bucharest (June 13, 2007).

Rose, Nikolas. "The Death of the Social? Re-figuring the Territory of Government." *Economy and Society* 25, no. 3 (1996): 327–356.

Rose, Max and Frank R Baumgartner. "Framing the Poor: Media Coverage and U.S. Poverty Policy, 1960–2008." *Policy Studies Journal* 41, no. 1 (2012): 22–53.

Rosenau, James. "Strong Demand, Huge Supply; Governance in an Emerging Epoch." In *Multi-level Governance*, ed. Ian Bache and Matthew Flinders, 75–89. Oxford: Oxford University Press.

Rovny, Jan. "Where Do Radical Right Parties Stand?" *European Political Science Review* 5, no. 1 (2013): 1–26.

Rudmin, Floyd. W. "Critical History of the Acculturation Psychology of Assimilation, Separation, Integration, and Marginalization." *Review of General Psychology* 7, no. 1 (2003): 3–37.

Rughiniş, Cosima. "The Forest Behind the Bar Charts: Bridging Quantitative and Qualitative Research on Research Roma/Ţigani in Contemporary Romania." *Patterns of Prejudice* 44, no. 4 (2010): 337–367.

Ruhs, Martin and Philip Martin. "Numbers vs. Rights: Trade Offs and Guest Worker Programs." *International Migration Review* 42 (2008): 249–265.

Rydgren, Jens. *Från skattemissnöje till etnisk nationalism. Högerpopulism och parlamentarisk högerextremism i Sverige.* Lund: Studentlitteratur, 2005.

———. *From Tax Populism to Ethnic Nationalism: Radical Right-Wing Populism in Sweden.* Oxford: Berghahn Books, 2006.

———. *The Populist Challenge: Political Protest and Ethno-Nationalist Mobilization in France.* Oxford: Berghahn Books, 2004.

———. "Radical Right Populism in Sweden: Still a Failure, But for How Long?" *Scandinavian Political Studies* 25 (2002): 27–56.

———. "The Sociology of the Radical Right." *Annual Review of Sociology* 33 (2007): 241–262.

Rydgren, Jens. and A. Widfeldt (eds.). *Från Le Pen till Pim Fortuyn – populism och parlamentarisk högerextremism i dagens Europa.* Malmö: Liber, 2004.

Sainsbury, Diane. *Welfare States and Immigrant Rights: The Politics of Inclusion and Exclusion.* Oxford: Oxford University Press, 2012.

Sassen, Saskia. *Globalization and Its Discontents. Essays on the New Mobility of People and Money.* New York: New Press, 1998.

Schain, Martin A. "Managing Difference: Immigrant Integration Policy in France, Britain, and the United States." *Social Research* 77 (Spring 2010): 205–236.

———. "Why Political Parties Matter." *Journal of European Public Policy* 15, no. 3 (2008): 465–470.

Schattschneider, Elmer. *The Semisovereign People: A Realist's View of Democracy in America.* Hinsdale, IL: Dryden Press, 1960.

Scheffer, Paul. "Het multiculturele drama." *NRC Handelsblad,* January 29, 2000.

Schmidt, Vivien. "Reconciling Ideas and Institutions through Discursive Institutionalism." In *Ideas and Politics in Social Science Research,* ed. Daniel Béland and Robert Henry Cox, 47–64. Oxford: Oxford University Press, 2011.

———. "Taking Ideas and Discourse Seriously: Explaining Change through Discursive Institutionalism as the Fourth 'New Institutionalism.'" *European Political Science Review* 2, no. 1 (2010): 1–25.
Schnapper, Dominique. "Immigration and the Crisis of National Identity." *West European Politics* 17, no. 2 (April 1994): 127–139.
Scholten, Peter. *Framing Immigrant Integration: Dutch Research-Policy Dialogues in Comparative Perspective*. Amsterdam: Amsterdam University Press, 2011.
Sciarini, Pascal, Alex Fischer, and Sarah Nicolet. "L'Impact De L'Internationalisation Sur Les Processus De Décision En Suisse: Une Analyse Quantitative Des Actes Législatifs 1995–1999." *Revue Suisse de Science Politique* 8 (2002): 1–34.
Searle, John. *The Construction of Social Reality*. New York: Free Press, 1995.
Secretary of State for the Home Department v Nasseri [2009] UKHL 23.
Sev'er, Aysan and Yurdakul Gökçeçiçek. "Culture of Honor, Culture of Change: A Feminist Analysis of Honor." *Violence against Women* 7 (2001): 964–998.
Shapiro, Robert Y. "Public Opinion and American Democracy." *Public Opinion Quarterly* 75, no. 5 (2011): 982–1017.
Sheldon, George. "Foreign Labour Employment in Switzerland: Less Is Not More." *Swiss Political Science Review* 7 (2001): 104–112.
Sigona, Nando. "Locating 'The Gypsy Problem.' The Roma in Italy: Stereotyping, Labelling and 'Nomad Camps.'" *Journal of Ethnic and Migration Studies* 31, no. 4 (2005): 741–756.
Simmel, Georg. "The Stranger." *Georg Simmel on Individuality and Social Forms*. Chicago: University of Chicago Press (1971[1908]).
Smith, J. "Towards Consensus? Centre-Right Parties and Immigration Policy in the UK and Ireland." *Journal of European Public Policy* 15, no. 3 (2008): 414–430.
Sniderman, Paul and Louk Hagendoorn. *When Ways of Life Collide:Multiculturalism and Its Discontents in the Netherlands*. Princeton, NJ: Princeton University Press, 2007.
Soini, Timo. *Maisterisjätkä*. Helsinki: Tammi, 2008.
Soroka, Stuart N. and Christopher Wlezien. "On the Limits to Inequality in Representation." *PS: Political Science and Politics* 41, no. 2 (2008): 319–327.
Sparke, Matthew B. "A Neoliberal Nexus: Economy, Security and the Biopolitics of Citizenship on the Border." *Political Geography* 25, no. 2 (2006): 151–180.
Squire, Vicki. *The Exclusionary Politics of Asylum*. Hampshire: Palgrave Macmillan, 2009.
Stammers, Neil. *Human Rights in Social Movements*. London and New York: Pluto Press, 1999.
Statens Offentliga Utredningar. *EU:s utvidgning och arbetskraftens rörlighet*. SOU 2002: 116.
———. *Svensk flyktingpolitik i globalt perspektiv* SOU 1995: 75.
Statewatch. "Immigration Law Amendment to Turn Expulsion of EU Nationals into Routine," available at http://www.statewatch.org/news/2010/sep/02france-expulsion-routine.htm (Accessed October 10, 2010).
Statham, Paul and Andrew Geddes. "Elites and the 'Organised Public': Who Drives British Immigration Politics and in Which Direction?" *West European Politics* 29 no. 2 (2006):248–269.

Statistics Norway. *Omnibus and Travel and Holiday Surveys.* Norway: Norsk Samfunnsvitenskapelige Datatjeneste, 2006-2008.

Stimson, James A., Michael B. Mackuen, and Robert S. Erikson, "Dynamic Representation." *American Political Science Review* 89, no. 3 (1995): 543-565.

Strom, Kaare. "A Behavioral Theory of Competitive Political Parties." *American Journal of Political Science* 34, no. 2 (1990): 565-598.

Sullivan, Paul. "Examining the Self-Other Dialogue through 'Spirit' and 'Soul.'" *Culture & Psychology* 13, no. 1 (2007): 105-128.

———. *Qualitative Data Analysis Using a Dialogical Approach*: London: Sage, 2011.

Suter, Brigitte. *The Different Perception of Migration from Eastern Europe to Turkey: The Case of Moldovan and Bulgarian Domestic Workers.* Prague: Multicultural Center, 2008.

Svenska Dagbladet. "Persson beredd bromsa EU-invandring från öst." (September 1, 2002).

———. "Utlänningar kan få med sig bidrag hem." (May 29, 2010).

Sveriges Radio, 2007, "Regeringen öppnar för arbetskraftsinvandring," available at http://sr.se/ekot/artikel.asp?artikel=1485607 (Accessed July 17, 2007).

Sveriges Television, "S-bud om övergångsregler avvisades," available at http://svt.se/svt/Crosslink.jsp?d=1804&a=202589 (Accessed July 17, 2007).

Swedish Ministry of Justice. *Cirkulär migration och utveckling*, Dir 2009: 53, 2009-

Sweeney, James. "Credibility, Proof and Refugee Law." *International Journal of Refugee Law* 21, no. 4 (2009): 700-726.

Swenson, Peter. *Capitalists against Markets: The Making of Labor Markets and Welfare States in the United States and Sweden.* Oxford: Oxford University Press, 2002.

Swiss Statistics Office. *La Population Etrangère en Suisse 2009*, available at http://www.bfs.admin.ch/bfs/portal/fr/index/themen/01/07/blank/key/01/01.html (Accessed September 27, 2012).

Tages, Anzeiger. "FDP, CVP und SP beschliessen neues Schwarzarbeitsgesetz." *Tages Anzeiger* (June 18, 2005): 3.

Taggart, Paul A. *The New Populism and the New Politics: New Protest Parties in Sweden in a Comparative Perspective.* London: Macmillan, 1996.

T. C. Başbakanlık Türkiye Istatistik Kurumu. "Hanehalkı iş gücü Istatistikleri." *Haber Bülteni* 38 (2009).

Thomas, Kathrin. "Policy Responsiveness? Evidence for One Side of the Thermostat." In "ELECDEM Workshop on Content Analysis." Amsterdam, 2011.

Thomas, Robert. "Assessing the Credibility of Asylum Claims: EU and UK Approaches Examined." *European Journal of Migration and Law* 8 (2006): 79-96.

Thränhardt, Dietrich and Michael Bommes. *National Paradigms of Migration Research.* Osnabrück: IMIS Schriften, 2010.

TI v UK. Immigration and Nationality Law Reports 211. 2000.

Tichenor, Daniel. *Dividing Lines: The Politics of Immigration Control in America.* Princeton, NJ: Oxford: Princeton University Press, 2002.

Togeby, Lise. *Man har et standpunkt: om stabilitet og ændring i befolkningens holdninger*, Magtudredningen. The Danish Democracy and Market Study. Århus: Aarhus Universitetsforlag, 2004.
Tops, Pieter. *Regimeverandering in Rotterdam: hoe een stadsbestuur zichzelf opnieuw uitvond*. Atlas: Amsterdam, 2007.
Toshkov, Dimiter "Public Opinion and Policy Output in the European Union: A Lost Relationship." *European Union Politics* 12, no. 2 (2011): 169–191.
Travail Suisse. "Svp Will Arbeitgeber, Die Ausländische Schwarzarbeiter Anstellen, Finanziell Unterstützen. Ein Skandal!" 2005, available at http://www.travailsuisse.ch/fr/node/366 (Accessed November 2011).
TT Nyhetsbanken, TT Nyhetsbanken. "Kd vill att Sverige ska vara ett föredome," February 6, 2004a.
———. "Maud Olofsson: Regeringen närmar sig dansk invandringspolitik," February 6, 2004b.
Uitermark, Justus and Jan Willem Duyvendak. "Civilising the City: Populism and Revanchist Urbanism in the City of Rotterdam." *Urban Studies* 45, no. 7 (2008): 1485–1503.
Uitermark, Justus, Jan Willem Duyvendak, and Reinout Kleinhans. "Gentrification as a Governmental Strategy. Social Control and Social Cohesion in Hoogvliet, Rotterdam." *Environment and Planning* 39, no. 1 (2007): 125–141.
Uitermark, Justus, Ugo Rossi, and Henk Van Houtum. "Reinventing Multiculturalism: Urban Citizenship and the Negotiation of Ethnic Diversity in Amsterdam." *International Journal of Urban and Regional Research*, 29 no. 3 (2005): 622–640.
UK Government. *Nationality Immigration and Asylum Act 2002* (c.41) (NIAA). 2002.
———. *Asylum and Immigration (Treatment of Claimants Etc) Act 2004* (c.19). 2004.
———. "Asylum Process Instruction." *Nationality Doubtful Disputed and Other Cases*. Home Office. October 5, 2010.
United Nations. *The Convention Relating to the Status of Refugees*. Geneva, July 28, 1951.
United Nations High Commissioner for Refugees (UNHCR). *Handbook on Procedures and Criteria for Determining Refugee Status*, September 1979, 2nd ed. 1992, reissued (with Guidelines on International Protection). Geneva. December 2011.
———. *Quality Initiative Project, Fourth Report to the Minister*. London, January 2007.
———. *Position on the Return of Asylum Seekers to Greece under the Dublin Regulation*. (April 15, 2008a).
United Nations High Commissioner for Refugees (UNHCR). *Quality Initiative Project, Fifth Report to the Minister*. London, March 2008b.
———. *Improving Asylum Procedures: Comparative Analysis and Recommendations for Law and Practice: A UNHCR Research Project on the Application of Key Provisions of the Asylum Procedures Directive in Member States*. Craig Odofin, Staffans Fraser, and Sikosek Hartwig. Brussels, March 2010.

Van Baar, Huub. "The European Roma: Minority Representation, Memory and the Limits of Transnational Governmentality." PhD Thesis, Amsterdam: University of Amsterdam, 2011.

Van den Bent, Els. "Proeftuin Rotterdam: bestuurlijke maakbaarheid tussen 1975 en 2005." PhD Thesis, Erasmus University Rotterdam, 2010.

Van der Welle, Inge and Virginie Mamadouh. "Territoriale identiteiten en de identificatiestrategieen van Amsterdamse jongvolwassenen van buitenlandse afkomst: over evenwichtskunstenaars en kleurbekenners." *Migrantenstudies* 25, no. 1 (2009): 24–41.

Van Oudenhoven, Jan Pieter, Karin S. Prins, and Bram P. Buunk. "Attitudes of Minority and Majority Members towards Adaptation of Immigrants." *European Journal of Social Psychology* 28, no. 6 (1998): 995–1013.

Veenman, Justus. *Sturen en gestuurd worden, De geschiedenis van het migrantenbeleid in Rotterdam*. Rotterdam: Gemeente Rotterdam, 2001

Vermeulen, Floris and Rosanne Stotijn. "Local Policies concerning Unemployment among Immigrant Youth in Amsterdam and Berlin: Towards Strategic Replacement and Pragmatic Accommodation." In *The Local Dimension of Migration Policymaking*, ed. Tiziana Caponio and Maren Borkert, 109–134. Amsterdam: Amsterdam University Press, 2010.

Vink, Maarten. "Dutch Multiculturalism: Beyond the Pillarisation Myth." *Political Studies Review* 5 (2007): 337–350.

Von Beyme, Klaus. "Right-Wing Extremism in Post-war Europe." *West European Politics* 11, no. 2 (1988): 1–18.

Walgrave, Stefaan, Stuart Soroka, and Michiel Nuytemans. "The Mass Media's Political Agenda-Setting Power—A Longitudinal Analysis of Media, Parliament, and Government in Belgium (1993 to 2000)." *Comparative Political Studies* 41, no. 6 (2008): 814–836.

Warwick, Paul V. "Representation as a Median Mandate? A Response to Best, Budge and McDonald." *European Journal of Political Research* 51, no. 1 (2012): 57–63.

Weaver, Ole. "Identity, Integration and Security." *Journal of International Affairs* 48, no. 2 (1995): 389–431.

Weil, Patrick. *La France et ses étrangers; L'aventure d'une politique d' immigration 1938–1991*. Paris: Éditions Calman-Lévy, 1991.

Weinfurt, Kevin. P. and Fathali M. Moghaddam. "Culture and Social Distance: A Case Study of Methodological Cautions." *Journal of Social Psychology* 141, no. 1 (2001): 101–110.

Weyland, Petra. "Gendered Lives in Global Spaces." In *Space, Culture, and Power: New Identities in Globalizing Cities*, ed. Ayşe Öncü and Petra Weyland, 82–97. London: Zed Books, 1997.

Wlezien, Christopher. "Patterns of Representation: Dynamics of Public Preferences and Policy." *Journal of Politics* 66, no. 1 (2004): 1–24.

———. "The Public as a Thermostat: Dynamics of Preferences for Spending." *American Journal of Political Research* 39, no. 4 (1995): 981–1000.

Wolff, Rick. "Minorities Policy in the City of Amsterdam and the Amsterdam Districts." Paper presented at the MPMC Workshop in Liege, October 30–November 2, 1999.

WRR, *Allochtonenbeleid*. SDU: The Hague, 1989.

Yeates, Nicola. "Global Care Chains: A Critical Introduction." *Global Migration Perspective* 44 (2005), available at http://www.gcim.org/attachements/GMP%20No%2044.pdf. (Accessed September 14, 2013).

Yeoh, Brenda S. A., Shirlena Huang, and Gonzalez Joaquin III. "Migrant Female Domestic Workers: Debating the Economic, Social and Political Impacts in Singapore." *International Migration Review* 33 (1999): 114–136.

Young, Iris Marion. *Inclusion and Democracy*. Oxford: Oxford University Press, 2000

Zaslove, Andrej. "The Dark Side of European Politics: Unmasking the Radical Right." *Journal of European Integration* 26 (2004): 61–81.

———. "Exclusion, Community, and a Populist Political Economy: The Radical Right as an Anti-globalization Movement." *Comparative European Politics* 6, no. 2 (2008a): 169–189.

———. "Here to Stay? Populism as a New Party Type." *European Review* 16, no. 3 (2008b): 319–336.

———. "The Populist Radical Right: Ideology, Party Families and Core Principles." *Political Studies Review* 7, no. 3 (2009): 309–318.

Zetter Roger, David Griffiths, Silva Ferretti, and Martyn Pearl. *An Assessment of the Impact of Asylum Policies in Europe 1990–2000*. London: Home Office Research Study, 2003.

Zimmerman, Mary K., Jacquelyn S. Litt, and Christine E. Bose (eds.). *Global Dimensions of Gender and Carework*. Stanford, CA: Stanford Social Sciences, 2006.

Zincone, Giovanna and Tiziana Caponio. "The Multilevel Governance of Migration." In *The Dynamics of International Migration and Settlement in Europe*, ed. Rinus Penninx, Maria Berger, and Karen Kraal, 269–304. Amsterdam: AUP, 2006.

Zolberg, Aristide and Long Litt Woon. "Why Islam Is Like Spanish: Cultural Incorporation in Europe and in the US." *Politics and Society* 27, no. 1 (1999): 5–38.

Zwaan Karin, Maaike Verrips and Pieter Musken (eds.). *Language and Origin: The Role of Language in European Asylum Procedures: Linguistic and Legal Perspectives*. Nijmegen: Wolf, 2010.

Zylinska, Joanna. "The Universal Acts Judith Butler and the Biopolitics of Immigration." *Cultural Studies* 18, no. 4 (July 2005): 523–537.

Contributors

Alexandre Afonso is a Lecturer in the Department of Political Economy at King's College, London. His current research interests are the political economy of immigration politics, radical right parties and the welfare state, and institutional change in times of economic crisis. His articles have been published in the *Socio-Economic Review*, *Governance*, and the *European Journal of Industrial Relations*. His book *Social Concertation in Times of Austerity: European Integration and the Politics of Labour Market Reforms in Austria and Switzerland* has been published by Amsterdam University Press in 2013.

Gregg Bucken-Knapp is an Associate Professor in the School of Public Administration at the University of Gothenburg, Sweden. He received his PhD from the George Washington University in Washington, DC. His research interests are immigration, prostitution, and trafficking policies, chiefly within a Nordic context. His books include *Defending the Swedish Model: Social Democrats, Trade Unions and Labor Migration Policy Reform* (Lexington, 2009) and *Elites, Language and the Politics of Identity: The Norwegian Case in Comparative Perspective* (SUNY Press, 2003).

Sarah Craig is a Lecturer in Public Law at the University of Glasgow, Scotland. Her areas of research and publication are in immigration and refugee law, with a particular focus on administrative and judicial decision-making procedures in asylum cases. Previously a legal practitioner, she has published in the *International Journal of Refugee Law* and the *Edinburgh Law Review,* among others, and she has conducted research for a range of bodies including the Scottish government and the United Nations High Commissioner for Refugees.

Helen Drake is a Professor of French and European Studies at Loughborough University. Her research focuses on French politics, society, and culture; French relations with the European Union; and matters of political leadership and legitimacy. She is currently chair of UACES (University Association of Contemporary European Studies) and coconvenor (with Alistair Cole) of the French Politics Specialist Group of the PSA (Political Studies Association).

Hande Eslen-Ziya is a Lecturer at the Sociology Department of Bahçeşehir University, Turkey. At the time of writing, Dr. Eslen-Ziya is a postdoc scholar at the University of Kwazulu-Natal, South Africa. Her current research focuses broadly on social policy, religion, and gender rights, as well as the constructions of femininity and masculinity. Her work has been published in *Social Politics, Totalitarian Movements and Political Religions, Journal of Sociological Research*. Since 2011, she has been the project coordinator of "Construction of Family, Masculinity, Femininity and Population Issues in Friday Mosque Prayers in Turkey."

Frøy Gudbrandsen, PhD, has focused her research on immigration policy and immigration flows, and on their various determinants. She has published articles on influence of political parties and press coverage of immigration in the Scandinavian countries. She is currently working as a journalist in Bergens Tidende, Norway.

Jonas Hinnfors is a Professor of Political Science at the University of Gothenburg, Sweden. He is also a Honorary Senior Researcher at the University of Stirling, Scotland (Division of History & Politics). His research, publications, and teaching focus on immigration, social democracy, political parties, and welfare policies. Currently, he is working on a project concerning immigration policies among mainstream political parties and is the leader of the Swedish partner of the Urban Europe "Imagination" comparative project (2013–2016) on Central and Eastern European (CEE) migration in the European Union.

Umut Korkut is a Lecturer at Glasgow School for Business and Society at Glasgow Caledonian University. He was admitted to the degree of Doctor of Philosophy with magna cum laude at the Central European University in Budapest in 2004. He was awarded the "Doçent" degree by the Turkish High Education Authority in 2009. His current research focus is, broadly speaking, social policy, liberalization, religion and gender rights, democratization and Europeanization in Central and Eastern Europe and Turkey. He is a follower of discursive institutionalist and ideational approaches in research. Among many, he has published in *Eurasian Geography and Economics, Social Politics, Parliamentary Affairs, Nationalities Papers, Economic and Industrial Democracy*, and *East European Quarterly*. His book entitled *Liberalization Challenges* *in Hungary: Elitism, Progressivism, and Populism* has been published by Palgrave/NYU Series in Europe in Transition in 2012. Currently, he assists in coordinating a project entitled "Construction of Family, Masculinity, Femininity and Population Issues in Friday Mosque Prayers in Turkey." Dr. Korkut is the coconvenor of Political Studies Association Comparative European Politics Specialist Group.

Mikko Kuisma is a Senior Lecturer in International Relations at Oxford Brookes University, UK. He received his PhD in Political Science from the University of Birmingham where he also held an Economic and Social Research Council (ESRC) Postdoctoral Research Fellowship. He has also worked at the University of Wales, Aberystwyth, and the European University Institute in Florence. His main research interests lie in the comparative political economy of European welfare states, with a special focus on the constitution of citizenship in welfare capitalism. He is the editor of a symposium "Role of Ideas in Welfare Crises and Transformations" for *Public Administration*. His work has been published in, for example, *Cooperation and Conflict*, *New Political Economy*, and *Citizenship Studies*.

Kesi Mahendran is a Lecturer in Social Psychology, at the Open University, UK. Previously a senior researcher in International Relations in the Scottish government, she has an interest in migration, the European Union, and the dialogue between governments and citizens. She is the codirector of the Enactments program in the Centre for Citizenship, Identities and Governance. Her current research is centered on mobility, nonmobility, integration, and citizenship.

Aidan McGarry is a Senior Lecturer in Politics at the University of Brighton. His research focuses on minorities, political representation, Roma, the European Union, and social movements. His research findings have been published in *Nationalities Papers*, *Social Movement Studies*, *Critical Social Policy*, *Ethnopolitics*, *and Ethnicities* (forthcoming in 2014), among others. His book *Who Speaks for Roma? Political Representation of a Transnational Minority Community* has been published by Continuum in 2010.

Peter Scholten is an Associate Professor of Public Policy & Politics at Erasmus University, Rotterdam, and associate research at the Center on Migration, Policy, and Society of the University of Oxford. At Erasmus, he is the coordinator of the interdepartmental research cluster on the Governance of Migration and Integration. His research focuses on the multilevel governance of migrant integration, research-policy dialogues on migration, social media and integration, citizenship and admission policies, and Central and Eastern European (CEE) migration within Europe. He is also the editor of *Comparative Migration Studies* and the *Perspectives on Europe*.

Andrea Spehar received her PhD from the University of Gothenburg, Sweden. She is currently a Senior Lecturer in Political Science at the University of Gothenburg, and researcher at Centre for European Research at University of Gothenburg (CERGU). Her fields of interest comprise the political, social, and gender equality developments in Central and Eastern Europe, gender approaches to public policies and theories of Europeanization, migration, and political parties. Among other publications, her work has appeared in *Journal of European Public Policy*; *Journal of Women, Politics & Policy*, and *Eastern European Politics & Societies*.

Index

10-point migration continuum 111

Acculturation Theory 116–17
AKP (Justice and Development
  Party) 47
Amsterdam 14, 154, 156, 160–2
  Diversity Policy 161
  Van Gogh, Theo 161, 166, 167
Antiglobalization 102
Anti-immigration 21–6, 34, 37, 40,
  46, 93–4, 96, 98–100, 104, 108,
  110, 143, 160, 171, 172, 176, 184,
  192, 195, 196
Assimilation 14, 97, 116–17, 124, 127,
  129, 130, 152, 153, 156, 159,
  164, 166–8
Asylum 1, 2, 5, 7, 10, 14, 27, 41,
  53–70, 98–9, 107, 119, 135–51
  access to process 54, 65–70
  claims and credibility 61–3
  Common European Asylum
    System 54–9
  deflection techniques 59–61
  Dublin regulation 59–61, 63–5, 67–9
  EURODAC 57
  interpretation and translation 65–6
  linguistic analysis 61–3
  minimum standards 53–6
  policy 135–6, 139–41, 149–50
  Procedures Directive 53–6, 59–61,
    63–4, 67–8
  safe countries of origin 60–1
  safe third countries *see* Dublin
    regulation

Bakhtin, Mikhail 112
Balkan Wars 139
Bavul ticareti 44
Belgium 21, 25, 55, 64–5, 66, 67
Belonging 11, 73, 74, 76, 80, 85–6,
  90–1, 102, 116, 119, 153
Blair, Tony 101
Blocher, Christoph 25
Bulgaria 27, 41, 73, 78–9, 81,
  84, 86

Capitalism 105
  crude 105
  free-market 104
  global 102, 104–5
  laissez-faire 105
  regional 105
Care drain 45
Childcare 45, 51
CHP (Republican People's Party) 47
Citizenship 2, 4, 11, 83, 89, 106, 109,
  129, 130, 153, 158–9
  access to 23
  equal 9
  EU/European 84, 119–20
  Nordic 120
  Russian 128
  social 101
  Swiss 26
Class 9, 18–23, 50, 81
  lower 50
  middle 44–5, 51, 193
  working 18–25, 34–5, 176
Common good 2

Competitiveness 12, 29, 106, 108
  competition state paradigm
    105, 108
Costello, Cathryn 59
Council of Europe 56, 81, 83, 87, 90
Court of Justice of the European
  Union 54, 67–70, 196

Dansk Folkeparti 143
Denmark 87, 135–6, 139–40, 143,
  146, 150
Dialogical 110, 118
  analysis 112, 130
  approach 11, 113, 121, 161, 163
  capacity 113, 114, 116
  I-positions 123
  positioning 114
  self 118, 128
Discourse analysis 95, 110, 196
Downs, Anthony 18
  Downsian policy adaptation 189

Edinburgh 11, 109, 114, 116, 119,
  120, 123, 127–9
Epistemic communities 2
Equality 106
  of opportunity 106
  of outcome 106
Erdoğan, Recep Tayyip 49
Ethnic Category:
  conflation with migration 112
Ethnic/Ethnicity 2, 5, 73, 76, 80–1,
  89, 95, 98, 100–1, 105, 157–8
European Convention on Human
  Rights 56
European Court of Human Rights 55,
  59, 63
Europeanization 3, 111, 118
European Pact on Immigration and
  Asylum 6–7
European Union:
  Charter of Fundamental Rights 67
  Commission 85, 88
  Common Basic Principles for
    Immigrant Integration Policy 7
  Common European Asylum System
    see Asylum
  common market 104
  Enlargement 28
  enlargement transition rules 178–80
  Euro bailout packages 95
  European elections 2009 95, 106
  Framework on Roma Strategies
    73, 89
  free movement of workers 28–30
  intervention of 73, 79, 83, 87, 90
  "irregular" migrants 57
  Maastricht Treaty 140
  monetary union 104
  protection of asylum seekers 10;
    see also Asylum
  Race Equality Directive (RED) 74,
    84, 88
  Treaty on the Functioning of the
    European Union 56

Family 11, 45, 49, 95, 114, 183, 193
  immigration policy 136, 140
  party 102–3, 107
  policy 97
  reunification 30, 99, 140
  roles 50
Filipino 43
Finland 1, 192, 193
  2003 parliamentary election 97–8, 100
  2007 parliamentary election 95
  2011 parliamentary election 94–6,
    100
  Association of Finnish Culture
    and Identity (*Suomalaisuuden
    liitto*) 99
  Eduskunta 100
  Finnish Rural Party (*Suomen
    maaseudun puolue*, SMP) 95, 104
  Finnish Sisu (*Suomen sisu*) 99
  Finnish Supreme Court (*Korkein
    oikeus*) 96
  Parliamentary Administration
    Committee (*Eduskunnan
    hallintovaliokunta*) 96

Sour Election Manifesto (*Nuiva vaalimanifesti*) 100
True Finns Party (*Perussuomalaiset*) 11, 93–108
Fortress Europe 38
Fortuyn, Pim 164, 166
Framing 103, 110, 111, 113, 118, 129, 151, 152, 155, 156–7, 159, 192, 193
  dilemmas 176
  mechanisms 191
  policy 160, 167–8, 195
France 1, 11, 21, 73–91, 153, 193–4
Front National 82
Fremskridtspartiet 143
Fremskrittspartiet 143

Gagauz 43
Gender 1, 9–10, 12, 37–52, 81, 193
  of immigrants 10
  and informality 38, 46
  labor 39–40, 43, 44, 49, 51
Ghetto 89
Ghettoization 107
Government responsiveness 136–7, 141
Guest-workers 3
Greece 54, 55, 63–8

Hague 119
  Programme 7, 120
Halla-aho, Jussi 96, 99–100
Halme, Tony 98–9
Halonen, Tarja 96
Homma forum 99
Host nation 2, 9–10, 193

Identity 3, 9, 13, 18, 115, 197
  and belonging 86
  cultural 159–60
  and culture 19, 117
  documents 62
  group 90
  national 151, 156, 159, 162
  politics 76–83
Immigration systems 1, 2, 4, 193
Income transfers 106

Individualism 105, 189
Informal economy 1, 38–9, 43, 49
Informality 10, 38, 40, 43–5, 48–9
  and gendered labor market 39
  and illegality 44
Integration 89, 90
  canonical individualized 116
  Dutch 192
  EU 6
  Europeanization of 118
  and migration/immigrants 3, 10, 74, 81, 90, 168
  migrant perceptions 127
  and multi-level governance 1
  national models 14
  nonmigrant perceptions 121
  perceptions of 109–10, 191
  of Roma 74, 79, 86, 88, 89
Integration policy 4, 5, 7, 93, 105–7, 153–5
Internal supply-side analysis 95
International Political Economy 102
IOM 41
Iraq 41, 42, 183
Islam 4, 48, 96, 158, 164
Istanbul 39, 46

Keynes, John Maynard 103

Labor market 79
Labour Party:
  Britain 4
  The Netherlands 164–5, 167
Language 2, 61–3, 65–6
Left 13, 17, 19–20, 32–3, 65, 79–80, 94, 95, 102, 105, 138
Liberalism 102–3, 106
  economic 104
  ideology 182, 188, 189
Lipponen, Paavo 101
List, Friedrich 103–4

Median voter 138, 142
Mercantilism 104
  neomercantilism 103

Middle East 41, 42
MIPEX 109
Moreno-Lax, Violeta 68
Multiculturalism 93, 97, 100–1, 106, 129, 159, 167
  thin 97–8
Multi-level governance 1, 155–7, 168

Natasha 43
Nationalism 93–4, 96, 102–3, 106, 108
  economic 93–4, 101, 103–7
  holistic 97, 105
  nativist 94, 96, 98, 100–2, 105–7
National language acquisition 123, 125, 129
National models of integration 153–5, 159, 168–9
Naturalization 105
Neoliberalism 18, 21, 25, 28, 34, 35, 101–2
Netherlands, the 1, 152–3, 157–67
  Ethnic Minorities Policy 157–8, 165
  Integration Policy 158–9
  pillarization 157, 167
  Scientific Council for Government Policy 158, 163
Nordic countries 94
Norway 135–6, 139–40, 146, 149
Ny Demokrati 143

Ontology:
  cosmopolitan 102
  nationalist 94–5, 103–4, 107
  particularist 102
Otherness 9–12, 81, 113

Party identification 143
Party politics 5, 19, 20, 138, 143, 164–5
Peers, Steve 61, 69
Persson, Göran 101
Policy preferences 138
Problem definition 7, 8, 156–7, 192
  migrant 127, 130

Process tracing 190
Progressive's dilemma 101
Prophet Mohammad 96
Protectionism 103–4, 176
Public:
  debate 110
  opinion 135, 137–9, 148
  philosophy 2, 5, 6, 11
  sphere, communicative 110, 116
  sphere, coordinative 110, 116
Populism/populist 13, 93–5, 104, 164
  new 95
  old "agrarian" 95
  political economy 102
  radical 95

Racism 85, 95–6
Refugee 98, 107
  deflection techniques 59–61
  "life standard" 99
  UN Convention 55, 56
  protection struggle 53, 55–9, 65–6
Roma:
  deportations 82–4, 86
  inclusion 75
  migrants 73, 75, 79–80, 82
  migration 1, 78
  responsibility for 11, 73, 76, 85, 87, 89, 91
  security threat 73, 74, 80–7, 88–90
  stigmatization of 77–8, 80, 87
Redistribution 20, 101, 103
Religion 2, 9, 156
Responsibilization 101
Right:
  extreme 13, 14
  far 12
  mainstream 96, 146
  populist radical 93–5
  radical 14, 20, 21, 95–6, 146
Rights:
  civil 4, 23
  ethnic 4
  fundamental 9, 67
  human 4, 13, 56

linguistic 9
migrant 4, 6, 23
refugee *non-refoulement* 56, 65–6, 69
social 4, 5, 23
Romania 73–4, 76, 78–9, 85
Rotterdam 14, 154, 156, 162–5
  Diversity Policy 163
  Liveable Rotterdam Party 164–5, 166, 168
  Rotterdam Law 164, 166
Russia 42, 43, 48, 112, 128

Salience 22
Scandinavian States 1, 14, 101, 136, 139–40
Schengen 78–9
Securitization 1
Sex workers 43–4
Smith, Adam 103
Social Representations:
  of cohesion 129
  definition of 110, 115, 129
  of diversity 129
Socialism 102–3
Soini, Timo 98, 104–5
Solidarity 12, 42, 43, 101, 105, 106, 119, 176
  Roma 83
Somali 99
Sovereignty 57, 67–8, 151
Soviet Union 38, 48, 99
Squire, Vicki 60
Stockholm 11, 109, 114, 115, 119, 120–2, 125–7, 129
Sweden:
  Bosnian refugees 172, 182–3, 189, 139
  Christian moral values 189
  circular migration 180
  individual rights 189
  labor migration policy debates 177 ff
  Lucia decision 139, 181
  public opinion 136, 142
  refugee migration policy debates 181 ff
  socialist parties ideology 189
  Sweden Democrats 171, 143
  TCN (third-country nationals) migration 172, 177–80, 185
  welfare state 182, 189
Sweeney, James 61
Switzerland:
  immigration policy 26
  Swiss People's Party 10, 17–35

Taxation 96, 106, 108
  progressive 103
Technocratic problem solving 188
Third Way Social Democrats 101
TISK 48
Transnational 1, 2, 74, 75, 80, 83, 91, 104
Transcultural Language 125
Turkey 1, 10, 37–53, 193
  family 50
  gendered and informal 43–6
  legal framework 41–2
  migration regime 38
  official indifference 37, 40
  patriarchal culture 49
  residency 42, 48
Turkkila, Matias 99

Ukraine 42
Undeclared work 18, 26, 27, 32–4
United Kingdom 1, 59–62, 193
United Nations High Commissioner for Refugees 54, 58
United States of America 13, 101

Vennamo, Veikko 95

Welfare 12–14, 98, 176, 189
  benefits 2
  chauvinism 11, 13, 94, 100–1, 107
  cuts 11
  nationalism 179
  Nordic 106–7, 176

Welfare—*Continued*
　policy 4
　programs 101
　reform 167
　regime 4, 5, 100
　services 51
　state 4, 5, 13, 20, 50, 51, 96, 102, 106–8, 182
　system 30, 181

Swedish 176–7
universal welfare state 96, 103
visa-waiver 41
Wilders, Geert 21
Workfare 101

Xenophobia 14, 83, 95–6

Yugoslavia 99

GPSR Compliance

The European Union's (EU) General Product Safety Regulation (GPSR) is a set of rules that requires consumer products to be safe and our obligations to ensure this.

If you have any concerns about our products, you can contact us on

ProductSafety@springernature.com

In case Publisher is established outside the EU, the EU authorized representative is:

Springer Nature Customer Service Center GmbH
Europaplatz 3
69115 Heidelberg, Germany

www.ingramcontent.com/pod-product-compliance
Lightning Source LLC
LaVergne TN
LVHW011812060526
838200LV00053B/3756